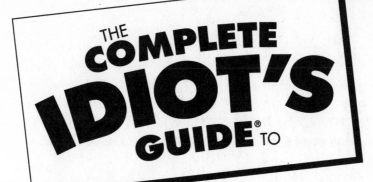

THE COMPLETE IDIOT'S GUIDE® TO

Journalism

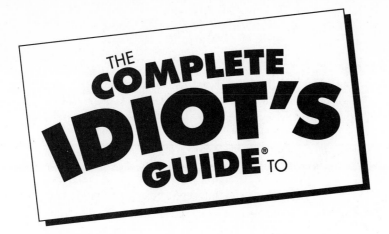

Journalism

by Christopher K. Passante

ALPHA

A member of Penguin Group (USA) Inc.

ALPHA BOOKS

Published by the Penguin Group

Penguin Group (USA) Inc., 375 Hudson Street, New York, New York 10014, USA

Penguin Group (Canada), 90 Eglinton Avenue East, Suite 700, Toronto, Ontario M4P 2Y3, Canada (a division of Pearson Penguin Canada Inc.)

Penguin Books Ltd., 80 Strand, London WC2R 0RL, England

Penguin Ireland, 25 St. Stephen's Green, Dublin 2, Ireland (a division of Penguin Books Ltd.)

Penguin Group (Australia), 250 Camberwell Road, Camberwell, Victoria 3124, Australia (a division of Pearson Australia Group Pty. Ltd.)

Penguin Books India Pvt. Ltd., 11 Community Centre, Panchsheel Park, New Delhi—110 017, India

Penguin Group (NZ), 67 Apollo Drive, Rosedale, North Shore, Auckland 1311, New Zealand (a division of Pearson New Zealand Ltd.)

Penguin Books (South Africa) (Pty.) Ltd., 24 Sturdee Avenue, Rosebank, Johannesburg 2196, South Africa

Penguin Books Ltd., Registered Offices: 80 Strand, London WC2R 0RL, England

International Standard Book Number: 978-1-59257-670-8
Library of Congress Catalog Card Number: 2007924620

09 08 07   8 7 6 5 4 3 2 1

Interpretation of the printing code: The rightmost number of the first series of numbers is the year of the book's printing; the rightmost number of the second series of numbers is the number of the book's printing. For example, a printing code of 07-1 shows that the first printing occurred in 2007.

Printed in the United States of America

Note: This publication contains the opinions and ideas of its author. It is intended to provide helpful and informative material on the subject matter covered. It is sold with the understanding that the author and publisher are not engaged in rendering professional services in the book. If the reader requires personal assistance or advice, a competent professional should be consulted.

The author and publisher specifically disclaim any responsibility for any liability, loss, or risk, personal or otherwise, which is incurred as a consequence, directly or indirectly, of the use and application of any of the contents of this book.

Most Alpha books are available at special quantity discounts for bulk purchases for sales promotions, premiums, fundraising, or educational use. Special books, or book excerpts, can also be created to fit specific needs.

For details, write: Special Markets, Alpha Books, 375 Hudson Street, New York, NY 10014.

Publisher: *Marie Butler-Knight*
Editorial Director: *Mike Sanders*
Managing Editor: *Billy Fields*
Executive Editor: *Randy Ladenheim-Gil*
Development Editors: *Susan Zingraf, Jennifer Moore*
Senior Production Editor: *Janette Lynn*
Copy Editor: *Lisanne Victoria Jensen*

Cartoonist: *Shannon Wheeler*
Cover Designer: *Bill Thomas*
Book Designer: *Trina Wurst*
Indexer: *Tonya Heard*
Layout: *Brian Massey*
Proofreader: *Aaron Black*

Contents at a Glance

Contents

Appendixes

Introduction

At the root of journalism is basic storytelling: those in the know sharing information with others who want to know. This practice has taken place since cavemen sat around fires communicating what one man saw on his hunt earlier in the day. The information is merely broken down for the next guy to understand.

Today, that very concept remains intact, although greatly enhanced. We pop a quarter into a box at the newsstand and become informed and entertained. We turn to a news channel on TV and our world becomes just a little bit bigger with each story. We flip through the glossy pages of a magazine and discover cultures we once knew nothing of. We spin the dial on our radio and catch the sports talk or weather report. Or we surf the Internet and watch the culmination of these media flourishing into one giant melting pot of information.

Those producing all this information are journalists—reporters, editors, producers, photographers, artists, and anchors who are trained to report fairly, accurately, and timely.

Journalists are governed by strict ethical codes that they must adhere to in order to remain reputable and trusted. There may be degrees of these ethics from medium to medium, however, and it's becoming more important today to understand what they are as those lines become more blurry in certain media.

It takes a lot to be a journalist. In what other field do you have to be an expert in such a vast array of subjects—government, the environment, business, medicine, the military, education, the judicial system …. Training to become a journalist takes a lot of education and practice, but it's one of the most fulfilling careers a person can have.

How This Book Is Organized

This book is divided into five parts that discuss the world of journalism. Storytelling is the very root of good journalism, and nowhere in this discipline is storytelling more prevalent than in newspapers. Good storytelling is the very essence of informing readers, commenting on our world and chronicling news events. **Part 1, "Newspapers,"** discusses the role of newspapers, how journalists write and report, and how what they write affects our everyday lives.

Magazines go far beyond simple entertainment; they are the very essence of journalism. But the spectrum is wide. From niche publications to broad-ranging publications, the words found within those glossy covers are enterprising, investigative, and, yes, very entertaining. In **Part 2, "Magazines,"** we'll look at what it takes to work in this medium and how magazine journalism is done, start to finish.

Often overlooked and underestimated, radio is a powerhouse in the world of journalism. Portable, immediate, and extremely relevant, radio has made, and will continue to make, a mark. **Part 3, "Radio,"** discusses the ins and outs of journalism on the radio waves.

Since the first news broadcast, television has taken the world of journalism by storm. This medium has exploded since the 1950s and today remains a journalistic force. In **Part 4, "Television,"** we'll show you how TV journalism all began, and what it's evolved into.

Perhaps the most dynamic of all mediums, Internet journalism is a convergence of print, TV, and radio all in one infinite medium—and it's still in its infancy! Internet journalism is growing faster than any other form of journalism out there. In **Part 5, "Internet,"** we'll show you where it came from and where it's going.

Notes of a Journalist

Throughout the book, you'll find notes and sidebars full of interesting nuggets of information to help you understand the world of journalism. There are three kinds of notes:

Breaking News

From the off-beat to the unexpected, this note will show you some of the more quirky and interesting side of journalism.

Extra! Extra!

Newsrooms are jam-packed with information and facts. Some very interesting tidbits are found under this heading throughout this book.

---

def•i•ni•tion

The jargon in newsrooms can be overwhelming sometimes. Tricky terms are defined throughout this book to help you negotiate through those odd phrases, puns, and terms that journalists use every day.

Acknowledgments

In researching for this book, I found out something about myself, and it caught me a little off-guard: I found out just how many colleagues and friends I have worked with over the years.

As a journalist, I've bounced around more than a few newsrooms and rolled up my sleeves beside more fine reporters, editors, and photographers than I can recall. Many of them I have tapped to add their unique and critical insights to this book. And for that, I would like to thank this solid core of working journalists in all media: Christopher Zurcher, Brian Dearth, Peter Guinta, Ken Palmer, Edward Woodward, Laura Powell Fritz, Julie Bologna, Sheila Conolly, Geoff Ziezulewicz, Jason Ryan, Jeff Kidd, Jill Coley, Kendall Bell, Michael R. Shea, and Miranda Bender.

I thank those who've worked to make this book possible: Kimberly Lionetti at Book Ends for getting this idea off the ground; Executive Editor Randy Ladenheim-Gil at Penguin for her patient guidance and incredible insight; Jennifer Moore, Susan Zingraf, and Lisanne Victoria Jackson for very capable editing; and everyone at Alpha Books who has worked hard on this project.

I also would like to thank my family and friends for their amazing love, support, generosity, and belief in me, and God for the everyday miracles and blessings in my life.

I would mostly like to thank my amazing bride, Robyn, who inspires me to be the best I can be, and I dedicate this book to her.

Trademarks

All terms mentioned in this book that are known to be or are suspected of being trademarks or service marks have been appropriately capitalized. Alpha Books and Penguin Group (USA) Inc. cannot attest to the accuracy of this information. Use of a term in this book should not be regarded as affecting the validity of any trademark or service mark.

Part 1

Newspapers

Newspapers initiated the mass communication revolution, and the power of the printed word is here to stay. Despite fierce competition from other media, newspapers have remained strong throughout the years and continue to hold their own.

In this part, we'll explore the evolution of newspapers including the newsroom ins and outs, who does what, how to write and structure good news stories, newspaper design, ethics in print, and how to launch a career as a newspaper journalist.

Chapter 1

All the News That's Fit to Print

In This Chapter

- ◆ The news on your doorstep
- ◆ Writing for success
- ◆ The Jobs in a newsroom
- ◆ Newsroom departments
- ◆ Niche publications

Never before has the world of journalism been so explosive, so global, so competitive. Forget hourly news flashes—we live in a world of 24-hour breaking news, with radio and TV stations and Internet news sites updating stories by the minute. Although there are fewer newspapers, TV, and radio stations in the United States today than there were even 10 years ago, the number of Internet news portals has grown precipitously in the past decade. In this climate of constant change, newspapers must constantly adapt to stay relevant to an increasingly media-savvy audience.

But in no way do these changes suggest that any aspect of journalism—especially newspapers—is becoming obsolete. Never before have Americans been so interested in all manners of news and information—from the results of a vote at a local school board meeting to elections taking place halfway around the globe, from the latest Britney Spears mishap to a British royalty scandal—and they rely on a wide variety of mediums to satisfy their insatiable appetite for knowledge. They also rely on a highly-trained, quick-thinking, and fast-acting core of workers called journalists. In this chapter, we explore the power of the printed word that we find when we open our favorite newspapers.

Good News About Newspapers

Journalism has become more global-minded, and the level of the global consciousness of everyday people has never been greater. We're no longer talking about a three-day-old newsreel from Vietnam or day-old interviews at the Kremlin. At our fingertips are volumes of stories on any subject—from a skirmish in Syria to a club football game in New Zealand to a feature on the Cloud Train running from China to Nepal.

You want it now? You got it. And the folks who give it—report, write, compile, edit, illustrate, shoot, and post—are journalists.

While employment news from the print medium has been gloomy—more than 2,000 job losses in 2005 alone—this reduction is simply a "de-bloating" of this media staple as boardrooms watch the bottom line in tumultuous economic times. So, say goodbye to the synergy editor, the assistant perfume columnist, and the assistant prep football editor and say hello to leaner and meaner newsrooms that blend and peddle their wares on TV, radio, websites, and even handheld personal digital assistants (PDAs).

Gary Pruitt, CEO, president, and chairman of the board of the McClatchy Company, forged the second-largest and one of the most successful and reputable newspaper chains in the United States by purchasing 20 Knight-Ridder newspapers in 2006, then selling 12 of them in a landmark move. Pruitt talks extensively about creating "athletic"—think leaner and meaner—newspapers by keeping newsrooms stocked with the best and brightest writers and editors to ensure that the papers produce high-level journalism. Many leaders industry-wide are following McClatchy's lead in order to stay aggressive.

Extra! Extra!

The number of U.S. daily newspapers has dropped steadily since 1950, when there were 1,772 dailies, to an estimated 1,410 today.

But as large newspaper chains have gobbled up more and more small newspapers, they've also swallowed up the competition—leaving many newspapers as the only game in town. This trend concerns many media pundits, who worry that these newspapers will lose their journalistic edge without competition. After all, what's the rush to break a story if no one else is going to scoop you?

Who's the Competition?

No need to worry too much, though. That's because even in communities where there's only one newspaper, the paper still faces plenty of competition—from TV, radio, and the Internet, to name just a few. Even most small towns have some sort of television news coverage, and while many smaller radio stations read their news from newspapers and Internet news sites, network radio's news reporting is strong.

We'll talk a whole lot more about those other mediums later in this book. For now, all you need to know is that although there is reduced competition among newspapers, there is actually quite a bit more competition coming from other mediums. Whereas a little more than a quarter-century ago the only source of TV news came from three networks—ABC, NBC, and CBS—today there are more TV news sources than ever imagined. Cable news, such as CNN, has proliferated. Just turn on the TV and start counting. With more than 200 channels to choose from, entire blocks in your TV listings are dedicated to 24-hour news channels. Along with mainstream news sources such as ABC, CBS, NBC, Fox News, CNN, MSNBC, many networks have added news programming or news networks, such as MTV News and ESPN News, and many local or regional markets have formed 24-hour news networks, such as Bay News 9 in Tampa, Fla. Also, foreign-language news stations have proliferated in major metropolitan areas, such as Spanish-speaking Telemundo. And speaking of big cities, there may be more than one network affiliate broadcasting in major metropolitan areas.

> **Extra! Extra!**
>
> There's an implied understanding between newspapers and their readers that the newspaper will disseminate important news as quickly as possible. This expectation not only keeps newspapers relevant but credible. We'll chat more about journalistic ethics in Chapter 5.

So Why Do We Still Need Newspapers?

Many readers assume that newspapers are "institutions of truth" that will never disappear. Sure, the print competition has decreased—but readership levels haven't tapered off as much as many doomsayers have predicted. As a matter of fact, compared with other media, newspapers have held pretty steady.

That's not to say that newspaper circulation hasn't dropped in the United States. Between October 1, 2005, to March 31, 2006, the Newspaper Association of America (NAA) reported that average weekday circulation fell 2.5 percent, with Sunday circulation dropping 3.1 percent. The *San Francisco Chronicle* experienced a particularly sharp circulation drop of 15.6 percent. The *Los Angeles Times'* circulation dropped 5.4 percent, and that city's *Daily News* plummeted 11.9 percent. But it wasn't just the West Coast that saw a decline in newspaper readership. *The Boston Globe* lost 8.5 percent of its circulation, and the *Boston Herald* dropped 9.1 percent.

> **Breaking News**
>
> In a world of minute-by-minute breaking news, are newspapers still relevant? You bet. A very large audience still wants the analysis and variety that print publications provide.

Do You Have the Write Stuff?

The continuous battle for circulation, the layoffs, and the doomsday proclaimers haven't stopped students from majoring in journalism. As a matter of fact, they're rushing into the field in record numbers. In 2004 alone, more than 50,000 journalism graduates were estimated to aspire for a career in the industry. The problem is, there were only an estimated 66,000 newsroom positions—most of which were already filled.

Peter T. Guinta, senior writer at *The St. Augustine Record* in Florida, has seen a lot of changes in his 26 years in newsrooms. Inspired by combat journalists reporting from his Vietnam foxhole, Guinta decided to major in journalism and has an admiration for reporting that's nearly unparalleled in the business. But that doesn't mean he'd necessarily recommend a career as a newspaper reporter.

> **Breaking News**
>
> There are 72 journalism schools in the United States, and that doesn't include the journalism programs in many other schools. For a list of top journalism schools and programs in the United States as well as their contact information, see Appendix C.

"Actually, I would recommend choosing some other field," Guinta says. "But if someone is really determined to do this, try writing beat stories for a while, like for the city commission. That nails the form and hones one's writing craft. Make yourself valuable. There's a whole crew out in the newsroom. Be the utility fielder, the one enthusiastic person the editor calls on to cover something after hours, something complicated or disgusting, or when something odd happens, like a plane crash. Learn how to use a camera. Afterward, try to specialize in something. I cover the county commission. Borrrrring! But I paid enough dues and got sent to El Salvador, Panama, Iraq, Qatar, and Oman as well as Washington, D.C., Tallahassee, and covering the aftermath of Hurricane Katrina."

It takes years in a newsroom—or blind luck early on—to be tapped to cover the good stories. But as Guinta notes, there are tricks to help tilt the scales in your favor.

"I'd also suggest that reporters get to know the military or National Guard units in their home city," he adds. "When a crisis calls, all those little briefs about a general being promoted or a new F/A-18 being assigned to the base could turn into an invitation to join them in a deployment. I once got to ride over Saudi Arabia in a C-5A, the largest cargo plane in our Air Force. And I've just been invited to go to Afghanistan with the Florida National Guard. If I weren't such a girly man, I'd tell my wife to expect me back in a month."

Hard work and blind luck aside, employers are no longer willing to take a chance on the local kid who is willing to work long hours for little pay. Top journalism programs, graduate schools, multiple internships, and big-name fellowships supply newspapers with work-ready employees. Sure, those new hires will still need to learn on the job—but they're much better prepared than their predecessors.

Extra! Extra!

Want to know how to get a leg up on the competition? Experience and a willingness to relocate top newspaper recruiters' lists of desirable qualities.

Invaluable Internships

J-schools are spitting out droves of eager job candidates. So how do you make yourself stand out from the crowd? Edward Woodward, a former reporter at *The Tampa Tribune* in Florida, preaches the value of practice. His number one suggestion? "Internships, internships, and internships. Early and often."

Woodward, who has written for newspapers and magazines, got an early start at a local newspaper while attending Florida State University.

"The summer after my freshman year in college, my dad suggested I try an internship at *The Gadsden County Times*, my hometown weekly newspaper. English and writing were my strong suits. And though I was a bit nervous about the deadline deal, I dove in and dug it," Woodward says. "I covered a little bit of everything: a murder trial, community meetings, a feature about firefighters when the movie *Backdraft* debuted."

Putting in the Time

Internships are never a bad thing, and any editor looking for a new reporter will tell you as much. But a willingness to try an unpopular beat, *stringing* for the hometown daily, or working at a small daily or weekly might just get you a leg up, too. After all, it's experience we're talking about.

def•i•ni•tion

A **stringer** is a freelance reporter or photographer who works for a newspaper when needed and is paid per story.

Internships, in most cases, are paid and count toward credits in a degree program. Students in these programs will apply for internships—which may last from a few weeks to a full semester or over a summer—through their schools or may apply directly to newspapers if their schools don't have established internships. We'll discuss internships more in Chapter 6.

"From my experience, so much of it is chance, being in the right place at the right time ...," says Jill Coley, a news reporter for *The Charleston Post & Courier* in South Carolina. "You'll meet people who fell out of bed one day and landed a job at *USA Today* and then others with an Ivy League Master's degree slogging it up the circulation ladder 10,000 at a time."

In Coley's case—like so many others—it was perseverance, a willingness to try different beats, and ... well, talent.

"I studied English and creative writing and soon after graduation learned there aren't many ways to get paid as a writer," Coley admits. "So I got a job as an indexer and researcher cataloging content from *Harper's Weekly*. As that project came to a close, I continued to work in research in a newsroom library. I knew I could report; it combined my writing and research background. So I freelanced and worked my way into the newsroom."

We'll talk more about interviewing tricks and what sparks an employer's interest in a candidate in Chapter 6, but for now it's important to realize that newspaper journalists are a tough breed. It takes a special kind of person—a special combination of artist, lawyer, scientist, philanthropist, and perfectionist—to be a journalist. And getting into the field takes gumption and a thick skin. After all, in what other field is your day's work published for all to read and judge?

Who Does What in a Newsroom

More good news: you're a good writer, you pay attention to detail, but you hate county government. There are still newspaper jobs for you. And good ones, too.

I know reporters and editors who would rather chew off their own hands than attend a city council meeting or write a story about school taxes.

Some people who are interested in journalism don't want to write at all. Photography and graphic illustration are two mediums that involve entirely different journalistic palates, while copy editing and researching are among other in-demand newsroom posts.

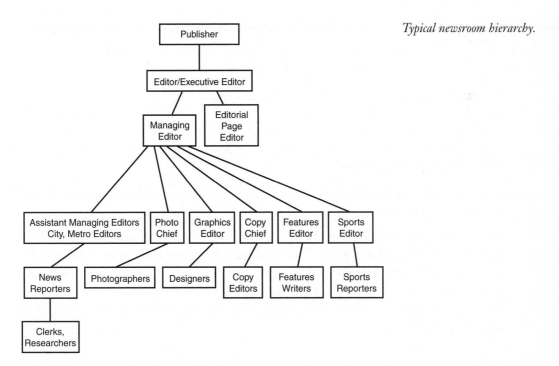

Typical newsroom hierarchy.

Note: New media staff may fall under a number of managers or be its own department.

It takes a lot of people doing many different jobs to put together a newspaper. Outside the nonjournalism jobs—display and classified ad sales, prepress and press, distribution, accounting, human resources, and other administrative positions—newsrooms are abuzz a good portion of the morning, day, and night putting together the latest and most interesting information for their audience. So let's take a walk through a typical newsroom to see who does what and how each component is integral in putting an edition "to bed."

Executive Editor: The Buck Stops Here

There are a whole lot of names for the same positions at different newspapers. Some papers employ *executive editors* as the top dogs in the newsrooms, while others call themselves plain ol' editors. In either case, they typically report directly to the publisher, who oversees every facet of a newspaper—ads, press, newsroom, and so on, and would report to a president, CEO, or board of directors (unless he or she owned the newspaper).

def•i•ni•tion

The **executive editor** is typically the top dog in the newsroom, answering to the publisher.

The executive editor sets the tone for the newsroom and is responsible for making the toughest decisions—whether they are financial ("Can we afford to send a reporter and photographer to Iraq to cover the war?"), ethical ("Do we name the juvenile suspect of a murder case?"), or practical ("Does this headline make any sense?").

In the end, many of the decisions made in the newsroom come out of the executive editor's corner office. At most mid- to large-circulation newspapers, the executive editor doesn't do much in the way of actually editing anything. Instead, they manage the staff that does the actual writing and editing. They join in on newsroom meetings and are in constant contact with managing editors and sections editors. They also must balance the newsroom budget, represent the paper at community functions, and protect the newspaper from lawsuits.

Executive editors usually achieve that status through years of training and experience in different newsroom jobs. An executive editor at a small rural weekly might earn less than a starting reporter at a mid-size daily—maybe a salary in the mid-$30,000s—but an executive editor at a large metro daily could earn hundreds of thousands a year and have many bonuses and perks.

Managing Editor: Controlling the Chaos

Some folks would call the managing editor (ME) post the best job in the newsroom; others, the worst. Answering to the executive editor and sometimes publisher, the ME controls every facet of the newsroom without having the entire weight of ultimate accountability on his or her shoulders. Others say the middle-management aspect of the job stifles that very control by leading the newsroom, but still under the auspices of an executive who might want a different direction. In the end, however, this post is accountable for the entire daily edition.

The managing editor is the hub of the newsroom. Each section and line editor reports to the ME and will do so several times in a day. The ME runs most of the newsroom meetings and makes or signs off on most of the decisions that journalists face daily.

Among some of those decisions are ...

♦ What story will lead the paper?

♦ Does this photo show too much blood?

♦ Is it too early to write a feature on Christmas?

♦ Is this column in poor taste?

♦ What is the best way to handle this lead?

♦ Should we go after the mayor for using tax dollars to fund his campaign?

♦ Can you meet with the governor or police chief about a complaint?

♦ Should we break this story on the website or wait until the print edition comes out?

> **Breaking News**
>
> Hundreds of decisions are made every day in the newsroom, and most are made or approved by the managing editor.

The ME's office is often busier than an air-traffic control tower!

At a small daily or weekly, nearly every single decision is run across the managing editor's desk. At larger papers, editors below him or her make some of the decisions.

Managing editors, like executives, have worked a plethora of jobs in a newsroom and have been trained to lead. Generally, they can earn very small salaries at small weeklies—$30,000 a year or less—to more than $100,000 in larger newsrooms, along with bonuses and perks.

def•i•ni•tion

An **ombudsman** serves as a go-between for the newspaper and community without being part of the news staff, and handles complaints or other suggestions from readers.

Managing editors are like *ombudsmen* (in other words, representatives) at many newspapers, too—answering complaints, explaining processes, dissecting why a story was written the way it was … and, occasionally, an ME will write an editorial or even a story.

A managing editor must have a solid understanding of every job in a newsroom—design, writing, and photography—along with good management skills. Also, they are often involved in doing payroll, hiring personnel, and reviewing employees

Assistant Managing Editors: On the Front Lines

Assistant managing editors and metro or city editors manage the reporters and often the artists beneath the managing editor. These frontline editors work with reporters and photographers, decide what stories and art to run, edit the copy, and coordinate placement of the stories on a page or section. These are the editors who are closest to the reporters, and many a city editor will write an occasional news story as well. City editors also are in charge of *budgeting*, or ordering, the newspaper for the week and often for the weekends.

The salaries for these positions vary widely. At very small dailies, these positions might come in just above reporter salaries—in the mid- to upper 20s—but can reach into the 60s or even 70s at larger metro dailies.

def•i•ni•tion

Budgeting stories doesn't have anything to do with finances. Instead, it involves making a list of the day's or weekend's stories and ranking them based on their value for that edition.

The daily news budget begins days before the edition. Reporters often will list the stories that they will be working on for the week. Those story ideas are usually written in paragraph form with a date and time element, a proposed length and deadline, and an indication of whether art is being considered for the piece. In its finished form, the item is appropriately called a budgetline. A budget is made up of all the budgetlines for the day.

Example of a Budgetline

SHOOTING: A man was injured in a drive-by shooting Tuesday night in front of a diner downtown. Police said the victim is expected to be released from the hospital on Wednesday with only a minor wound. No suspects.

REPORTER: Doe

ART: Map of the area; photo of police working the scene

DEADLINE TO EDITOR: 4 P.M.

LENGTH: 500 words

The city or metro editors compile the budgetlines into one daily budget and update them throughout the day before presenting the main budget to the other editors in a budget meeting, which sometimes occurs more than once a day.

The city and metro editors who work during the day are called dayside editors. Those who work at night are nightside editors. The nightside editors begin compiling the next day's budget before they sign off for the night.

Many newsrooms also employ news or *wire* editors to coordinate wire service news from around the world. During budget meetings, wire editors compile their own budget consisting of wire stories. They choose those stories based on each story's importance and the paper's readership.

Larger newspapers might even employ more specific wire editors, such as a national or international editors.

def•i•ni•tion

The **wire,** short for wire service, is a group that collects news reports for newspapers and distributes it electronically. Examples include The Associated Press and Reuters.

Reporters: A Newsroom's Bread and Butter

The folks who actually produce the majority of the stories you read in the newspaper are the reporters—trained journalists who write everything from local government stories to recaps of last night's game to features on food, health, or entertainment.

There are various types of reporters in a newsroom, working many different beats. A beat is an area that a reporter works specifically, such as town government or business. Beats include:

- Government
- Environment
- Cops and courts
- Military
- Education
- Community
- General Assignment
- Health
- Business
- Transportation

- Weather
- Lifestyles
- Food
- Fashion
- Entertainment
- Fine Arts
- Sports
- Recreation
- Medical

Reporters can write anywhere from one, two—even three—stories a day at a small daily newspaper down to one or two stories a week or fewer at major metro papers.

To become a reporter, a Bachelor's degree in journalism is standard fare, along with an internship or two to get real-life experience before trying for a pro job. Salaries range wildly, depending on the size of the paper and the experience of the reporter, but in general, a small daily may pay $20,000 to $30,000 to start, while a large metro daily will be more than double, and possibly, triple that.

Clerical jobs also keep a newsroom running. They include receptionists, newsroom librarians, researchers, records reporters (births, obits, police and fire records, etc.) and typesetters. All of these jobs can be good starting places for getting into news-paper journalism.

Copy Editors: Last Line of Defense

We'll talk about the role of the copy editor in detail in Chapter 4, but for now you should know that this position is the last line of defense. Simply put, when the reporter has turned in a story, made any changes the editors have suggested, and that story is ready to be put on the page, the copy editor is the last person to check it.

In most newsrooms, copy editors are the real word weenies. If there's a comma out of place, a fact that seems suspect, or a sentence that reads awkwardly, the copy editor is going to send it back to an editor for clarification. Only after a copy editor signs off on a story is it ready for print.

In recent years, the role of copy editor has been extended into designing the pages, writing the headlines and cutlines—or photo captions—and even posting the stories onto the website.

Extra! Extra!

The role of a copy editor has been transformed since newsrooms have started using design programs to lay out pages. Now, editing copy might be just a portion of the job, while building pages has become a significant part.

It's a tough gig, having to be an expert editor and designer—but it's also one that's in very high demand at newspapers around the country. Copy editors often are putting together newspapers right up until deadline. At most papers, that could be midnight or later. That means copy editors are working a late-night shift, if they are working in news or sports departments. Other departments, such as features or business, have earlier deadlines, and the copy editors adjust to meet those deadlines.

It's also a great field to get started in if you want to become a more senior editor someday.

Generally, copy editors have a Bachelor's degree in journalism or English, and can earn anywhere from $20,000 at a small daily to nearly $100,000 at a large metro.

Photographers and Graphic Designers: Newsroom Artists

Last but not least, several artists are involved in putting together a newspaper. The artists who are critical in this genre are the photographers, the ones who take the pictures. The people who coordinate a staff of photographers are called photo chiefs.

Make no mistake, the folks who shoot pictures may be artsy types, but they are highly trained journalists as well—often having obtained degrees in journalism and photojournalism.

Photographers work very closely with reporters and editors, too. A common question in the newsroom is, "How can we best illustrate this story?" It takes good conversation and thinking outside the box to come up with that answer.

Photographers generally have a Bachelor's degree in photojournalism, but real-world experience is acceptable, too. A photographer's salary can range from the $20,000s to $75,000 a year or more at large papers.

More and more newspapers are employing graphic artists or entire graphics departments to work in the newsroom. When a story needs to be illustrated to help the reader through it or to attract more attention to it, the graphic artist enters.

Say you have a story about the recent turnip crop. It's a bumper-crop year, and the reporter shows that in the past 10 years, turnip production has never been higher. Well, instead of bogging down the story to show the increase in both whole numbers and percentages, a graphic can be used to break out that information. It might show 10 years of turnip production and the increase drawn like a fever chart or a linear graphic. A creative artist might incorporate some sort of sketch or icon into the graphic, such as numbers falling off a turnip truck …

Graphic artists help readers make sense of important statistical and numerical data that might otherwise clutter a story.

Generally, graphic artists are trained in their fields, typically earning degrees in art disciplines as well as journalism. A starting salary at a small daily would be in the $20,000s, while a metro daily could pay as much as $75,000 a year.

Section Interjection

Most newspapers contain multiple sections. Typically, they are lettered in order, A, B, C, and so on. Each section usually has its own title, but some are shared. For instance, just about every major daily U.S. newspaper has news as its A section. After all, it is a newspaper. The next section, the B section, generally has either more regional news in larger markets, or it can go right into sports. Generally, a sports section is followed by features, or lifestyles, which could also contain games, comics, TV listings, and calendars.

> **Breaking News**
>
> What we now call the features, or lifestyles, department evolved from the days when newspapers had a society page full of gossip. These were usually written by and for women. We've come a long way, baby.

Not all newspapers are organized as such. Some have complete business sections with stocks, while others have business news following the regular news or sports.

In general, a newspaper's various sections are managed as follows:

◆ The news section is overseen by a host of editors, from the executive editor right down to the assistant city or metro editors. There may be more than one news section with individual wire editors for each, such as international desk, national desk or state desk, as well as editors for specific pages such as education, cops and courts or military desks.

◆ The opinion or editorial pages are generally found in the news section and are managed by the editorial page editor. He or she might fly solo or have a staff of writers and assistant editors. Features of the editorial pages include the main opinion piece(s), letters to the editor, outside columns, op-ed commentary, and editorial cartoons.

◆ The sports section is run by the sports editor, who oversees assistants, reporters, and sometimes page designers and copy editors. Like the news section, stories are budgeted, plans for coverage of games are made, and stories are written and edited. While the managing editor oversees the entire section, what ends up on the sports pages is driven by those in the sports department.

◆ The business section has its own staff of business editors and reporters that cover business-related news and industry trend stories. This section contains stock market information and listings.

◆ The features department is also an auto-nomous group, like the sports section, led by a features—sometimes called a lifestyles—editor. Typical features sections include content on food, arts and entertainment, and health but can be as niche as military, automotive, society, or religion. Often, these sections include TV listings, comics, puzzles, and *syndicated* advice columns and horoscopes.

def•i•ni•tion

A **syndicated** item in a newspaper is an editorial piece that is written by one person and sold individually or packaged with others for publishing in other newspapers.

Finding Your Niche

So far I've told you all about daily newspapers. But there are many other kinds of newspapers that reach all sorts of readers. These are specialized, or niche, publications. They range from all sports all the time, such as *The Sporting News*, to alternative weeklies such as *Creative Loafing*, to pro-military papers such as *Stars & Stripes*, to pure tabloid sensationalism like the *National Enquirer*.

Not All Tabloids Are Created Equal

Let's break it down. There are more types of newspapers than you can shake a stick at. Consider the *New York Daily News*. It's a *tabloid*-sized newspaper; that is, it's half the size of a big—broadsheet—newspaper, folded in half and printed on its side. Some people equate tabloids with *sensational* papers such as the *National Enquirer*, but some tabloids are highly respected, such as the *Christian Science Monitor*.

def•i•ni•tion ───────────────────────────────

There's more to **tabloids,** or **tabs** for short, than alien abductions. The tab is just a format—half the size of a regular broadsheet newspaper—and can be as journalistically solid as *The New York Times* or as sensational as the *National Enquirer*.

Sensationalism is a term used to describe exaggerated or modified news. "Aliens Abduct Elvis" is an example of a sensational headline, but so is "Woman Makes Sign of Cross Before Leaping to Her Death." Although the latter incident probably happened, it's presented in an overly dramatic fashion.

Why the smaller format, then? Well, in most cases it's cheaper to produce, not to mention much easier to hold in your hands while on the subway. You see, many tabs are called commuter papers. Folks grab a bagel and a "cuppa joe" along with the newspaper and get on the train or grab a cab ride to work in the morning. It's much easier to read a tab-sized paper than a big broadsheet. No bumping knuckles with the guy sitting next to you, for one thing, and no pages falling out of the middle. They're much easier to fold, too.

Not that the size of the paper is what dictates where you might want to work someday, but be aware that not all tabs are sensational and not all sensational papers are tabs ....

Local A&E Tabs

Do you feel more compelled to write about arts and entertainment? Take a stroll down any city's main street, stop by the newspaper racks, and you'll probably find at least one arts and entertainment (A&E) publication. Many of them even dabble in politics and social issues and have an edgier take on the news. They may tackle important local and national issues like homelessness, sexually transmitted diseases, unfair taxes, corporate greed, and other local controversy. Many of these publications don't have paid subscriptions and are free at the newsstands. They make their money from advertising. Think about it: their circulations are enormous because they're free and available in scores of newsstands, racks, stores, restaurants, and clubs. And the audience is enormous—usually young readers with a voracious appetite for interesting and informative stories.

On the very fringe of A&E publications is *The Onion.* A parody on newspapers, *The Onion* is published weekly online and in print and claims a print circulation of nearly 600,000.

The spoofs on mainstream news know no boundaries, from President Bush to the Playboy Playmate of the month, recent headlines read "Conspiracy Theorists Insist Barbaro Still Alive" and "Hillary Clinton Tries to Woo Voters by Rescinding Candidacy."

All Sports, All the Time

Also a hit with younger readers are niche sports publications. *The Sporting News* has created an empire out of baseball, football, hockey, and basketball. Weekly sporting publications are scooped up by thousands of readers who want expanded box scores, stats, scouting reports, and more interviews than mainstream daily sports sections can offer. Fantasy-leaguers have even further boosted interest in *The Sporting News.*

The Biz News

The same goes for business publications. Many urban areas employ top journalists to cover just business, cutting through business lingo and creating editorial catered solely to the business reader. Again, it's more information than could be squeezed into a six-page business section in the metro daily.

Examples of business-oriented publications begin with the granddaddy of them all, *The Wall Street Journal*, published in New York. But smaller niche journals exist in most major metro areas, such as the *Baltimore Business Journal*, the *Tampa Bay Business Journal*, the *Minneapolis/St. Paul Business Journal*, and the *Los Angeles Business Journal*.

Neighborhood Weeklies

Perhaps one of the strongest and oldest niche mediums is the weekly or neighborhood newspaper. Sustained by cheaper ad prices and inexpensive classifieds, these papers

Extra! Extra!

Small neighborhood weeklies are a good place to get your feet wet in journalism, whether as an entry-level employee, contributor, or intern. They're always looking for content, so don't hesitate to contact them about article ideas.

focus on news that is relevant to small towns, bedroom communities, or specific geographic areas not often covered by the mainstream newspapers.

Most weekly newspapers don't compete with dailies—it's hard to scoop a seven-day-a-week machine when you publish once a week. But that's not the modus operandi of a weekly. Weeklies fill in where the dailies leave off. They can spend the week writing more in-depth, almost magazine-length, stories without having to worry about the tick of the daily deadlines.

The Least You Need to Know

- Despite naysayers, newspapers have a strong future.

- There are a wide variety of positions in a newsroom for many different personalities.

- Newspapers cater to the masses, so it's important that their sections are diverse.

- Niche publications have a stronghold in the print journalism world.

Read All About It

In This Chapter

- Understanding the boundaries
- Playing fairly
- Knowing the reader
- Owning up to mistakes

Who do we write for, how do we write, and where do we draw the line between our own opinions and the opinions of our readers?

Putting the news into our readers' hands isn't as easy as pecking away on a keyboard and sending the edition to press; hundreds of decisions are made in communicating information effectively, ethically, and interestingly. Reporting fairly, accurately, and timely and doing so in a compelling and honest way are goals journalists strive for. And keeping the reader at the forefront with every editorial decision made is essential to success.

"That story you have on the front page is nothing but a blatant plug for your advertisers!"

Too many times, newspaper editors receive this very complaint. Rest assured, no reputable newspaper would publish stories to promote business for an advertiser. But it's one of the most common misconceptions and criticisms. For instance, consider the following scenario:

A story appears on page 1A about how the real estate market in a southern coastal town seems to be immune to the home sales slowdown that the rest of the country is experiencing, and it quotes a variety of sources—including a local Realtor. That Realtor's competition calls with the aforementioned complaint. What he or she is really saying is, "Why didn't you call me?" Instead, the allegation comes out that the quoted Realtor must have paid to be in the story.

It's just silly, but it happens.

Complete volumes are written on the ethics of the dynamics between news versus advertising, because—let's face it—there would be no newspaper if no ads were sold. That quarter or half-dollar that you plink into a newspaper box for *The Daily Bugle* doesn't pay for the coffee editors gulp in the morning news huddle, let alone for the staff salaries and production costs. The ads make the newspaper profitable. On the other hand, there would be no readers if there were no news in a paper, and no one's going to advertise if there's no audience.

Other typical complaints are about the liberal or conservative slant of a story or of an entire newspaper. In this chapter, we'll look at the ethics of news reporting and what happens when lines are blurred or crossed.

Buying Into the Argument

News cannot cater to *advertising* just as advertising cannot cater to news. That is, if a newspaper is on shaky financial footing, its ad people can't strike a deal with the editors: "If you run a positive story about Big Roy's Used Cars this week, he'll buy a full-page ad and that will keep us from going in the red this month."

def•i•ni•tion

An **advertisement**, or ad, is a paid spot in the newspaper that says whatever an advertiser wants, within reason. It is not a news story, nor can it resemble a news story to dupe the reader.

Many readers believe that newspapers work this way. Has it been done in some form, perhaps less blatantly? Probably. Should it? Definitely not.

Why? Ethics, for one. We'll talk a bit more about this topic in Chapter 5, but for now look at it this way:

A guy walks into a bar where you're sitting and having a drink after attending a particularly interesting town council meeting. He taps you on the shoulder and says, "So, what happened with the vote to increase our taxes?"

You begin to tell him all about it. But while you're telling the story, you look up to see a growing number of folks standing around listening. The subject drifts a little bit to the county council meeting the night before and how they discussed the tax and its outcome, too. You were there, so you talk about that to give the story you're telling some context.

You're a smart cookie, so you also highlight the last three tax increases the town has seen, tell the folks how much money they've contributed with those increases, how much the city has collected in total, and how much more it will collect over the next year with the new tax. With a good degree of authority, you tell the crowd what the town has spent the money on, but you don't give your opinion. You let them decide.

"The town has spent all the money on raises for themselves," you say. "None of the tax collections have gone anywhere else." Now you've got them good and angry. Some make comments, and you say, "Well, the mayor, for one, said that the town sees residual benefits from having a higher-paid staff. The council can attract a higher-caliber candidate with more knowledge who needs more money to govern, so we would have wiser and more prudent decision-making."

What you've just done is told an accurate story—unbiased and fair. You've outlined the action of the meeting and the impetus for it; you told both sides of why the tax was passed; and you did it without using your opinion. This is what a good reporter does every day.

Your colleagues, as a result, nickname you *Scoop.*

def•i•ni•tion

The term **scoop** means getting the exclusive story and breaking it before anyone else does. The term comes from an Evelyn Waugh novel by the same name about the rush of reporters to an area for a story.

Setting Your Journalistic Jaw

Now imagine that the town is a major advertiser. Often, governments are. Come again? That's right. Ever notice the *Legals* sections in the classifieds? They generate a lot of money for local papers. Also, governments run regular spots that advertise meeting notices.

def•i•ni•tion

> **Legals** are paid ads from a government body or publicly funded organization and must be published, according to law, in a large-circulation publication, such as a newspaper. Usually, legals contain information on meeting schedules, court cases, or government findings, such as water quality reports.

So what happens if the mayor calls the reporter and says, "If you run that story about how we've been taxing the heck out of people, we'll pull all of our advertising from your newspaper and give it to your competition, you so and so …!"

Hopefully, your ethics stick. You tell him to pound dirt. Once you sell out to just one person, no one's going to plink a quarter into the news box to read your story. You're no longer a credible source of balanced, fair news, and your career is shot.

Scoop is dead.

Live to Fight Another Day

Early in my career, I was an overconfident and arrogant reporter. I got into the reporting field to be a hard news reporter, to uncover dirt, to help the common folk, and to scoop the big guys. In my overzealousness to prove myself, I acted on a tip without first running it by my editor.

Turns out the sanitation department in town was having a storage problem at the sewage plant. And because it had nowhere to store the sludge it was collecting at a frantic pace, dump trucks were commissioned to store the sludge on a hill in the outskirts of town.

Problem was, at the base of the hill was a mobile home park, complete with wells that served as the community's drinking water. One resident called and wondered what those trucks were dumping and why it smelled so bad. He also said it was raining and that stuff was coming down the hill and percolating into his neighborhood's wells.

A couple weeks on the job and I thought I was going to win the Pulitzer.

So I interviewed several residents, town officials, and the health department (which, by the way, began launching an immediate investigation). Later, sitting at my desk typing up my notes into story form, I heard the slamming of doors, the pounding of fists on desks, and loud voices behind the closed door of my editor's office. I thought, "Hooray for me!" Boy, was I wrong.

When the slamming, pounding, and yelling had ceased, a very red-faced mayor and sanitation director marched out of the editor's office, scowling at me as they stormed past my desk. It scared me—I was green as grass—but the adrenaline was surging through my journalism-or-die veins. That is, until my editor screamed for me.

"Passante!"

Turns out this small newspaper's main advertiser was the town. Those legals were our bread and butter. I wouldn't have a paycheck if it weren't for that account. That was a journalistic battle that I couldn't win. The ball was in a higher court. The story wouldn't run, and within a few weeks I had resigned and taken a job at a bigger paper—the sting of disillusion still sharp.

Being the publisher of a newspaper is a tough racket with tough decisions, but it was clear to me early on that some newspapers would allow themselves to be bullied by advertisers. And while the majority of American newspapers have rock-solid ethics, some papers' ethics, unfortunately, can be bought and sold.

Putting It in Writing

So what does it take to report, write, and edit a good, well-balanced story? For the answer, let's turn to my grandma. My grandma knows that I am a managing editor of a daily newspaper. But when I bring home a stack of newspapers to show her the work I've done, she always says, "Well, I don't see your name in the newspaper." I take that to mean, "… so you must not be working too hard." When I try to explain what a managing editor does, her eyes glaze over. So I tell her, I'm like Lou Grant on *The Mary Tyler Moore Show*.

In other words, I'm the haggard-looking, crusty, loudmouth, call-a-shovel-a-spade editor who sits around yelling at young reporters from his glass office in the middle of the newsroom. In part, that's very similar.

Most folks don't really understand how a newsroom works or how a newspaper is put together. It's surely not just Lou Grant-like yelling and directing reporters; it's putting the reader at the forefront so that he or she can easily absorb a story and learn, feel, or react to it.

So what does this information have to do with my grandma? Everything. My grandma doesn't give a hoot whether I have a new reporter on staff who doesn't quite have the journalistic tools to craft a story about why her street is flooded after every hard summer storm. She wants answers. That's why she plinks her quarter in the box.

She also doesn't care whether two of my sports reporters are out with the flu on Friday night. She wants the write-up of how many touchdowns her great-grandson scored at the high school football game. And a photographer who misspells her neighbor's name in a photo caption should be keelhauled. Doesn't matter whether the neighbor wrote it down wrong.

In our quest to be relevant, comprehensive, accurate, compelling and timely, we also have to be in tune with the reader. Some of the best and biggest newspapers in the country ask this question of each story every single day: "What does the story mean to the reader?"

Breaking News

The cost of newspapers varies widely, but readers still get a good bang for their buck. Many weekday newspapers cost about 50 cents, with a good deal of them even charging a quarter. Some in major metro areas charge upward of $1.50, which helps offset publishing costs.

You can cover a county council meeting about a new road that will be built through a mostly rural community and discuss where the road will be put, what the speed limit will be, when the project will be completed, how much it will cost, how it will be paid for, and why it's being built—but if you haven't knocked on a few doors of the nearby residents to show how the road will affect them, you've not kept the reader in mind. One of those readers who will have a new road tearing up their petunia gardens could be—you guessed it—your grandma.

Step Away from the Soapbox

But writing for the reader doesn't mean dictating to them what their reactions should be. Remember, the key to being accountable and fair is telling all sides of the story and letting the readers make up their own minds.

"I think most people in the [newspaper] business see themselves as both conduits of information and advocates for the common man," says Jeff Kidd, sports editor at the *Island Packet* newspaper on Hilton Head Island in South Carolina. "I believe strongly in the former, because reliable and ordered information is a key to making a democratic, capitalist society work as it should … I think our profession suffers when it over-reaches to be the latter—at some point, we begin writing and reporting in clichés and rigging outcomes to please a perceived target audience (an audience to which we usually don't belong, I would add)."

Breaking News

For newspapers to be reputable, they must be consistent in their reporting, opinions, and even their design.

Staying true to the reader means consistently focusing on the reader in every story we write. But that doesn't mean we write to merely satisfy his or her opinions. If a newspaper is published in a GOP-heavy community, it doesn't mean that paper publishes stories that are pro-Republican merely to assuage those specific readers. Being consistent and fair means telling the truth and not catering to one side or another.

Kidd adds, "I believe journalists are at their best when they are advocates for the truth, not a particular demographic or social strata, and when they are not compelled to draw conclusions for readers. Objective and dispassionate dispensation of the news will always be relevant in free societies. Strictly speaking, this might be an unobtainable standard—but the integrity and health of the business depends upon the earnest attempt to meet this standard."

Journalism isn't all just stating the facts. Sure, we need to give readers information and provide them with the stuff that puts order in their world, makes it relevant, keeps them aware of what new taxes are coming down the pike and keeps them from driving through a new stoplight downtown or forgetting to change their voter registration when political districts are redrawn.

But there's much more. The stories themselves must be interesting, compelling, and make us feel good.

Howard Weaver, the vice president of news for the McClatchy Co., has often expounded on the merits of storytelling.

Like the story of the guy on the barstool earlier in this chapter, Weaver relates storytelling back to our most primal roots. He often speaks of our early ancestors sitting around a fire discussing the news of the day.

He's right. A hunter who comes back from a weekend jaunt over the mountains is going to share what he saw. He came from a place where most people don't venture, and he's seen things that most haven't or won't ever see. He tells his story, and those surrounding him listen and learn.

But if he has nothing interesting to say—no attack from a saber-toothed tiger, no news of vast fires that have destroyed the land, no conversation with a foreign tribe—chances are, folks will walk away. And if he can't get through his story without losing track and drifting off, fabricating, or bragging, chances are his neighbors will be turned off.

Although reporting is a very large part of journalism, writing is, too. There are methods and techniques that reporters can learn to make a dry subject more interesting. But there are also decisions about what stories to run, how long they should be, and where to run them. We'll talk about those tools in Chapter 3 as well as throughout this book.

Giving Your Two Cents

As humans, we are capable of an array of emotions. It's sometimes difficult for reporters to detach themselves from what they cover. However, good newspapers have no

def•i•ni•tion

Bias is the leaning or slanting of a story based on one's opinions, convictions, or feelings.

room for *bias*. Even seemingly innocent causes for emotion—such as the home team winning a championship game—should be handled with caution.

Fortunately, there is a place for sharing our opinions, and that place is the opinion page. Sometimes called an editorial or op-ed page, an opinion page is exactly what it sounds like: a place for opinion pieces. This page usually includes an editorial piece written by the newspaper, political cartoons, letters to the editor, and syndicated editorial columns.

Letters to the Editor

If you recall our fictitious mayor from earlier in this chapter, you'll remember that ol' Scoop quoted him as defending the new tax that the city would levy on its residents. But the mayor might have wanted to say more. News stories, being fair and balanced, aren't the venue for one individual to spout off in a lengthy diatribe. So where does one go? Not everyone with something to say is going to buy an ad, and they shouldn't have to. Most newspapers have a letters to the editor policy that allows the general public to state their opinion without money exchanging hands or fear of an editor making them look stupid in a retort.

Each newspaper has its own policy about how, when, and where to run these letters. For instance, letters might run in the newspaper in the order that they were received; be subject to editing for accuracy, conciseness, tone, grammar, and spelling; and be limited to one letter from an individual per month. They must be signed, too.

Editorials

Newspapers also employ editorial writers and editors. They are a bit more distanced from day-to-day newsroom operation. They don't usually attend news meetings and aren't involved in assigning stories. That's because newspapers want to avoid having the opinion editors dictating news coverage.

How do newspapers decide what editorials to write? In general, the paper's editorial board meets to hash out which issues affecting the readership need to get the newspaper's two cents.

But why do it? Well, while a news story is balanced, an editorial can tell a bit more of the story. For instance, a reporter can write in a news story that a school board member abstained from a vote and note that it was his third abstention in as many meetings. The reporter asks the school board member why he has abstained during the last three votes. The school board member can respond with whatever *spin* he wants to put on his answer.

def•i•ni•tion

Spin is a slant you put on a story or a comment to control reaction or deflect criticism.

In a news story, the newspaper has to report the member's explanation. And even though the reporter might not agree with the explanation, he or she can't say so in the story itself. However, in an editorial, a writer can flat out call the school board member a chicken for not voting or mention that this particular school board member doesn't vote because he doesn't understand the issues.

The editorial writer can spout off on all sorts of items: whether a certain candidate should get your vote, why it's important to ban smoking in restaurants, that a new tax is just another tactic to stuff the city council's pockets with more money … you get the idea.

And when the mayor's call comes in to say, "That editorial was wrong!" the editorial writer's reply should be the same as literary giant H. L. Menken's, back when he wore the columnist's hat: "Madam, you may be right."

Opinions aren't right or wrong. You might not like them, but in the end, they are simply opinions—and in that sense, they are no different than saying that chocolate ice cream tastes better than vanilla.

Columns

Columns also are opinion pieces, but rather than expressing the view of the newspaper, these commentaries express the view of the particular columnist. Columnists can completely disregard the facts if they so choose. Some political columnists give their two cents on just about anything they see as interesting. There are sports columnists who critique cheerleaders' uniforms. There are gardening columnists who will tell you how to grow a perfectly red tomato. There are even fragrance columnists at large metro newspapers who tell you what stinks.

Because columns are opinion pieces, newspapers must differentiate between news stories and columns—particularly because columns run throughout the newspaper, not just on the opinion pages (and sometimes they even appear on page one).

def•i•ni•tion

A **sidebar** is a story that runs secondary to a main story on a page, often giving a different dimension or perspective.

Occasionally, reporters and editors will write columns, whether they are regular features or just *sidebars* to a story.

A column "sig"—or signature—usually does the trick of distinguishing the column from regular articles. You'll notice advice columnist Abigail Van Buren's picture—what we call a "mug shot"—right there in clear view in the column with her name beneath it, or you might see a sig that's just a title of the column: "Dear Abby." Sometimes you'll see both.

In the end, the goal is to play fair because the livelihood of the newspaper is based soundly on its reputation. When credibility is breached, the reputation is tarnished and the newspaper probably won't be viewed as a fair and credible news source.

Owning Up

All this talk about sticking to the facts doesn't mean that newspapers always get the facts right. And there are a host of reasons why. A reporter misspells the name of a source he had quoted or, heaven forbid, misquotes him. Maybe a story doesn't have enough context to depict a clear picture of a subject, or maybe a fact in an editorial was just plain wrong.

When these things happen, in order for a newspaper to stay credible, the editors have to run corrections. And they have to be placed in a prominent or consistent place in the paper so it doesn't look like they are downplaying or hiding the fact that they erred.

Reporting errors is a serious business. If a newspaper doesn't quickly stand up and admit the mistake, its reputation can be destroyed.

The Least You Need To Know

- ◆ Fair reporting and writing are critical to a newspaper's success.
- ◆ Journalism goes far beyond simply feeding a reader what he or she wants to read.
- ◆ Ethics play a crucial role in good reporting.
- ◆ The opinion page is the appropriate place for expressing one's point of view.

3

Putting Pen to Paper

In This Chapter

- ◆ Leading off
- ◆ Keeping in context
- ◆ Setting the mood
- ◆ The editor-reporter relationship

If you recall, we talked about the importance of knowing your audience in Chapter 2. In addition to this fundamental rule of journalism, there are many other rules that all good journalists live by. In this chapter, we'll fill your journalistic toolbox with all the "write" stuff.

Leading Off

Who? What? When? Where? Why? Answering these five simple questions is the key to any news story, and they are equally as critical to the *lead* of your story. Most journalism professors and editors would argue that the question "How?" should also be included in this almighty opening paragraph. The key to a good lead is not only to answer those questions but also to order the information according to its importance. An added bonus is when the lead is also ordered in a way that makes the story compelling.

def•i•ni•tion

A story's **lead** (which is spelled *lede* in many newsrooms), is the introduction or entry point of the story and traditionally gives the reader a clear, and succinct idea of what the story is about but saves the details for the rest of the story. It is journalese for "lead-in."

Let's say you are covering a city council meeting for your local paper. At the meeting, the city voted to raise taxes by 3 percent next year to pay for four additional police officers to address the rise of crime in the city.

Crime has increased by 45 percent this year, the police chief told the city council, and he blames it on a new bridge that created an easy link between the big city over the river and your small city. As a result, crime has spread.

All good stuff. We might just put that on the front page. So being the well-trained journalist that you are, you go through your inventory of the five W's and "How?"

- ◆ **Who:** The city council

- ◆ **What:** Raised taxes

- ◆ **When:** Tuesday night

- ◆ **Where:** At the city council meeting

- ◆ **Why:** To add more police to fight the increase in crime

- ◆ **How:** By unanimous vote

You begin your lead:

> The city council unanimously voted Tuesday night to raise taxes by 3 percent next year to add more police officers to fight the recent increase in crime.

Not bad, kid. You have all the elements. It reads fairly well, and it's concise and accurate. You send it off to your editor, who asks whether you think that the city council voting unanimously is more important than either the tax hike or that we've seen a 45 percent rise in crime this year. Remember, ordering counts for a strong lead.

You scratch your head, think of what the reader wants to know, and answer, "the tax hike."

The editor nods approvingly. You write:

> A 3 percent tax hike in next year's tax bills will add additional police officers to fight the recent spike in crime, the city council decided unanimously Tuesday night.

Then, you'll go into the specifics—the 45 percent rise in crime and what 3 percent means to an average homeowner.

Let's look at another example. Say you are assigned to cover the big game. You have the score, reported on the highlights, and interviewed the coach. Back in the newsroom, any editor worth his or her salt will grill you: "What happened at the game?"

Extra! Extra!

Stories follow a certain order of importance. Don't save the best for last.

Before writing your lead, try writing it without your notes. This practice will ensure that the most interesting information begins your story.

The editor might actually care who won or what happened, but what he or she really is doing is having you describe the most important aspects of the event and indicate how they should be listed in the story. It's a good drill for journalists of all ages. Even if you don't have a seasoned editor, put aside your notebook or voice recorder and write your lead from memory before putting ink to paper. Then, go back to your notes and see whether you put the most interesting stuff in the lead.

Let's go back to the editor. Here's the typical conversation between the two of you:

Editor: "What happened at the game?"

You: "It was a clinic. The Giants couldn't move the ball at all, and the Eagles threw for 345 yards in the first half."

Editor: "What was the score?"

You: "Fifty-two to nothing."

Editor: "Wow. What did the coach say?"

You: "Not much. He was fired after the game."

All good stuff. Now, heading to your desk, you're looking through your notes and they back up what you told your editor moments ago. You pop open a soda, sit down in your chair, crack your knuckles, and think about the five W's:

- ◆ **Who:** The Giants and Eagles
- ◆ **What:** In a football game
- ◆ **When:** Friday night
- ◆ **Where:** Giants Stadium

- ◆ **Why:** Because they were scheduled to play

- ◆ **How:** One team played very well …

You write …

> The Giants lost badly to the Eagles 52-0 on Friday night at home during a regular-season football game.

It's accurate. But when we talk about putting those five W's into a compelling and well-ordered fashion, we should get something closer to:

> The Giants suffered more than a 52-0 loss to the Eagles Friday under their home lights; their longtime coach was canned after the team's fifth-straight loss.

Others might lead with the coach being fired. They would be equally right. It all depends on your editor's preference and what would be best for your readers. In this case, there may be no wrong way to go.

Another trick to writing a good lead is writing the headline before even attempting the lead. Because a headline, sometimes written as hedline in journalese, sums up the contents of the story in an even more brief and compelling way, it must represent your lead accurately. If your headline and your lead don't match, you've got a problem.

A headline for our example above might be:

> Coach Fired in Giants Rout

It's been said that while the story is a full-course meal, the lead is the appetizer. Keep that in mind before uncapping your pen or powering up the computer. You want to answer all the five W's in a clear, concise, compelling, and well-ordered fashion. Then, later in the story, you can elaborate.

Structuring the Rest of Your Story

When newspapers first hit the scene, they were printed on presses that were ingenious for their day—but by today's standards, those presses were labor intensive and tedious.

Those early presses involved setting type one character at a time. Each letter had to be put into a form, and once an entire page was assembled, it was inked and blotted onto a piece of paper. Imagine going through this process for each letter of each sentence on each page of a newspaper, and you might begin to get a sense of just how grueling and time-consuming publishing was.

Once typewriters came onto the scene, reporters could type their stories and hand them off to
editors who would mark them up. Then, they'd
retype them. Once retyped, the stories would
be pasted onto a page, which would be plated—
burned onto a metal plate—and put onto the
press. If a story was too long, and couldn't fit
into the spot allotted on a page, it had to be cut
quickly, usually from the bottom-up. So it was
important for reporters to write in what's known as a descending order of importance,
the almighty "inverted pyramid" shape, for editors to be able to cut from the bottom.

> **Breaking News**
>
> In the early days of newspapers,
> each letter had to be painstak-
> ingly set by hand onto a press
> before a page could be cranked
> out. Talk about making dead-
> lines!

Inverted Pyramid

The story starts off with a great lead.

Then, a nutgraf (a short summary of the story
and sometimes a little history for context).

Important stuff goes here.

Becomes unimportant here.

Even more unimportant.

Downright dull.

Can be cut now.

Often cut.

Cut.

Why work like this? Well, space constraints, mostly. An editor would get halfway into
your story and decide another story on the page is more interesting and will get more
ink. Yours gets slashed three-quarters of the way down.

In this day of computers and programs designed exclusively for newspaper editing and
writing, the inverted pyramid should have been thrown out with the typewriters. Still,
many young journalists are taught the technique early in their training, and many
retain and use it today. While the inverted pyramid is fine to use, it's a very basic form
of journalism.

Other Important Story Elements

Correct ordering of a news story is important, but equally important are a few key elements of any good story: the nutgraf, transitions, quotes, and the ending.

Nutgraf

The nutgraf (or nutgraph) has a silly-sounding name, but there's nothing nutty about it. The nutgraf is used to place important information near the top of the story, usually in one paragraph, giving a bit of history and other helpful context. It tells the reader the intent of the story and summarizes it by adding context. It generally follows the lead and often is one paragraph, but two are acceptable, too.

> **Breaking News**
>
> *The Wall Street Journal* mandated the use of nutgrafs back in the 1950s, and the esteemed publication still uses them today. Stories generally have one theme or point, usually put into a one- or two-paragraph nutshell summary high up in the story.

Let's take another look at our city council example. The lead summed up the five W's, so now we're ready to delve into our story. But we want the reader to know a few things. In the second graf, we might continue our lead to say that a handful of residents voiced opposition to the increase and said the money should be found elsewhere, and the council debated alternate funding sources for an hour before voting in favor of the tax.

But before we get into discussing the tax and the crime situation with our color and quotes, we need to provide some context, which is the nutgraf:

> Sleepy Hills witnessed a 45 percent jump in crime since the Edgar J. Washington Sr. Bridge, which links Metro City to Sleepy Hills, was opened earlier this year, allowing much quicker access into the city. Police data show that 79 percent of the arrests involved Metro City suspects.

That pretty much sums up the situation. Now we know that there wasn't a whole lot of crime in our beloved Sleepy Hills until the bridge was opened. And we have a little data to support that. We know the impetus for the action, and we get a dose of history in the numbers. Now it's time to add some color to the story.

Quotations

Quotes are a good way to support data or add a splash to a story without having to add the reporter's two cents (which, as we all know, is against our ethics). Our color might go a little something like the following:

> Mayor Joe Fish called the tax a much-needed measure to help the city cope with the increase in crime.

> "Voting for new taxes is never easy, but I see no other way around it," Fish said. "If we want to get a handle on the crime spike, we need to put more cops on the street."

That's more good stuff. Good job on your notes! We actually got an outside opinion—a side of the story—that supports what we had written higher in the story. One note, though. While we want to bolster the point and elaborate with the use of quotes, we never want to repeat information with a quote.

Extra! Extra! _____

Quotes are an easy and instant way to add color to your story.

In other words, we wouldn't want to say:

> Mayor Joe Fish called the tax a much-needed measure to help the city cope with the increase in crime.

Then follow it with a quote that says:

> "The tax is a much-needed measure to help the city cope with the increase in crime," Fish said.

That would be cheap, not to mention a waste of space.

Next in the story, you would want to add more background. You would want to mention how, when, and why the bridge was built and how much of a timesaver it is driving to and from Metro City, and you'd want to address some of the crimes that the police chief has outlined—especially some of the bigger ones that show a change in the city's crime scene. Perhaps you could also talk a bit about how the town has grown over the past decade since the new pickle factory opened its doors, bringing in 1,000 new jobs. Don't forget to use quotes to bolster the claims.

Transitions

Every time you make a new point or mention a new fact, you need to introduce it with a *transition*. You want to avoid bumpy transitions. Following the mayor's quote with another quote on a different topic, for instance, would be a rough transition.

def•i•ni•tion

A **transition** eases the reader from point to point in a story without abrupt changes in information or thought.

Suppose you want to tell the reader about the pickle factory. You don't want to follow the mayor's quote with:

> A new pickle factory brought 1,000 new jobs to Sleepy Hills.

That means nothing because it's out of context. Transition into it with something like the following:

> Sleepy Hills has seen a growth spurt since the Freewill Pickle Company opened a packaging plant just outside of the city last year. Fish said 1,000 new jobs had been created, but Freewill needed to tap into Metro City for workers because Sleepy Hills didn't have a large enough labor pool.

Eventually, you'll want to quote those who had opposed the new taxes and maybe add more facts about the last three tax increases. In your search for that, you might have found a little gem in your notes:

> Sleepy Hill's last tax increase was 10 years ago and was implemented to build a bridge ...

Ending

At some point, you'll want to end the story. Although most would love to just stop writing when the thoughts run out, a good writer will tie in some key points:

> The city council will sign the new tax law on Monday, and it will go into effect January 1.

Or look for a good end quote:

> "With this new measure, Sleepy Hills will finally see liberty and justice for all," the mayor said.

Or bring the story full circle:

> "A search to fill the four police positions will begin immediately," said Lt. Bill McGoo.

Using Alternate Sources

So far, we've covered a meeting, a crime spree, and a football game. As we all know, there's a lot more to reporting than just breaking news. There are news features, profiles, advances, humor pieces, short *"brites,"* enterprises, and more.

But no matter what the story, there is an opportunity to break away from going to the same people—the officials—in every story. Look at it this way: if you're the city hall reporter, the mayor is going to be an integral component of many of your stories. Sure, you'll mix it up with the other city council members, but in outlining your story—a story on crime, for instance—the top folks you're going to interview will probably be those in every other crime story you've written at the paper. By going to secondary sources, not the "usual suspects," you add a new dimension to your story and bring it closer to home for the reader. Journalism may be a discipline with some pretty rigid rules, but there's room for creativity.

def•i•ni•tion

A **brite,** or bright, is a very short, punchy story that stands on its own, usually just a couple of paragraphs long.

Extra! Extra!

When writing even a dull town hall story, look for an alternate source. A community leader, such as a pastor, the head of the local NAACP, or the Chamber of Commerce president adds dimension without sacrificing a valid, trustworthy source.

When I was a young sports reporter in Catskill, New York, prep sports was pretty much the bulk of what I covered. There were four high schools, which meant a whole lot of games to cover for an afternoon daily. My day would start at 6 A.M. with buckets of coffee beside me as I rushed to churn out four stories on high school baseball games before my 10 A.M. deadline.

After a couple of weeks on the job, I realized the only way to get in all the games, stay accurate, and make deadlines was to write at blinding speeds. I created a template for my stories in my head.

I could spew stories out faster than you could spell "Poughkeepsie."

> The _____ beat the _____ X-X ____day afternoon at home/away in Region X high school baseball action.
>
> _____ _____ went X-for-X which included a _____ in the Xth inning to allow the _____s the win.
>
> The _____s move to a record of X-X on the season with the next game _____ at home/on the road.
>
> "Quote from coach."

This wasn't my sort of journalism. I wanted to write about the kid who battled leukemia and came back to earn a college scholarship to UCLA or the coach who had to get a second job to keep the team afloat after budget cuts axed the sports program. Those pieces came and went, but more often than not I was a slave to the deadline grind.

Eventually, you begin figuring out ways to get to better stories or ways to take routine stories down a different path. The more experience you have, the easier it is to spot the not-so-obvious. You begin looking for peripheral sources. Sure, the coach can give you all the stuff to fill in between the quote marks, but it's going to be cliché 9 out of 10 times ("We really gelled as a team," "I'm proud of my guys," "I told the guys, 'Hey, just do the best you can …'"). Obviously, you're going to talk with the pitchers and star batters, but how about the catcher? You might get:

> "Johnny pitched an awesome game tonight. He came up to me in practice before the game and said tonight he was pitching this game for his little sister, who just had her appendix out and is in the hospital. She's been to every single one of his games, so they hooked up a radio in her room so she could listen to the game."

Hey, you never know …

And don't think that you have to limit yourself to a single story about an event. You might want to consider following the breaking story with one that looks at the problem a bit more in-depth. Or if you've been assigned to cover a scheduled event, you might want to preview the event in another story a day or two in advance. For our final tax vote story discussed earlier in this chapter, you could collect the data ahead of time; chat with the sources; maybe even poll the city council members to see how they are going to vote; and beat the streets to talk with business owners who have been robbed, the old lady who has walked her dog at night since she moved here in 1965 and won't anymore for fear of being mugged, or the high schoolers who say that crack is easy to get on the streets. Who knows? Your crime-tax story might have ended up having a different lead:

> Hundreds of residents packed the city council chambers Tuesday night to protest a 3 percent tax increase …

Again, the idea is to arm the reader with the most accurate and balanced information that you can present so that they can make an informed decision or react or not react, depending on the conclusion that they have drawn from your reporting.

The Artist's Palate

There's more to the story than a list of the facts. After all, the thread that connects all journalists, whether they work in sports, features, or hard news, is that they are writers. And while journalism is formulaic in its rules, it isn't stunting in its creativity. Not altogether, anyway. And even the best reporters in some of the most dry news situations—covering White House press conferences, for instance—can find a way to weave good prose.

Just like all of the journalistic techniques mentioned so far, knowing your audience is key to gauging the most appropriate style, color, and tone. For instance, no White House press corps reporter is going to comment on Bush Press Secretary Tony Snow's pinstriped suit or wingtip shoes. Could you imagine?

> White House Press Secretary Tony Snow in a gabardine jacket and tweed trousers said Tuesday that President Bush is meeting with British Prime Minister Tony Blair …

The fashion coverage is simply unnecessary.

Also, the press corps isn't going to lead the story with something anecdotal, to create a certain tone:

> Silence descended on the press corps quarters in the White House like a funeral pall on a snowy Wednesday morning in January. Under the soft green glow of the florescent lights precariously perched above an uncharacteristically sullen group of journalists, Press Secretary Tony Snow said President Bush will meet with British Prime Minister Tony Blair …

Ugh.

What we've just talked about are a few of the techniques—style, color, and tone—which set the mood of a story. Judgment rules here, and it's important for a writer to know how to set the right mood.

Just because the creative-writing tools are in your toolbox doesn't mean you should use them with reckless abandon. But let's take a look at them individually.

Keeping the Newspaper's Tone in Check

When planning a front page for the next day's edition, an editor takes a lot into consideration. Where the story "plays," meaning where it's positioned in the newspaper or on the page, dictates to some degree how the story can be written. The story, too, dictates its position on the page throughout the edition as well, so there's a good deal of thought that goes into this process.

For instance, suppose a reporter breaks a story about a police cover-up where an investigator intentionally threw away critical evidence gathered at the scene because the

suspect paid him off. Man, what a story! The reporter also finds out that this practice has been going on for at least five years. The police chief, the city council, and the state district attorney have confirmed the allegations, and the investigator has been arrested. That's a story that would lead the newspaper.

Police Scandal Rocks City Hall

Wow. Other stories that would make page 1A for the day might be:

U.S. Soldiers Ambushed in Iraq Shootout

Hurricane Peter Bears Down on Keys

Downtown Parking Plan Scrapped

Abuse Victims Gather for Candlelight Vigil

So how do we play, or order, these stories?

The top story, we've established, will be the scandal. We'll run another story—say, the Iraq shootout—right below it, and maybe to soften the blow of all the hard news, something softer: the candlelight vigil. We'll talk at length in Chapter 4 about designing pages, but for now let's go with this lineup.

Writing for Page Position

Now that we've established where the stories will play on the page, the reporters get busy writing. Sue is on the scandal story, and Alvin covers the vigil. Sue's story better not have a flowery lead. It's a hard news story that demands a very serious tone so that readers immediately understand the seriousness of the incident.

> The city's lead investigator has confessed to taking bribes from suspects in exchange for their freedom …

Pretty good stuff.

And on Alvin's computer screen, we see:

> In the flickering glow of the candle that she struggled to steady in her trembling hand, Carol Brown stood among her weeping peers listening to the names of more than 1,000 domestic abuse victims being read over a loudspeaker during an emotional candlelight vigil Tuesday evening.

It's soft, succinct, and paints an emotional picture. It uses color—flickering glow, trembling hand—and style—the cadence of the lead, the length, the action behind the preposition—to set the mood. The tone—sullen, dark—represents what actually happened that night.

> **Breaking News**
>
> By mixing soft and hard news stories on a page, a newspaper satisfies more types of readers.

That story will soften the page. Those words will set the mood for the rest of the story. A rookie mistake would be to write it in a matter-of-fact sense:

> More than 100 people gathered downtown Tuesday for a candlelight vigil to remember domestic abuse victims.

Is it accurate? Sure. But it's too generic. The lead is void of any emotion. It stinks.

Tone can also be set in the verb tense. Most stories in a newspaper will take on the journalistic past tense.

> The mayor told a group of business owners Friday that the city supported installing parking meters downtown.

But if you want to make the reader feel like he or she is part of the story, you would move the tense to present:

Pvt. Jeremy Figgs' stare is locked squarely at the tops of his jet-black combat boots as the Black Hawk chopper dives below the cloud line, but what he's really looking at is a million miles away in his mind.

The verb tense puts you right beside Pvt. Figgs. A good writer is going to make you feel every shake in that helicopter, smell the fumes from the turbine, hear the click of the M-16, and feel the heat of the damp jungle when those combat boots step down on enemy soil.

Again, there's a right time and place for color and flair. The type of story you're covering and it's position in the paper will help you determine whether to play it straight or spice it up.

Nip and Tuck: The Edit

Every writer needs an editor. There are no two ways about it. Besides catching a misspelling or a misused word, even the best writers could use a different perspective on what they write. Some writers don't like the editing process. They might see themselves as artists like Leonardo Da Vinci, who finished a piece and waited for the accolades to come. Had the master artist had an editor, there would be no confusion over whether there were actually 12 apostles in *The Last Supper*.

Editor: "Say, uh, Leo …"

Da Vinci: "Yeah?"

Editor: "Can we clarify who is sitting to the right of Jesus? Looks like a woman."

Da Vinci: "No prob. Back to you."

An editor has to prove his or her mettle from time to time while also giving reporters room to be creative in their reporting. Journalism may be a one-size-fits-many job; however, that one size doesn't fit all. But once an editor has a sense of how each of his or her reporters works, the editing process becomes easier and trust is built. When that respect is given, it has to be earned every day—and that accountability becomes a privilege that no good reporter wants to risk losing.

Extra! Extra!

Even editors need editing. Never let your work go unedited.

Other writers want to be right in their editors' back pockets when being edited. They want instant feedback, and they want to learn by seeing the edits as they are being made.

They tend to gasp at occasional edit marks and wish to negotiate every one of them. That's okay, too. It's a great idea to learn how editors edit and be able to ask questions during the process, rather than simply answering those that the editor had written in the markup.

As we mentioned earlier, editors keep the audience in mind at all times. They must also be attuned to a story's tone, color, and mood as well as its balance and bias.

> **Breaking News**
>
> Every reporter has different editing needs. While the basics may remain similar, some reporters want more hands-off … others more hands-on.

When writing a story, a reporter becomes very close to it and might not always see the bigger picture. I've read sports stories that didn't include the record of the teams who just competed, news stories that didn't have a nutgraf, and features articles that never identified the story's subject. Then, there are the misspellings, disjointed facts, awkward vocabulary, jargon, misplaced modifiers, and libelous reporting (we'll talk about libel in Chapter 5). Editors also look at design (see Chapter 4) and headlines.

As we mentioned earlier, the editing process doesn't begin once the story is turned in; it begins when the idea for the story comes up. It will make an editor's job a heck of a lot easier if the editor's expectations of what the story should accomplish synchs with the reporter's plan. An editor who goes into launch-pad mode when his or her reporter turns in a story that's 180 degrees different from what the editor thought it would be is an editor who didn't communicate with that reporter. It's the editor's fault, unless the reporter truly is a knucklehead.

> **Extra! Extra!**
>
> Reporters aren't always to blame if they come back with a different story than what was planned. The editing process starts before pen is put to paper.

There needs to be a conversation before the story. Think of it as a "contract" between editor and reporter so no one gets blindsided.

That's not to say the story can't change. Suppose a reporter goes out to cover a basketball game in which, during the game, the coach announces his forced retirement because the school stopped funding athletics. If the reporter turns in a story with a headline that says, "Vikings Beat Lions, 67-65," you've got yourself a problem.

Instead, the reporter must communicate with the editor—preferably from cell phone the minute he or she hears the information—so the editor and reporter can plan a new sports story with a different angle.

The Least You Need to Know

♦ The lead of the story sets the stage for what's to come, enticing the reader to read the story.

♦ Readers need a little bit of history and context as they delve into a story; the nut-graf accomplishes this task.

♦ A writer's toolbox includes color, tone, and style to set the mood of the story.

♦ The editing process begins before the story is written.

The Visual Appeal

In This Chapter

- ◆ Learning good design
- ◆ There's more to copy editing than proofing copy
- ◆ Different design elements add zest to pages
- ◆ Fonts make a strong statement

Have you ever taken a look at newspapers from the 1950s? Besides the fact that holding them open took the full breadth of your wingspan, they were design nightmares—with stories thrown onto the pages without any thought put into how the papers looked.

Well, times certainly have changed, and while content is still king in the newspaper business, the design of that content shares the throne.

Intelligent Design

There are many different design elements on any page of a newspaper. The front page is the granddaddy of them all. On this page, you will find a host of different design elements, and as this page is what sells the newspaper, designers like to put their best foot forward here.

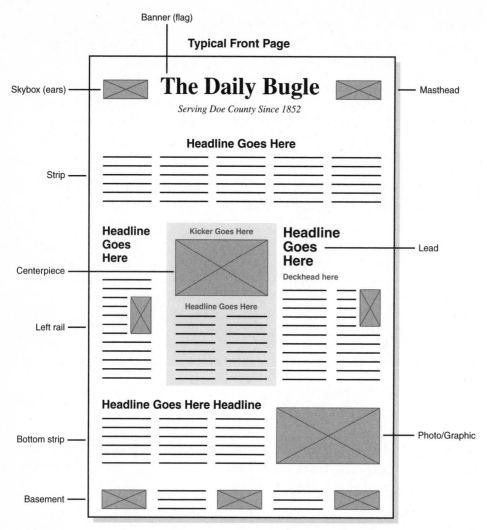

The front page.

Placement of stories, sizes of headlines, and an array of layers—different design items, such as kickers, pull quotes, refers, subheads, and summary boxes—are available to help readers negotiate the page as well as find it visually appealing.

Starting from the top:

- The masthead is the entire box that contains the name of the newspaper and other visual elements atop the front page.

- The banner is the nameplate of the newspaper. Sometimes it's called the flag. It lets readers know what paper they are reading.

- The skyboxes are a clever way of describing the elements that appear beside, above, or below the banner but still in the masthead. Skyboxes on both sides of the banner are called ears.

- Below the masthead begin the stories and art elements (photos or graphics) on the page. If there is a full headline running straight across the top of the paper beneath the masthead, it's called a striphead. The story beneath it is the strip. A story placed here is meant to attract readers at the racks—those mechanical boxes scattered all over town where folks by their papers.

- Beneath the strip in the center is called the centerpiece. This is a story and art package that usually contains softer or enterprising news. It doesn't have to scream at you; the art usually gets your attention.

- On the right side of the page running down a couple of columns and starting above the fold is the traditional lead of the paper. Many studies have shown that this is the place that the human eye goes to first on a page, because we read left to right. This space is usually reserved for the hardest news story of the day.

- Opposite the lead, the left rail is the other story that flanks the centerpiece. This story isn't as prominent as the lead or the strip, or even the centerpiece, but editors want readers to know it's important enough to warrant placement above the fold.

- Below the fold, a term in itself, is home to either a bottom strip story, or just at-fold or below-fold stores.

- The very bottom is appropriately dubbed "the basement." Usually you will find index items, refers, short stories, briefs, or brites in this area. Not all newspapers use the basement, but a good bunch do.

Once upon a time, an editor would choose the stories for the front page based on each story's journalistic weight. Editors still do, but what makes up that weight is more than the story's subject; it's also how the story "plays" off other stories on the page, what it feels like emotionally to readers, and whether the entire story package is visually pleasing.

A breaking or strong story won't be relegated to an inside page because it doesn't have a cool graphic or photo to accompany it, but a photo or some other artistic element accompanying a more marginal story could very well improve its chances of making the front page.

Consider the following headline, which accompanies a breaking news story:

Train Jumps Tracks; 5 Dead

This story demands art: a map of where the incident happened and photos of the scene. But what about the art possibilities for this next story:

Test Scores Plummet in Hoke County

def•i•ni•tion

The **centerpiece** is the story and art package in the center of the page, usually just below the **strip** story or the story that appears just beneath the masthead.

Why not include a graphic that takes a look at test scores over the past five years and compares them to other counties and the state and/or national average. How about adding a photo? Sure. We can take a picture of students studying or playing, although that adds art for art's sake and not a whole lot of journalism. The combination of the elements might get you a *centerpiece* or a *strip* with a photo.

Generally, the article that runs as centerpiece can be hard, breaking news (such as our train derailment or our piece on test scores) or a feature (such as a candlelight vigil or a profile of a mailman who is retiring after 50 years on the job). What you don't want is four or five stories on the front page that are about the mailman. Instead, you want to mix them up.

Back in the dark days of newspaper design, *The New York Times* motto, "All the News That's Fit to Print" was taken quite literally. On my office wall is an old, yellowed front page from a broadsheet paper from the '50s. Among the headlines are, "Fire Destroys Plant," "Worst Fire Seen in City History," "Crew Fought Blaze All Night," "Tomato Prices Up 11 Percent," and "100 Girls Attend Homemaker's Meeting."

Breaking News

The Wall Street Journal has made it a practice to remain old school in its design. Its columns, black-and-white sketches, and comparatively small headlines are a throwback to early days of newspaper design.

Maybe those stories would have worked in today's newspapers. The fire story was a big story for any era, and maybe an 11 percent hike in tomato prices means something in an agriculture-rich area. And homemakers? Well, that could still be news, albeit in a much different way.

But as for design? Well, none of the fire stories actually touched the other; that is, one ran down two columns on the left with a big photo, the second was tucked into a bottom corner, and the third was in the upper left corner (also with a photo). The tomato price hike story was a single column running down the middle of the page, and the women's forum filled the rest of the page on the right between the fire stories in the corners. It looked as if someone just blindly threw the stories on the page.

Newspaper design today must accommodate readers' shorter attention spans and preferences for stories accompanied by photos and surrounded by pillowy rows of *white space*. Today's newspapers are design-rich. Newspapers spend a lot of money and time on their design. And while changing the look of a newspaper was a sin back in the '50s, today newspaper design is changed every few years and modifications are added as needed.

def•i•ni•tion

White space is the area on a page that has no words or art—no ink—on it. It's white because of the color of the paper on which the publication is printed. In early newspapers, it was taboo to have much white space. Now, it's an important design element to draw attention.

Breaking News

In 2005, the Minneapolis *Star-Tribune* heralded its new design, with fresh approaches to design and elements that were duplicated by newspapers coast to coast. The *Star-Tribune* compiled much research, surveys, and data to best know how to represent itself to the market audience—a process that took two years to achieve! Think redesign is a second thought now? Nope. It's a very big part of the game.

It's a Brave New World

As I pointed out in Chapter 1, the role of copy editors has changed immensely in the past 50 years. There was a day when those on the copy desk would simply proof the stories and pages, looking for typos, bad headlines, abrupt page breaks, and misspellings. These folks were word weenies and took a lot of pride in sending a story that contained bad syntax or grammar back to an editor or reporter. Although they still might relish correcting journalists' bad grammar, today's copy editors not only copy edit articles—they also assemble the stories on the page. That's a practice in the business known as *paginating*.

def•i•ni•tion

Paginating is just fancy lingo for putting pages together—that is putting all of the components onto them and ordering the pages.

And the job got much harder. Now, a copy editor spends his or her time thinking about the story and what it looks like on the page, complete with headlines, decks, photos, graphics, layers, jumps, subheads, and entry points—terms we'll review in a moment—all while on deadline.

It takes nerves of steel to perform this job, because while copy editors are very dynamic, they are also usually the last line of defense on the edition. The night copy desk staff is the last to see the paper before it goes onto the press. However, if a procedure is in place, the errors will be minimal or nonexistent day to day.

Putting It All Together

Earlier, we talked about how in the early days typesetters painstakingly picked out each character to put onto a press. Today, computers do all the work for us.

Templates of what the page will look like have been created, as well as library items—formatted elements that an editor can drag from the library right onto the page, such as a photo box, in order to save time. Everything is digital, including photos, graphics, and illustrations.

How does it all work? Well, just as an editor assigns a story to a reporter, a copy chief and editor discuss how the stories will play and which stories and art elements are needed on the page. Copy editors receive that information and create a page lineup—which is an inventory of all these items in order. Then the copy editor "imports" the stories onto the page. Importing is the electronic way of selecting the stories and putting them into the designed area, or box, on the newspaper page. Once the story is on the page, the copy editor writes a headline—sometimes with a deck, which is a smaller, secondary headline or subhead that further summarizes the story.

If any art accompanies the story, it is added along with a photo caption (often called a cutline), bylines, and photo credits. Other layers—items like a quote from the story (called a pull quote), another entry point or refer (a sentence that refers to a related story inside the edition), and—if needed—a jumpline, which is located at the end of the story and tells the reader it is continued on an inside page. Multiply that process by how many stories are on the front page, and the general body of that page is complete.

All Those Little Extras

But wait—there's more! Those pictures and words above or beside the *masthead* need to be placed. That area of the newspaper is called the skybox.

Lastly, any other *refers*, such as pictures or words that direct to stories inside the paper or stories that will be published at a later date, and item refers, such as what the weather will be like or how the stocks performed yesterday, are included on the page.

def•i•ni•tion

The **masthead** is the area at the top of the front page where the newspaper's name appears. It often includes the publication date, the cost of the edition, **refers**—elements that refer readers to stories inside—and the volume number. The banner, or flag, is the newspaper's name, written in its fancy style.

The copy editor then sends the assembled page to another editor (or editors) to be proofed, and it is returned to the copy editor for any corrections or modifications. When that process is complete, the copy editor says four Hail Marys and sends the page to the press to be printed, then moves on to the next page.

At a small newspaper, a copy editor does it all—he or she might even write stories, take photographs or create graphics. At most papers, however, copy editors paginate pages and proofread stories. At very big newspapers, a copy editor might just be tasked to designing one page or proofreading.

Elements of Style

Like bell-bottom hip-huggers, if you're in this business long enough, some design items from days gone by will become popular again. It wasn't that long ago that color—as in the rainbow kind, not words—became mainstream on presses. Only a few stodgy traditionalists have held out on using full color in their newspapers.

Color

But when color came on the scene, you can bet that just like bell-bottoms in the summer of '69, the rainbow available to us was overused. Newspapers began looking like cereal boxes, with blocks of color beneath text in text boxes, colored symbols serving as bullet points, color photography, colored headlines, and colored graphics. It was color overload.

It didn't take long for designers to realize that in their zest for the new design frontier, they fell off the edge of the design world. So, thankfully, off went the colored bullet points, color bars, red headlines, and orange screens—and we all survived the '80s with only a small part of it caught on tape.

As the pendulum swung back, though, many of the items from the rainbow days stuck. Designers became selective about which they could incorporate and which items would be forever banned.

One forever banned, or so it seemed, was the *color screen*. Many newspapers believed that using a color screen was among the worst offenses a designer could make. Yet, here we are and the screen is making a comeback. (Like bell-bottoms …)

def•i•ni•tion

A **color screen** is a box of color, usually in a gradient—10 percent, for instance—of the color, which is light enough that text may appear over it without it being illegible.

The Charticle

But new items have evolved, too. One of my favorites is the charticle, which is also sometimes referred to as a billboard. These are independent graphics and stories in a tight, visual box. They can be light or serious, can be used in any section, and they are generally easy to put together. They provide a quick-hit look at a subject or give us a strong refer point to an inside story. It's the combination of a chart and an article. Plopping a larger text size over a color screen with a cutout of a photo or a drawing, such as a graphic, can give readers the scoop on a new cancer drug in a space the size of a dollar bill.

Like the color-crazy '80s and the charticle, design tricks of the trade are generally stolen, not invented. Or they may be a culmination of a few different designs. When one paper does something innovative, then other papers soon follow. The Minneapolis *Star-Tribune* was among the first to wheel out the charticle, although many other papers would claim they were the first.

Font

Just as graphics and photographs must have a strong journalistic message, so too must the specific type used for the letters, or *font*.

Imagine a strip headline:

Terrorists Kill 4 in Embassy Bombing

The journalist in you might be thinking of a bold font, maybe in all capital letters—something that says serious.

What we don't want is a skinny or wimpy font. In order to determine what font to use, designers must ask themselves a series of journalistic questions:

- How much weight do we give this story?

- How serious is it?

- How are we playing it?

- Is it a feature or a news story?

- Do we want to soften the blow or give it more impact?

def•i•ni•tion

A **font** is a specific family of printing type where all typefaces have uniform characteristics.

A serif font has hooks and curves, as in this common font called `Courier`. While some fonts are without the curves, called sans serif fonts, such as this font, **Arial**. Notice the difference?

Breaking News

We've all seen newspapers with a headline consisting of a single word in a bold, menacing font and large type size: **WAR!** Such headlines tell readers all they need to know. In newsrooms today, any font that is big—usually too big—is jokingly referred to as "the war font."

Layout

But good design goes far beyond color and fonts—or any other individual design element, for that matter. It's all about balance, good use of white space, practical layout, and easy-to-negotiate jumplines, refers, and other items. And it's a good mix of stories that help accomplish that.

Easy enough, right? Not exactly. Not so long ago, a features page proof hit my desk a couple of hours before deadline. Features pages tend to be bolder in design and run one or two stories very big, unlike a news or sports page that shoehorns a couple more stories onto it.

def•i•ni•tion

An **enterprise story** doesn't necessarily react to an event or action, such as news from a city council meeting. Instead, it explains an idea, trend, or issue, such as the rising homeless population since the steel factory closed.

The features sections are slower reads. They might contain need-to-know information, but it isn't need-to-know-right-now (in other words, "breaking") news.

Features pieces and *enterprise stories* tend to be more leisurely reads. The design must reflect the stories and art elements. A light feature about choosing the right preschool for your child might use a chalkboard-type font, maybe even in color.

But on this particular day, the editor slipped me a feature proof that was very compelling. The story was about how police are undergoing sensitivity training to deal with a growing mentally ill population. While many mentally ill people are not dangers to themselves or others, police can't always tell that.

The graphic illustration that the designer employed for the page was terrible. It looked like a pencil-drawn sketch of a person cowering from a police officer whose baton was drawn in striking position.

My first reaction was Rodney King. The picture seemed to accompany a headline along the lines of, "Dealing with the Mentally Ill." In my mind, the story and its design were disconnected. Was it compelling? Sure. Was it accurate? No.

I discussed the page with the editor and designer, who each conveyed what the page was trying to say. With time slipping away, we couldn't rebuild the page. We could, however, tie a headline in like "Sensitivity Training" to better illustrate the stigma and tie it to how we have to break it.

In the end, we clearly conveyed that message and used a summary head to further clarify and bring the elements together in a unified front. But not without a lot of thought.

The Least You Need to Know

- Good newspaper design is putting the right stories in the right place with the right accompanying elements.

- Today's copy editors are an integral part of the newspaper design, they do much more than proofread stories nowadays.

- Appropriate use of color, font, graphics, and layout are tenets of good design.

- Good design is good journalism.

Chapter 5

It Comes Down to Ethics

In This Chapter

- ◆ Understanding the ethics of print
- ◆ Treatment of sources
- ◆ Information access
- ◆ Responsible reporting

So you're ready to write the great American news story? Not so fast.

First, you need to understand that what you write can—and occasionally, *will*—be held against you in a court of law. It's this threat of legal action that helps keep journalists and newspapers honest.

Fortunately, most journalists subscribe to a higher law: ethics. In this chapter, we'll look at the ethical ties that bind us and some of the legal trouble that can land a good journalist in a bad jail cell.

Ethics for All

Judging by what you read in the paper each morning, you might think that professional *ethics* have gone the way of movable type. What with Wall Street scandals, doctors switching water for chemotherapy, developers

def•i•ni•tion

In general, journalists follow a code of **ethics**—a set of moral principles—to ensure truthfulness, fairness, accuracy, objectivity, and accountability.

building on toxic dump sites, politicians trading votes for cash, and reporters fabricating stories, ethics in any profession can seem like an empty promise and a hard sell.

But the profession of journalism has been hit particularly hard by scandals in the past few years. The situation has gotten so bad that recent polls have shown that the public trusts lawyers more than journalists.

That's scary, because without credibility, news reporters might as well be writing stories about aliens abducting Elvis. Ethics is the very core of our product.

But what's all the fuss about? As we've seen from previous chapters, a journalist's job is to accurately report a balanced and timely story. No big thing, right? And photographers aren't supposed to manipulate or skew photos to fit a story, and designers should make a clear and accurate statement in their layouts.

Why Journalists Get Such a Bad Rap

Former *New York Times* reporter Jayson Blair became a household name when he admitted to lying in and plagiarizing his stories about the war in Iraq in 2003. He duped readers into believing he was reporting on location throughout the United States. He also admitted to stealing other reporters' work and making up quotes and details. Blair's ethical misdeeds served to further erode public trust in journalism.

Blair wasn't the first journalist to make an ethical blunder. Ben Bradlee, the esteemed editor of *The Washington Post* when Woodward and Bernstein broke the Watergate scandal, had a pretty big blemish in his newsroom during his reign. In 1981, his reporter, Janet Cooke, won a Pulitzer Prize for her story on an 8-year-old crack addict named Jimmy. The story was fabricated. The Pulitzer was returned.

And former *New York Times* correspondent and Pulitzer Prize winner Rick Bragg also ran into his own troubles. In 2003, he was suspended for using an intern's reporting without giving credit. He later resigned, but maintained his innocence.

Judgment lapses happen from time to time, and no newspaper is immune. Also in 2003, the *New York Post* was caught in a scandal when freelancer Robin Green was fingered for lifting a *National Enquirer* article about Kathie Lee Gifford. Green was banned from contributing to the *Post*.

Ethical Gray Areas

But ethics in the newsroom isn't always so cut-and-dry. It's not always about whether I should make up a quote or a source to add some zing to a story or lie about an event that never happened; rather, it's often the smaller decisions that get caught in the gray area between black-and-white issues.

Take a situation that editors must unfortunately deal with all too often: a few days before an election, a candidate calls in a tip that his competitor has done something immoral or illegal. It might be a judge who fixes parking tickets, a House member who cheated on his wife, a council member who hasn't paid his taxes ... The details might differ, but each allegation can damage the candidate's reputation so close to the election that he won't be able to recover. Heck, even if it turns out to be false or no conviction is handed down, the truth will probably only come to light after the election.

What's an editor to do?

And what about running a photograph of a soldier killed in battle? It's journalism—the shot depicts a scene in a war. These are tough decisions that editors must make. The conversation of ethics will arise—do we run it on the principle that it's good journalism but risk being called sensational or do we not run it? Each newspaper might handle the situation differently.

For instance, a fair number of reputable newspapers ran photos of people falling from the World Trade Center towers after the September 11, 2001, terrorist attacks. They felt that depicting these scenes showed the true magnitude of what happened on that fateful day. Many other papers refused to use these photos, however—deeming that the people could possibly be identified, which would horrify and hurt the families of those victims.

Right or wrong? This issue is largely debated, and many editors disagree. In all instances, erring on the side of caution—playing it safe—is certainly easier. But is it right?

As you can see, there may be no clear-cut right or wrong answers for these situations; however, it's important that debates and consideration of your paper's code of ethics take place before publishing the edition.

In deciding ethical issues, accuracy, truthfulness, objectivity, sensitivity, fairness and public accountability are the principles that must be accounted for. Journalists should ask the following.

Is the piece of journalism, whether it's a story, photo, or even a cartoon, accurate? A story should be edited with a fine-tooth comb—the words that comprise an allegation, for instance, dissected to ensure each word's meaning is direct as well as each sentence's meaning.

Is the story or photo truthful? The facts must be grounded in truth and triple-checked. If an allegation is made, that allegation must not only be called as much but verified and documented to ensure it is truthful.

Is the story or photo sensitive? Identifying a minor or releasing the address of a person who identified a dangerous suspect must be considered carefully. Running an intense photo must be justified as well. What journalistic value does it portray or is it just for shock-effect?

Is the story fair and balanced? Did we give all sides a chance to respond? Even the timing of the story is critical: Ethically, journalists have a responsibility to disseminate information as quickly as possible. But they also must ensure that the timing of an article or photo gives fair and ample time for a response before a decision, such as a council vote or an election, is made.

Is the story accountable to the public? Journalism should strive to achieve a good purpose for the public. If there is no redeeming value, then journalists aren't doing their jobs. Stories should engage and teach people, help them to understand the issues that affect their lives and even help enrich their lives. Public service stories such as investigating contaminated drinking supplies or finding out whether recalled spinach is still being sold in grocery stores or used in school children's lunches are examples.

> **Breaking News**
>
> As a journalist, what you write may affect countless people. Ask yourself: "Am I potentially harming any innocent people?"

Other ethical points include:

- Identifying sources whenever possible; the public should be able to decide whether that source is reliable. If using an anonymous source, tell the reader why. If there is an agreement between the source providing information for his or her anonymity, let the reader know that.

- Avoid going undercover to get a story unless all other methods have failed and only when the information sought is vital to the public. Explain to the reader why you needed to go undercover.

◆ Be sure all display type—headlines, refers, quotes, summaries, graphics, and photo captions accurately and fairly represent the stories they augment.

◆ Be sure that photos or video don't distort the content. Color-correcting is acceptable, but distorting a photo to enhance a point is not. If a photo is changed, let the reader know so. Call it a photo illustration.

◆ Never reenact or stage an event for a photo.

Still, the level of debate in print journalism is very strong and ethics is among the strongest topics of debate in all of journalism. Pictures and live newsreels of people falling from the World Trade Center towers were much more prevalent on TV news and even more so on Internet portals.

The difference in the type of media often blurs the lines between newspapers and broadcast news.

Sports editor Jeff Kidd says, "What concerns me about the industry at this time is that the public isn't drawing distinctions between the mainstream press and outlets such as the *National Enquirer* or what I would call pulp television. And there are good reasons for this … people who make it up or steal as they go along," he says.

Kidd raises an important point. The mistake of one high-profile journalist could spoil the industry.

"The vast majority of journalists I've encountered take ethics, morals, and professional standards seriously," Kidd adds. "But no matter how big or small their biases, all have been sullied by high-profile reporters (such as Blair), who have operated outside industry law because of the willful disregard of high-profile editors and publishers."

Michael R. Shea, a news reporter at *The Modesto Bee* in California, says a heightened level of consciousness is needed to be aware that every detail matters.

> **Breaking News**
>
> Much has been made about the fictitious reporting of former *New York Times* reporter Jasyon Blair, but Blair wasn't the first reporter to violate his paper's code of ethics. There have been thousands of cases of fiction in journalism that have marred the industry's reputation. And Blair's won't be the last.

"Honesty, integrity, and unbiased reporting are the working maxims for the local reporter. Across the industry, indeed, there's a sliding scale—what flies at the *National Enquirer* wouldn't at *The [New York] Times*. But in most mainstream newsrooms, most people aren't hung up on the black-and-white issues—the Jayson Blairs are rare.

Editors are always around to discuss the gray areas. And in that lies the most important rule: if you don't know, ask."

The industry surely has taken some hits, and if any good came from the Blair debacle, it's that ethics again came to the forefront and a social intolerance for unethical practices was strengthened. Still, it remains to be seen whether journalists will stick to their true guns.

Naming Names

As we mentioned above, being accountable to the public sometimes means making ethically tough decisions. Identifying sources, suspects, and victims are among those decisions.

Identifying Victims

An elderly man is robbed and beaten on a downtown street. Any citizen can get the police report with the victim's name on it. Should the local newspaper protect the victim's privacy? Most would say no, that it's a matter of public record. Newspapers generally print information from police reports anyway.

But what if the victim is a 14-year-old boy or an 18-year-old woman who is sexually assaulted? Most newspapers will protect a victim's identity for special conditions—if there is a possibility for retaliation, if the victim is a minor, or the crime against him or her will hurt his or her reputation or result in added anguish, such as with a rape victim.

There are many victims that newspapers will protect, and many cases are different and must be treated as such. Victims of sexual attacks and any crime involving a minor are among those most protected.

Extra! Extra! _____

Every newspaper should have a code of ethics. If you are not familiar with your newspaper's code, ask your editor for a copy.

Beyond a newsroom's code of ethics, most states have laws that protect victims. Police also have rules and follow those laws in redacting or omitting victims' names from their reports in accordance with that policy or law.

That's not to say a reporter won't get the name from another source .... But, again, if a peripheral source—such as a family member of an assault victim or the foreman of a racially discriminated employee—is used, be sure he or she is reputable and that you tell the reader why you are using that source.

Sometimes withholding the name of the victim isn't enough to protect his or her identity. Earlier in my career, a newspaper carried a story about a young female athlete who claimed that her coach sexually assaulted her. She was a 16-year-old junior on the junior varsity tennis team of a private school in the county. To protect her anonymity, the editors of the paper would not print her name, her age, or the name of the school. Turns out that the girl was the only junior on the academy's tennis team, and only one private school in the county had a junior varsity tennis team. Sometimes you have to be more careful.

Identifying Suspects

Recently, one of my reporters wrote a story about a group of girls who ganged up to beat another girl and then doused the victim with gasoline, threatening to light her on fire by flicking a cigarette lighter. The girls, all 17 years old, were named in the paper as suspects and their addresses were listed, as per the newspaper's policy. The paper didn't disclose the victim's identity, also a policy at the paper. Imagine my surprise when I picked up the phone the next day and heard an angry suspect who asked why I named her and printed her address. I told her it was a matter of public record and that any citizen could have that information by going down to the police station or looking at her jail mug shot online. Besides, it was our policy.

Her beef? The victim's friends now knew where she lived and would retaliate. I told her that she should have thought about that before she tried to light another human being on fire. But did we fuel that fire? Gangs have been known to retaliate.

Public record is public record; anyone can go to the police department, for instance, and ask to see a police report and a suspect's name will be available to them. Some police departments will withhold the name of a juvenile suspect—depending on the crime. The name of a 14-year-old boy who kills his parents will most likely be available, while the fourth-grader who stole an Xbox might not. In each case, reporters should be familiar with their state's Freedom of Information laws and always question when information isn't released.

But when it is available, journalists must decide whether to use that information. Ethically, journalists have an obligation to not withhold information. But when releasing that information endangers someone's safety, a discussion should be held among editors and the reporter whether to use that information. In most cases, a suspect's name will be published.

Identifying Sources

Naming or not naming victims and suspects is different from not naming sources. Perhaps there was no greater protected source than "Deep Throat," the insider who tipped off *Washington Post* reporters Bob Woodward and Carl Bernstein to a clear path of evidence that would bring down the Nixon administration in a scandal the world would forever know as *Watergate*.

def•i•ni•tion

Watergate refers to the scandal in which Nixon White House officials hired 50 agents to perform tasks that would sabotage the Democrats' chances of winning the 1972 presidential election, including stealing files and wiretapping the committee headquarters. The term comes from the name of the Washington, D.C., hotel that housed the Democratic National Committee headquarters.

Only at the time of his death in 2005—more than 30 years after Watergate—would the world discover Deep Throat's true identity. It turned out to be W. Mark Felt, former FBI deputy director.

Although the FBI was actively working the Watergate scandal, *The Post* kept the case in the spotlight—and through its reporting was able to effect change. Had Felt not been assured that he would remain anonymous, he might not have disclosed information and the scandal might not have been uncovered. But using unnamed sources is traveling dangerous territory. It requires readers to put a great deal of trust in the reporter.

Breaking News

Protecting anonymity is, generally, a newsroom-by-newsroom policy, but some states have laws on the books for protecting a source from harm.

Obviously, Felt had much to protect in the high-stakes game of corrupt politics in D.C.—maybe more than just his career. Felt led reporters to the information cache with a series of cryptic tips and brief interviews, and that cache proved to be the evidence that backed up the claims.

But unnamed sources have gone very, and maybe dangerously, mainstream. More than 40 years after Watergate, a study reported in the *Christian Science Monitor* showed that in December 2003, 40 percent of *The New York Times'* A-section stories cited unnamed sources. A line must be drawn, especially after the media scandals and an erosion of public trust in journalism.

Just grab your local newspaper and you will find a front-page story that has the words, "Sources close to …," "Speaking on the condition of anonymity," or the most popular, "A senior official said …" It's gotten to the point that small-town newspapers even allow anonymous sources in noncontroversial stories: "One festivalgoer said this year's event was a disappointment …"

Lazy? Sure. But it also erodes credibility. Readers want names. Forget the old-school excuse that when a reporter gets an unidentified source, it makes him or her an insider. It doesn't; it merely cheapens the report.

But are there cases in which a reporter is justified in using unnamed sources? Absolutely. When that source leads to information that can be obtained and is credible, then we can use the source. Still, careful consideration must be given and every effort made to verify or find alternate sources.

> **Breaking News**
>
> In 2004, "unnamed officials" fed many newspapers the name of a man they said was a suspect in a string of Yosemite National Park killings in California. Many newspapers went with the information without significant verification, if any at all. The suspect was later cleared, but his reputation was ruined.

Reporters often make deals with their sources to maintain their anonymity, and it's a reporter's First Amendment right to protect those sources. Unfortunately, sometimes there are consequences. Many journalists have paid steep fines or spent weeks—even months—in jail for not revealing a source to a judge in a court of law.

Sometimes there's more than a source's job or reputation at risk. Their well-being or safety might be threatened if their identity is revealed. Newspapers must have clear ethics policies and guidelines but also must realize that it's not a one-size-fits-all world.

Let the Sunshine In

By now it must be obvious to you that journalism isn't as clear-cut as a lot of people think. All these rules, ethics, debates …

But the good news is that journalists have a whole lot of laws on their side, including the First Amendment to the *United States Constitution*, which grants U.S. citizens the freedoms of religion, speech, press, and assembly. For journalists, the government cannot censor their work. That, my friend, is a very large ally for a journalist and newspaper when you get a tip that the president is paying agents to break into party headquarters to collect damning evidence. It also means the mayor of your home-town newspaper can't throw you in jail for reporting that he voted on a land deal that directly benefited him.

Many a good journalist has spent a few nights in a jail cell instead of revealing his or her sources. But time and time again, the Bill of Rights has come to our rescue and even made states look harder at what the public and newspapers should and should not be able to report and what information should be available to them.

The so-called *sunshine laws* not only outline what information a journalist may obtain, but create a road map of how governments must operate. Since the federal *Freedom of Information Act (FOIA)* was signed into law in 1966, a stronger relationship between journalists and governments has been forged.

def•i•ni•tion

Sunshine laws generally refer to the Freedom of Information Act of 1966, which outlined what information is available to the public and the press and how government bodies, etc., should disburse it.

The **Freedom of Information Act (FOIA)** ensures public access to government records, with the burden on the government to substantiate what information may be released under nine specific exemptions.

The law has enabled citizens and journalists to obtain information that was previously unavailable. For instance, FOIA enables instant and free access to many police records—a key source of information when reporting about the bank robbery that happened overnight or the arrest record of a certain candidate running for office. The FOIA also mandates that government bodies keep minutes of their meetings, that information on government employee salaries (over a specified amount) be made available to the public, that public meetings must be posted at least 24 hours before they occur, and that nonprofit organizations must release their budgets to the public.

Of course, some states are better at complying with FOIA regulation requests than others, and a newspaper will often find itself dialing up the corporate attorney to step on the necks of public officials who want to close the books on the press. But other states choose to be more progressive.

Your state press association, which is a group of journalists who, together, fight for journalists' rights as well as meet regularly to discuss issues in the local or regional media, will have rules for its respective state's FOIA procedure along with a sample request form.

It was an absolute delight for me working in Florida as the editor of a string of north Tampa weeklies. In fact, it was downright easy. Walking into city hall each day, I would tip my hat to the clerks then head over to a press basket in the mail room that had copies of all the mail that came into the building for officials. Upon my request, copies of correspondence were made. The sunshine laws in Florida are among the best in the nation. Without them, I might not have known so early that a major "big-box store" was negotiating with city officials to build within the town limits. It was no Watergate, but to this small town, it was very relevant.

Other states need several reminders that they cannot pick and choose what information they make available to journalists. More often than not, we're not going to be dealing with sophisticated public information officers or press relations staffs. Instead, it's going to be the part-time clerk behind a desk in a police department who has never heard of the Freedom of Information Act. When the slick, college-educated reporter with a chip on his or her shoulder comes in waving the FOIA book, the clerk clamps down and the story smolders.

Other times, your requests for public information will be denied—even by a town attorney who should know better (and usually does). Your next step is to call your attorney.

Extra! Extra!

On a new beat, it's good to have a conversation with the officials from whom you'll be requesting information. During that conversation, talk about the importance of open government and find out how your requests should be handled. Also, drop off a copy of your state's FOIA guide; your press association usually provides these to members for free.

A tactic that newspapers can use is to write a story that outlines what information the paper is trying to obtain for the public, quote that officials have denied your request, cite the specific passage in the law that shows they are breaking it, include a press lawyer quote (your state press association can help) saying the officials are in the wrong, and publish the story. Sometimes simply letting the officials know your intent expedites the release of the information.

But why resort to bullying? Let's first remember that releasing information is in the public interest. A government agency refusing to disclose the plans for a giant development—say, a waste treatment plant proposed for your neighborhood—will affect the public. But FOIA laws often are barely enforceable, and any good press secretary knows that dragging their feet or outright denying to hand over public information won't land him or her in the state pen.

Worse yet, governments have tried to get judges involved in FOIA requests, preempting a newspaper lawsuit when that request is denied. What that could mean is a precedent that forces newspapers into a very expensive court case each time they request public information. Time and time again, judges have thrown out those cases—but lawyers are still involved, and that costs money.

In most cases, government officials will honor FOIA requests, but that doesn't mean they will do so in a timely manner. FOIA stipulates that a response to a request must be given within 15 days. That doesn't mean you'll get your answer in 15 days; it just means you'll get a note or a call in that time saying, "Yeah, we got your request; we'll get that to you …"

In a week, month, year? The timely release of information is written into the law, but I've waited three months for information before.

It also might not come cheaply. While FOIA stipulates that some information is free—like police reports—other information that must be compiled or gathered from a warehouse on the other side of town costs a clerk time and money, and the newspaper has to pay for that.

The trouble is that if officials really want to stick it to you, they will send the $24-an-hour clerk to retrieve that information, which could take 10 hours of work. At $24 an hour, that request is going to hit $240. The officials also can charge for copying and so on. A request for the salaries of all town officials higher than $50,000 now comes to $300.

Extra! Extra!

Before filing your FOIA request, let the agency you're querying know to expect a formal letter. Always make a copy of the request for your records, and be sure to call the agency to see whether they received it. The clock starts with their acknowledgment.

It's a great stalling technique, and often during a major project or series, the costs can reach into the thousands. If you encounter major obstacles in trying to obtain information, let your readers know how difficult the information was to obtain.

But play fair: if you are asking for an analysis of information that has to be compiled from a decade of cryptic data—how many nonfiction crime books were checked out of the public library from 1990 to 2000—it would be quite reasonable that the request might take a good long while to process, if it was processed at all.

In the end, most reasonable requests will be honored, but it's important to not wave the FOIA around like a baseball bat. Instead, try to achieve a good working relationship with your public officials and use the law as a guide or to formally request large chunks of information.

Of Libel and Lawsuits

What you write can get you into trouble if you're not careful. When newspapers are sued, it's usually for libel, which is the legal term for damage to one's character, reputation, or business. Libel is a false defamation of a person's character with or without a malicious intent. It is the written form of slander, which is spoken.

Walking a Thin Line

Writing a story about a construction company that has done some shoddy construction on city property or an assemblyman who is accused of taking bribes are two decent examples.

In the construction company example, if you don't have documents that prove the construction company is responsible for the shoddy work, then you're walking a tightrope. If the information's true, you're covered; if it's false, get that suit dry-cleaned—you're heading for the courtroom.

Can you report it if you do have documents and other sources to back up your claims? Sure. Can you still get sued? Of course. Can you win in court? That's unknown.

In this case, you're taking a risk. Why? Because when the mayor and two council members, unhappy with work that's being done on the new city hall building, blast the contractor in the paper for being crooked and you quote them in your story, you are broadcasting that this contractor is irresponsible. That's likely to have a negative impact on the contractor's business. Those are real damages, and a judge may offer a handsome reward for the damage of the contractor's reputation and livelihood.

Some judges may look at your notes as evidence supporting your claim, but again, it's a slippery slope. On the other hand, if the contractor was cited and penalized for the work and that information is documented, a decent judge will throw out the case.

The same goes for the assemblyman example. In a case like this, the burden of proof switches over to the newspaper and journalist (he or she will be named) when the assemblyman files a libel suit. Where is your proof that he has accepted bribes?

Or what about the guy arrested downtown last night for breaking and entering? So long as we don't convict him by going beyond the facts and calling him guilty we're alright. But it's an easy mistake.

Police reporting is usually cut-and-dry, but there are pitfalls. Early on in my career, I had to write my share of cops' briefs and did so accurately:

> A Poughkeepsie man was arrested by city police Tuesday for breaking into the corner mart and stealing three cases of Snickers bars, police said. James B. Doe, 29, of 244 Main St., was charged with breaking and entering and robbery, felonies, according to police reports.

Notice I said *arrested*. In the next sentence, I said what the charges were. Then, a copy editor would plop a headline on the story—and it was off to the courts:

> Doe Steals Candy Bars from Corner Mart

Breaking News

Actress Nicole Kidman was awarded a boatload of money from London tabloid *The Sun* in 2003 after the paper printed that she had an affair with actor Jude Law. The article was said to have prompted Law's wife, Sadie Frost, to file for divorce. The claims were unfounded, but Law lost his wife.

Note the difference between my story and the copy editor's headline. The story simply states that he was arrested and charged with stealing candy bars. The headline, however, says that he actually stole the candy bars. He hasn't been convicted yet, but the headline implies that he is guilty. So if those charges are dropped, guess who's coming to see you ...

Whenever you write a story, you must always consider its implications. Will someone lose his or her business, spouse, or inheritance because of what you write?

Sourcing and Attribution

Nine out of ten times, you can eliminate any chance of losing a libel suit by being scrupulous about your facts. An old editor once told me to print out my story after I've written it and circle all the words or passages that could get a newspaper sued, then make sure those statements are accurate, have good sources, and are attributed.

Works like a charm. The discipline will get you thinking about what pitfalls could exist in your story. By consciously searching them out and fixing them properly, you will avoid a potentially costly error.

The Least You Need to Know

- ◆ Without ethics, journalism couldn't exist.

- ◆ Be careful when using unattributed sources.

- ◆ Although journalists have the right to inspect public documents, many are off-limits.

- ◆ Sourcing and attribution are paramount to avoiding libel lawsuits.

Chapter 6

Getting Started in Newspaper Journalism

In This Chapter

- The personality for working in the news
- Learning the ropes
- Getting the skills and experience
- Selling yourself

Landing a job in journalism is a tough gig. Working the job is even tougher. It's a very competitive market, and newspaper openings are generally filled quickly. If you live in Connecticut and the entry-level job you want is in New Mexico, don't expect your prospective employer to foot your round-trip ticket and hotel bill.

Starting wages are comparatively low, the hours are generally long, and the accountability and responsibilities are larger than jobs in just about any other field. And be prepared to move around: having a career in journalism generally means leaving your hometown and moving for promotions or to bigger newspapers.

You Know You're a Newspaper Journalist If ...

Just about every reporter or editor I've worked with exudes a love of the written word, a passion for sharing important information, a pride in judgment, an instinct for knowing when the truth isn't being told, and an obsession with being right all the time. These are great attributes of a journalist. But it takes a lot of hard work, an eye for detail, and a passion for learning the craft to become a solid journalist.

Read! Read! Read!

If you like to read, chances are you'd make a great journalist. Author, veteran reporter, and editor Ken Bell says voracious readers make great writers. "Prospective journalists should begin by reading lots of newspapers, magazines, and books," says Bell, city editor at *The Item* in Sumter, South Carolina. "… I always ask potential reporters who their favorite author is. It doesn't matter who their favorite is; it matters that they *have* a favorite. Avid readers make the best writers."

Reading the stories of good writers is a great way to understand the nuances of the English language, and reading the works of good journalists is a good way of learning how to write. If you're embarking on a government-reporting career, check out how the big writers cover the White House and national politics scene. See how they write with authority and with tight, punchy leads and good context. Their form took years to perfect, and imitating those writers' styles will help craft your form, too.

Most important, however, one of journalists' strongest attributes is the knowledge they have in any given subject. The more you read, the more you learn—simple as that. Reading political journals will give you more knowledge, and that will give you more context when it comes to your own writing and reporting.

Natural Curiosity and "The Hunch"

Curiosity also is a critical characteristic a journalist must possess. And acting on that curiosity is what they do best. Journalists have instincts—a hunch—which causes them to seek out story leads, go after those gut feelings to see where the story takes them, and want to learn everything about what they are going to write about.

That hunch goes a long way. Without it, maybe journalists wouldn't have thought about questioning whether there weren't weapons of mass destruction being stored in Iraq—one impetus for the United States going to war.

Trust your instincts: chances are that if you think something's amok or someone's corrupt, it just might be. Follow up to find the truth. You never know—you could be the next Pulitzer Prize winner!

Wearing Many Hats, and Finding Your Favorite

Newspaper journalists need to know how to do a lot of things, and always be willing to learn. But journalism is a discipline, and the more disciplined you are, the farther you will go.

Some budding journalists want to uncover corruption in business and government; some want to tell dramatic stories about heroic individuals; others want to break down complicated information; and still others simply want to spin a tale. Some want to shoot photos in war zones, while others want to use their illustrative talents in a graphic design job. Some want to control every word that goes onto a page or into a story, while others want to make sure those stories use proper punctuation and grammar. There are all types of jobs in newsrooms for these people, but being good at more than one of these disciplines will greatly enhance your chances of landing the job and sprinting up the chain of command.

One of the greatest mistakes an editor can make is putting a person in a job that isn't suited for them. Sure, they may be a very strong writer, but do they want to cover car accidents and tragic fires? They might be able to shoot strong news photos, but how are they on the sidelines of a football game? They might understand Associated Press (AP) style (more on that in a minute), but can they design a page? Some budding careers have been ended excruciatingly early because the square peg doesn't fit the round hole. "Getting your foot in the door" takes on a different meaning when it goes against your grain, so it's important to know what your capabilities are when you agree to do a job.

> **Extra! Extra!**
>
> Be sure your job is the "right fit" for you. If it doesn't feel natural and is a struggle, you're probably in the wrong position. The more writing practice you can get, the more you will know what your niche is.

What You Need to Learn

So now you know in your heart that newspaper journalism is your calling (or not!). And come hell or high water you're going to be the best darn journalist west of the Hudson River.

Not so fast. There are a few things you should understand first—some harsh realities to be prepared for. If you learn about them now, you'll be better equipped to handle them when the time comes.

Competition Is Fierce

It's very important to be aware that the more selective you are about the position you want in a newsroom when you're just starting out, the more difficult it will be for you to land a job. For instance, most newspapers hire more news reporters than sports reporters, more sports reporters than photographers, and more photographers than graphic artists. So if you want to work at a newspaper that has four photographers on staff, you might be waiting awhile before a position opens. Then, you'll be competing with throngs of candidates for that one job. However, that same paper probably has 15 reporters on staff.

> **Breaking News**
>
> Newspaper journalism is a competitive field. In fact, there are more students in journalism school than there are newspaper jobs.

It's helpful to know how to do different jobs in a newsroom, or at least be familiar with them. Along with reporting and writing, learning how to shoot and process photos, copy edit and design pages, and even create graphic illustrations can only help you.

Studying a collegiate journalism curriculum will introduce you to many of these jobs, and an *internship* will give you practical knowledge in them.

def•i•ni•tion

> An **internship** is generally a hands-on, paid apprenticeship at a job that will teach you the craft and even earn you college credit in doing so.

No Comfort Zone, No Excuse

Reporting takes courage and insight. Too many times I've seen young reporters back away from good stories because they weren't equipped with the knowledge to handle them.

For instance, suppose that you're a first-year reporter at a small daily or a veteran cops reporter at a metro daily. Your assigning editor has asked you to cover a new surgery procedure that has been piloted in the medical center in your newspaper's readership area, but you've never written any medical stories before. Nonetheless, you're the only available body in the newsroom when the story surfaces, so you are assigned the story.

At the hospital while you're interviewing the doctors, they quickly realize that you don't know gout from a gall bladder—and they feel a bit robbed. After all, how do they expect that your reporting will be accurate if they aren't confident that you know what you're writing about? Some large dailies hire journalists with medical degrees or have reporters that specialize in certain fields so that they can write with a good degree of authority. But by and large, your first few newspaper jobs won't qualify you for these specific beats.

Well, don't give up. There's good news. You see, journalists are a bright lot, and this is what we're trained to do—think and learn on our feet. If you rely on your training— getting the important information, asking good follow-up questions, getting contact numbers for a source, using peripheral sources—you'll do fine. And you'll find you will learn more and more about various subjects, it just takes time and the courage to stick with it.

Still, that doesn't give you license to be unprepared. When tackling a story on an unfamiliar subject, look through your paper's archives to see how similar stories were written, what important points were made, and how sensitive issues were handled. Also, study the subject before you hit the streets. It's frustrating for an interviewee to have to explain the very basics to a reporter who should have learned at least a few things before the interview. Talk to your fellow reporters and editors to see how they think the story should be handled. Prepare some interview questions in advance. As business reporter Jason Ryan for *The State* finds, "Don't take your job seriously and you won't excel."

Extra! Extra!

A college minor in a practical subject—education, environment, medicine, urban planning, political science, or a foreign language—could give you the edge when trying to land a job.

Tools for the Trade

There are various reasons people want to go into newspaper journalism, and although you might have the desire, you will need the right tools and understanding to land the job. There are a few paths to landing a job at a newspaper. The most common is to pursue a degree in journalism, either at a four-year college or university or other institution. Another is to learn on the job rather than in a formal college journalism curriculum—much harder to not only do, but much harder to land a job. Also, you can learn the newspaper journalism ropes as you go while leveraging your expertise in another field.

Going to J-School

Becoming a poised and confident pro takes practice and training. That's where a good journalism school (J-school) comes in handy. The programs in J-schools can teach you the ins and outs of the field and provide you with a road map to a practical education and internship program.

Extra! Extra!

There were 463 journalism and mass communication programs around the country that enrolled 204,268 students in Autumn 2003.

Studying journalism, you will learn almost every facet of the field. You will learn the mechanics of writing a solid news and feature story, how to interview different kinds of people, and all about ethics. It is the best path to landing a job in the field.

More important, J-schools provide opportunities for practical training: practice, practice, practice. And when you've mastered the inverted pyramid, you will find yourself interning at a decent newspaper to get hands-on experience working with good editors who will offer you different perspectives than you learned from your professors. They will help you create good work habits and provide you with a strong sense of ethics. They will also arm you with the most important tangibles for your first job: the almighty *clips*.

def•i•ni•tion

Clips are cutouts of your published newspaper stories, art, or page designs. Although they were once physically clipped from the paper, most are now sent electronically or put on a disc.

"To get into a newsroom, you need a sheepskin and a stack of well-wrought clips," says Michael R. Shea, a reporter with *The Modesto Bee* in California. "Editors are more interested in, 'Can she write?' than, 'Where did she go to school?' or, 'What did she study?' Someone interested in science writing shouldn't shy away from getting that biology degree, but to get a science writing job you also need to prove you can carry a line. Having clips of previously published work is the only way to do that. For the person looking to change careers, the same applies. Whether you're 18 or 81, clips are king."

Shea continues, "I collected clips in college and took them to a regional magazine, where I collected clips and took them to a business weekly, where I collected clips and took them to a small daily newspaper. You must have the desire to grind out copy and the confidence to market that copy to bigger and better establishments."

So if clips are king, does it really matter where you go to school? While a stint at the J-school certainly helps, it's not necessary. In fact, I know more than a few journalists who never took a journalism class or don't have a journalism degree. Street smarts matter, and J-school can certainly help put the odds in your favor.

Alternative Routes

I've done a good share of hiring for all newsroom positions throughout the years. For me, the journalism school degree isn't the end-all, be-all. Many editors would agree. Give me a go-getter with a willingness to learn and a good B.S. detector, and I'll teach them how to write a story. It's important to know that there is more than one way into a newsroom, but it's a dog-eat-dog world—and you better be ready to stand up against 100 other candidates if you're going to land that job.

Sports Editor Jeff Kidd agrees:

"… there are few industries that seem to care so little for letters [of recommendation] and so much about real-world experience and earnestness as newspapering," says Kidd. "If you're willing to work hard, move early in your career to pursue opportunity, and endure the obstacles journalism presents to family life, you can move up the ranks fairly quickly."

Some people aren't looking for a full-blown journalism career, but they do want to contribute to the newspaper. Doctors, lawyers, environmentalists, historians, gardeners … these are just a few of the folks whose expertise can be useful to a newspaper and its readership. And generally they are not looking for money—just their article published or their name in print.

If a local veterinarian notices an increase in his office of blue-tick cases in dogs during an especially dry autumn, he might want to add some advice of his own, maybe that wasn't covered in a story. He calls the paper's managing editor and tells him or her about his idea. The ME tells him to write it up and he'll take a look at it. If the ME likes it, he'll negotiate a price or handle it as a free contribution. The piece, if well-written, is beneficial to everyone: the vet who gets published clips, the editor who gets a professional voice in his paper, and, most important, the readers who benefit from the knowledge of the vet.

Whatever route you choose, do so with confidence and proof. Look your prospective editor in the eye and let him know that you'll cover a story tonight—right now, if needed—and that you possess a body of work, as seen through clips.

Expect, too, that if you do land an interview the prospective employer will test you. Tests range from simple oral exams where an editor asks you how you would handle hypothetical situations to weeklong stints working in a newsroom, writing stories, and copy editing. Most tests, however, are written, take an hour or two, and test a range of journalism skills—from writing and reporting to spelling and grammar and facts about the world, such as important dates and people.

Many journalism foundations and organizations found online can help you prepare for these tests, but it's good to bone up on your history, work without a spell-check program, and know as much about AP (Associated Press) style as possible.

Published in a book and online, AP style is the style template that most newspapers have in common. For instance, if newspapers didn't adhere to a standard, the editing wouldn't be consistent, and that's important when you publish wire stories—stories from many other newspapers sent over the wire. If your paper uses the spelling of Al Qaeda to describe the terrorist group and another paper whose story you're publishing beside yours uses Al Qaida, then your paper looks inconstant, and your copy desk spends much time deciding which one works best. The AP Stylebook has thousands of terms and spellings and a solid protocol list of how to handle these inconsistencies.

The Associated Press is the foremost wire service that distributes and collects news from around the world. Therefore, newspapers often adopt its standards. You can bet that a large portion of any test you'll take will have a section on AP style.

Getting Your Foot in the Door

To land that job, or at least be considered, you'll need to put together a resumé package that includes a resumé stacked with education and experience in the field, at least five clips specific to the job you're pursuing, and at least three references who will vouch for your work ethic, skills, and experience.

A Solid Resumé

A good resumé should be clear, accurate, and thoroughly checked for grammar, spelling, and punctuation. Your name and contact information lead off the resumé, followed by a clear objective. This is a one- or two-sentence statement that generally declares what you are interested in applying for. Then list, in bullet form, your relative experience in chronological order followed by your education. If you lack much in experience, you may begin with your education.

And remember: Internships count. List them just as you would a job, but indicate that this was an internship. Follow by listing your accomplishments—awards, scholarships, honors, etc. If you have relevant affiliations, such as being a member in a journalism organization, then list them.

Remember, nothing corny or cute in a resumé. Stick to the facts.

Extra! Extra!

Take extra steps to ensure your resumé, cover letter, and references are perfect. Have your friends or colleagues look them over for spelling and grammar errors, and refer to resumé-writing guides to craft the perfect document.

Clips

Be sure the clips are as recent as possible. While an investigative piece that you did five years ago won all sorts of awards, it was, after all, five years ago. What have you done lately?

What if you don't have any clips? Call your local papers, public relations firms, or any organization that puts out a decent newsletter and ask them if you can contribute or freelance, even if it's unpaid. Chances are, you'll get some clips.

Christopher Zurcher, communications director for the Connecticut Fund for the Environment and former newspaper reporter, sums it up:

"Be willing to offer your skills and ambition to work at a newspaper on spec, or on speculation," he says. "This means the editor might not know anything about you. You might not have any writing samples to give him. But he may be willing to send you out to cover a local spelling bee or a town council meeting he doesn't have a staff reporter on hand to go cover. Since I left the field and went into communications for an environmental nonprofit, former bosses have suggested I write some articles for local newspapers if I want to get back into the field."

If you send your resumé package via e-mail, be sure to attach the clips; don't provide links to them. No editor wants to spend his or her morning surfing websites to find your work. Make it as easy as possible on your prospective employers.

References

References are a tricky thing. Most recent grads won't have experience other than collegiate. An internship really helps. Although many human resources policies don't allow employees to give negative references of former employees for fear of legal retribution, editors generally will discuss the strengths and weaknesses that a former intern possesses.

If you do have experience, have more than one editor in your reference camp. Strength in numbers is a good thing.

Also, if you have favorable performance reviews in hand, send them along, too, as well as any awards, achievements, or even kudos that you've collected inside and outside the newsroom.

Finally, be accessible. Offer every contact number that you have, and diligently check your e-mail. If you don't hear a response within a week, call or send an e-mail letting the editor know that you'd be happy to make the trip down for an interview.

While larger papers do have budgets to fly candidates in for interviews, when the job market is tight, those who are nearby and available with equal qualifications have a clear advantage. If you really want the job, you'd better do what it takes to get it.

Mastering the Interview

Once you land that interview from your great resumé package, don't be a blockhead. Wear appropriate attire (dress up), but don't deep-end it. Business attire isn't hard to figure out. And if you're unsure, ask. I worked at a paper in Florida whose office attire was very casual—golf shirts and khakis. I didn't want to be sweating in a three-piece suit while having lunch downtown, so I asked. The editor said no tie required (in fact, it'd be silly).

If you're going to hedge your bets, though, it's better to overdress than underdress. I'd rather wear a tie and a sport coat than be the only guy at the table without one.

So you look the part and you have the strong resumé package to boot. What now? Well, you'll want to be prepared to answer questions about your strengths and weaknesses, why you chose journalism, and what, exactly, it is that you can contribute to the newspaper. There are several "form" questions that you'll hear from newspaper to newspaper. In the end, though, just be yourself—a very respectful and polite yourself— and you'll do fine.

Most editors want just a few things: to know you're not a blockhead who is going to cause a whole lot of headaches and drama—and that you're someone who has the lights on, can plug in, and go to work without 80 seminar hours first.

Let the editor know that your journalism ethics are rock solid and that you're prepared to work long and hard to be the best reporter in the newsroom. If you're really feeling your oats, ask for a story to do on the spot. Even if an editor doesn't play along, he or she will admire your confidence. But never boast—you'll be a blockhead for certain. Finally, and this is key, find out as much as you can about the newspaper and its coverage area.

When applying for jobs, I make sure that I know the names of the mayors, legislators, county administrators, and school superintendents. I might even try to commit to memory the council and board members. Be sure you know how to pronounce those names, too. Read the stories, especially those on the beat for which you're applying. Nothing wows editors as much as talking about the issues that are on their desk or in their newspaper today. If nothing else, it shows you've made an effort to learn the territory and prepare for the interview. That alone shows a whole lot of respect. Otherwise, I guarantee that one candidate with the same qualifications as you did his homework—and that could be the difference between you standing in the unemployment line while he's on his way to becoming the new star reporter.

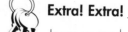

Extra! Extra!

Learn as much about the area and the newspaper as you can before going for your interview. A bit of local knowledge goes a long way with an editor.

The Least You Need to Know

- Knowing your strengths as a journalist is key to your success in a newsroom.

- A degree in journalism is the most direct route to landing a job with a newspaper.

- Internships are important for gaining experience, clips, and references.

- Be sure your resumé package is spotless and tailored to the job for which you're applying.

Part 2

Magazines

Magazines brought us the world of color, style, glossy pictures, and in-depth stories. Covering a spectrum of subjects, magazines give print the ability to reach audiences even more deeply.

In this part, we'll talk about the vast world and reach of magazines, how to write good stories for magazines, and the process of querying a magazine to get published.

Chapter 7

The Entire Spectrum

In This Chapter

- ◆ How magazines bucked the journalism trend
- ◆ The strength of the niche
- ◆ Advertising's stronghold
- ◆ The Life of *Life*

Think magazines are vehicles for soft journalism, or at least not as important as the daily newspaper or the cable TV news network? Think again. Nearing the end of his life, former FBI Deputy Director W. Mark Felt broke a 30-year silence in 2005 when he told *Vanity Fair* magazine—not *The Washington Post*, not CNN—that he was the famous "Deep Throat," the anonymous source who tipped off *The Washington Post's* Bob Woodward and Carl Bernstein to the secret dealings of the Watergate scandal, which led to the resignation of President Richard Nixon.

As the Felt example shows, magazines take on some pretty serious issues, and some of the best journalism—Pulitzer Prize-winning journalism—in the world is found inside their pages.

When folks think of the words *journalism* and *magazines*, they might think *Newsweek*, *Time*, or *Atlantic Monthly*. But *Sports Illustrated*, *Wooden Boat*,

Harper's Bazaar, Rolling Stone—even *Playboy*—have a good deal of journalism going on between their covers.

In this chapter, we'll take a look at how magazines fit into that broad spectrum of journalism.

Proliferation of a Medium

Most magazines have a more polished look than newspapers. Magazines are glossy and have thick covers, color galore, and smart design. They are fresh, have a ton of white space, and get the reader's attention with compelling ads.

The stories are longer pieces—often around 2,000 words—as compared to the 700-word newspaper stories, but they can run much longer and often have color photo spreads. The pieces are less formal and more in-depth. In short, magazines tend to stick around a household for more than the month or week for which they are published.

Extra! Extra!

There are four distinct groups of magazines: literary, consumer, trade, and Internet-only magazines (often nicknamed *zines*).

Generally, a newspaper reader will read an edition front to back in one or two sittings, and once the reader is done it's often a straight path to the recycle bin.

People don't read magazines for breaking news. In-stead, people who read news magazines such as *Time* and *Newsweek* are looking for analysis. Entertainment or lifestyles readers want to hunker down in an easy chair to check out a long feature that will engross them and take them away from the rest of the world for a while. Magazines are made to be comfortable, and we take great comfort in them.

Circulation numbers reflect our love for slick periodicals. Data show that in 1970, 174,504,070 magazines were sold via subscription—with only 70,231,003 in single-copy (newsstand and so on) sales. The total for all sales was 244,735,073. Interestingly though, in 2005, 313,992,423 magazines were sold via subscription—way more than 25 years prior—but single-copy sales were a meager 48,289,137. Still, the total number of magazines sold reached 362,281,559. Folks are buying yearly subscriptions more, which is good for this industry. Rack sales lag, primarily because of greater competition from print, broadcast, and Internet.

Breaking News

In 1970, 244,735,073 magazines were sold. In 2005, that number jumped to 362,281,559.

So it stands to reason that there is a healthy need for magazine journalists. The rub is that magazines rely heavily on contributing writers—those who sell their pieces but aren't on the magazine staff—and a relatively small staff of in-house writers and editors. Just look at the list of staff members in the reader's (or publisher's) box in the first few pages of a magazine. Even large magazines employ editorial staffs much smaller than newspapers.

An Internet scan of a few national job searches, however, shows a steady need for trained journalists—from contributing writers to researchers, editors, and copy editors as well as artists.

Extra! Extra!

Published in 1665, the *Journal des sçavans*, a French humanities journal, is believed to be the earliest example of magazine journalism.

Whatever your niche, finding a good full-time job at a magazine takes some time, just as it might in any medium. Contributing to a magazine is far easier and may be equally lucrative.

Writing for the Ages

So what kinds of magazines are out there? Part 1 of this book tackled newspapers. And boy, are there are a lot of styles of newspapers. But they share a very thick common thread: breaking news. Newspapers are just plain timely. Magazines, while contemporary, operate at their own pace, on their own time.

Certainly, magazines such as *Newsweek* or *Time* work on tight weekly deadlines to bring their readers relevant and current news and enterprise. It won't generally be breaking news, but it will be about a very current subject and generally will be covered in greater detail than in most newspapers. However, a piece on backwoods skiing for an outdoors magazine might be a year old before it makes print. You might write the skiing piece one winter and see it in print the next!

And magazines cover an array of subjects issue to issue. While there is certainly a niche for about 99 percent of all magazines—*Runner's World*, for instance, caters to everyone from the soccer mom who runs three miles four times a week to the marathoner who logs 100 miles in a single race—the types of stories may vary throughout a publication.

Breaking News

Magazines must have a strong niche in order for them to be successful. Even variety magazines, such as *People* and *Us Weekly*, target a certain readership—those interested in entertainment news and gossip.

Runner's World, for example, will offer tips on training for a race, a plan on how to lose weight, stories on overcoming a repetitive use injury, and inspirational pieces on those who have overcome great adversity to run.

The New Yorker has been tremendously successful. The dry, witty, and even snobby magazine has stayed true to its roots through the ages, writing with authority on everything from the war in Iraq to finding the perfect popcorn. Its reporters attack stories with integrity and discipline to produce a great read. Its journalism is lucid, sharp, and authoritative.

Time magazine generally covers the same kind of stories as *The New Yorker* but without the highbrow tone. Instead, *Time* relies on straightforward reporting without a lot of opinion. It, too, is among the most widely read and respected magazines, and its reach is enormous. *Sports Illustrated* has also made its mark by writing with authority, style, and substance. But rather than news or current events, it focuses on sports. Compare its straight-ahead writing style to one of its competitors, *ESPN The Magazine.* The latter is more light, familiar, and written in the youthful vernacular that its audience uses. ESPN has built a cable TV empire with its in-your-face knowledge and tongue-in-cheek humor. ESPN has successfully carried that tone into its magazine.

Generally, a successful writer can be selective in choosing which magazine he or she will write for. Contributors to the big news magazines, for instance, often "shop" around their stories to different magazines until they find a buyer (unless they are regular contributors to a magazine and receive special compensation). Famous folks who can write—let's say, tennis great John McEnroe—will probably have no trouble selling a piece to a tennis magazine. His name carries a lot of weight because he is wildly popular, and a large audience would want to read what he has to say, no matter how he says it.

Ditto for former Fed guru Alan Greenspan, rock guitar legend Pete Townshend, or interior designer Christopher Lowell. They probably won't have a problem getting published, let alone choosing their publication and writing in their own voice.

But John or Jane Doe? You'd bet that if they are writing for an extreme sports magazine, say on skateboarding, they better come equipped with a style, tone, knowledge, and vocabulary that uses skate-world vernacular. Gnarly!

This goes for tech publications, too. Computer programmers probably want to get into the nitty-gritty of computers, platforms, and software. Forget the survey stuff.

One thing is for certain in magazine writing: the stories have to come with a whole lot of authority and expertise. The opposite would be tragic: a 22-year-old bachelor (whose idea of cooking is pressing the Start button on the microwave) writing a 1,500-word article on baking a chocolate soufflé. Now that's a recipe for disaster.

We'll discuss writing style in detail in Chapter 8. But for now remember, what hooks readers on a magazine is the niche—who the magazine is geared toward—then the content.

A kid picks up a videogaming magazine because it has all the latest games and tricks. But if the content falls short, even if the magazine fills the niche, he or she won't buy it again.

Not All Glitz and Gloss

So far, we've limited our discussion to glossy, well-designed magazines targeted at a wide national audience. But certainly, there are many publications that don't fit this mold and yet have strong reputations. And—most importantly for our purposes—they hire journalists.

Magazines that take a more simple, straightforward approach are *trade publications*, how-to newsletters, academic journals, and reviews—niche publications.

def•i•ni•tion

Trade publications are publications that cater to a specific field of employment or industry, such as engineering, farming, nursing, or even journalism.

Take the *Journal of the American Medical Association*, often referred to simply as *JAMA*. Nothing fancy here. In fact, it's downright boring to most folks. The November 22–29, 2006, table of contents lists the following report: "Prevention of Nosocomial Infection in Cardiac Surgery by Decontamination of the Nasopharynx and Oropharynx with Chlorhexidine Gluconate: A Randomized Controlled Trial."

Uhhh …

That's incredibly niche, is it not? Still, the journal is widely known, and not just among doctors. When it publishes breaking medical news, other media outlets quote from the studies or conclusions found.

As far as the journalistic spectrum is concerned, *JAMA* falls way down on the niche end; however, its reporting might be the closest thing to pure journalism as one may find (that is, a complete report on a well-researched subject). Granted, it is the opinion of the authors that makes this type of journalism face a different sort of ethical criteria—a published report of medical findings is a far cry from entertainment reporting in a variety magazine—but the reporting and editing follow along the same general guidelines as all journalists follow.

Speaking of niche, ever peruse the magazine aisle at the grocery store or at a big-box bookseller and see a section devoted to auto magazines? Right there next to the super-slick, pinup girlie mags are a scattering of these comparatively ugly car magazines.

Some car enthusiasts might want to see all the classic or sports cars in glossy photos so that every last piece of chrome trim on the bumper of that '67 Camaro sparkles under the setting Malibu sun. Other publications are strictly nuts and bolts. Their readers want to find out how to torque that bolt to the recommended foot-pound or see a close up of how to tweak that four-barrel. Color? Doesn't matter. Thick, glossy page? No, sir. Printed on newspaper stock and no color inside, this publication is for serious motorheads.

def•i•ni•tion

> **Agate** is condensed information, such as advertisements or box scores, set in extremely small type (approximately 5½ points).

And that's no different from *The Sporting News*. Sure, its cover looks like a magazine, but it's strictly business inside. Its readers are stats hounds and fantasy league enthusiasts. The photos are in black and white. Mostly, it's a sea of gray numbers, *agate*, and short articles. So why is *The Sporting News* an enormous success?

Well, just as *The Wall Street Journal* has for years made its mark by remaining stalwart and "just the facts, ma'am," some periodicals are more about the information than the presentation. The previous examples illustrate that point, and many are often very successful (having been around for years).

Others, on the other hand, don't have the financial backing or ad or subscription revenue to present the publication they really want.

Money Makes the Mag Go Around

The editorial space in a magazine depends on the amount of ads sold and ad revenue. Subscriptions add up to guaranteed money for a magazine. Rack sales—those in the grocery or bookstores, newsstands, and so on—garner more money per magazine sold (because the per issue subscription price is always much lower than the individual copy price). But advertising is what pays the bills.

Ads generally can run from hundreds of dollars to thousands, depending on their size and placement. So a startup or a very niche magazine might not have all that money driving it, and it's either going to be very thin or on paper stock that isn't as high-quality as the publisher might prefer.

That creates a bit of a dilemma, because you won't get the subscriptions, rack sales, or ads without a good-looking product to sell. Your investors better have a large bank-roll or it's curtains!

Extra! Extra!

Magazines make their money from advertisers, paid sub-scriptions, and single-copy sales.

Lessons from *Life*

Here's a good example. Remember *Life* magazine? Its oversized format, comfortable-as-a-well-worn-sweatshirt feel, its apple-pie wholesomeness .... Sure, this magazine (which felt like an old friend) stumbled hard. Why is that, when virtually everyone knows *Life* and enjoys reading it?

Way back in 1936, *Time* magazine publisher Henry Luce knew there was an enormous market for a publication such as *Life*. To be more exact, Luce bought *Life* magazine, which had begun publishing in 1883 as a small, general-interest publication and turned it into a publication that was chock full of photos. The new and improved *Life* was wildly successful as a weekly magazine. At one point, it claimed to have sold more than 13.5 million copies a week!

But in 1972, circulation and advertising losses forced the magazine into a tailspin from which it couldn't recover. That same year, *Life* cut its circulation from 7 million to 5.5 million and ceased being published as a weekly. From 1972 to 1978, it ran 10 *Life Special Reports* that were met with some degree of success—enough so that *Life* started publishing regularly again (this time, as a monthly). *Life* stopped regularly publishing again in 2000. Dan Logan, *Time* chairman and CEO at the time, told PBS that, "*Life* didn't have a core of advertisers that needed to be in *Life* every month."

Life again reinvented itself, being published as a weekly magazine that would run in newspapers as an insert—like *Parade* did—with about 20 pages total. However, in 2007, the plug again was pulled as the publication again was not deemed profitable enough.

Life is a good example of how hard times can fall upon even one of the greatest of magazines. But what about all those startups? There are thousands of titles out there today—niche publications that fight tooth-and-nail for advertisers and subscribers.

Statistics show that half of all startup magazines fail in their first year, and only about 20 percent of them are alive and kicking by their fourth anniversary.

The reasons are many. The more niche the publication, the worse its chances of survival. Remember in-line skating? When was the last time you put on your 'blades? Or the 1980s country-look for home design? That mostly went the way of the dinosaur. Cigars? A fad, mostly. Still, at the time there were dozens of titles to choose from on the magazine rack. Today? It would be tough to find one or two, and they've probably reinvented themselves to stay successful. But there are perhaps dozens of tattoo magazines out there, right?

The Least You Need to Know

- ◆ Magazine subscriptions are still holding steady, but with more competition for readers and advertisers, the struggle to be successful is tougher than ever.

- ◆ Magazines are successful because they cater to a niche audience.

- ◆ Not all wildly successful magazines are glitz and gloss.

- ◆ Constant reinvention is key to keeping a magazine successful.

Chapter 8

The Write Stuff

In This Chapter

- ◆ Knowing your reader
- ◆ Setting the tone
- ◆ Structuring magazine stories
- ◆ Understanding voice of a publication

Ernest Hemingway was known as one of those authors who pored over every single word, studying it to see what better word could be used. Was there one even out there? How did it sound among the other words? Was it too long, too short, too vague? Every lead, transition, passage, and ending should be scrutinized equally as hard for magazine pieces.

Writers can be selfish at times. As artists, they also can be a narcissistic lot. But it's important to note that if you're going to write for a magazine, you're going to write for a wide spectrum of readers—not just yourself. Knowing what to write is half the battle; knowing *how* to write it—how to speak to your audience—is the other half.

In this chapter, we'll discuss how to talk to your audience and how to make your writing gleam.

Know Thy Audience

Magazine editors are busy guys and gals. Deadlines, story development, inch counts, and—good grief—where is the art? The last thing they want to see dumped into their inboxes is a *solicitation* from a writer who has no clue to whom who he or she is writing.

When we pick up a newspaper, we understand that there are only so many inches available for the story and that the reporter might have only had a few hours to assemble the piece. So although we expect the article to be accurate and insightful, we have limited expectations. When we read a magazine, however, we expect more: a longer story, a higher caliber of reporter, and better prose. We expect the magazine article to do what the other media can't—take us deeper into the subject matter and know who we are as readers.

def•i•ni•tion

A **solicitation** is a story and outline or a proposal for a story that you want to sell or contribute to be published in a magazine.

So who is your audience? Well, that's going to depend on what magazine you're writing for and the audience that it targets and attracts.

While many magazines have a strong niche, they want to grab all sorts of readers. Just look at most magazine covers—the range of stories promoted on them is meant to attract a wide variety of readers. For example, consider the December 4, 2006, issue of *Sports Illustrated*. This theme issue titled, "Football America" features a picture of Green Bay Packers quarterback Brett Favre on the cover, accompanied by the words, "For the Love of the Game." Love or hate the Packers, most folks agree this guy's got charisma—and that's a sell. Add to it a controversial year—should the future Hall of Famer have retired or not—and we're guaranteed an interesting read.

Other stories featured on the cover include, "Why Football Rocks" and "Photos From All Fields, Pee Wees to the Pros." Even under the "football-only" theme, the mix ranges from the players to an emotional piece on the excitement of the game to the "every man" photo essay.

Extra! Extra!

Your readers will demand a great degree of authority in your writing, so be sure to write with confidence about your subject.

Another example of strong content listed on a magazine cover is the January 2007 issue of *Runner's World*. The cover features pieces targeting everyone from beginners to experts: "New Year, New You"; "The Most Inspiring Runner Who Ever Lived"; "2007 Marathon Guide"; and tips to lose weight, stay motivated, and "Never Bonk Again." The cover photo shows a super-fit young woman caught mid-stride on a Malibu beach. There are even four other entry points teasers, in case those mentioned didn't do it for you.

The kinds of stories on these covers are meant to grab readers; they are anything but boring. The kind of writing you'll need to do should reflect what's on those covers.

If you wanted to write an article for *Runner's World,* are you seriously going to solicit a piece about running three miles a couple times a week through your suburban town or how you got your second wind running on the beach last summer? That's destined for the trash heap. No, your readers demand some degree of expertise, experience, and authority.

The last thing you want is a good majority of your readers to know more about the subject than you do. So, if you're writing a travel piece for a travel magazine, you'd better come off sounding like a seasoned traveler—having stayed in hostels to five-star hotels sea to shining sea. You will paint a wildly romantic picture of a faraway destination that will transport the reader to the locale. That's what the reader wants.

Capturing the culture, food, history, and essence of a travel destination is something you couldn't do if you didn't actually travel there yourself. But you have to be able to give practical advice, too: where to stay, where to eat, what to see, what to avoid, how to dress, and how to get there. That's what the reader *needs* to know.

So not only do you have to know what type of piece to write for a magazine, but what type of reader you are writing for. It's important, too, that you are knowledgeable in the subject and can write with authority.

Who reads *Berkshire HomeStyle, Vogue, Dr. Dobb's Journal, Playboy,* or *Outside?* That's a pretty diverse bunch. Some readers may read all of these titles each month. Most readers, however, expect their magazines to remain constant with their message and speak directly to them.

> **Extra! Extra!** _____
>
> One way to tell what kind of readers a magazine has is to look at its ads. If the ads are for Rolex, Mercedes, and Gucci, chances are the readers are affluent. If the ads are for Ziploc bags, Special K cereal, and Tide laundry detergent, chances are that the readers are stay-at-home moms.

To know your audience, you must become intimate with that magazine and its readers. Look at typical story length, the type of stories they publish regularly, and their tone, color, and voice. Analyze the entire magazine—its contents and design—from cover to cover.

Breaking It Down

Now that you know who your readers are and what they want to read, you're out of the woods, right? Well, not so fast. Knowing how to write for them is the next battle—and it's a big one, sometimes a 5,000-word one!

Your writing must reflect the tone, color, and point of view of the magazine. Magazine editors work very hard to ensure that their publication has a unified tone from cover to cover—even in their advertising. Just as you're not going to see an article about the five best cigar bars in Manhattan in *Outside* magazine, you're not going to see a cigar ad in it, either. In fact, what you will see are a bunch of ads for outdoor products and healthy ways of living: bikes, SUVs (not Cadillac DeVilles), tents, sports watches, running clothes, hiking boots, and so on. That's a good way to begin understanding what the magazine is all about.

Just as writing a novel is different from writing a short story, magazines have their own style. That style may feel more relaxed, casual, and conversational than a newspaper report, but that doesn't mean there aren't key rules to follow. The first point to remember is that while newspapers are immediate and necessary, magazines are casual and leisurely. Newspaper articles are read now, this morning, and today. By the end or even the middle of the day, they are pretty much left for fish and chips. With magazines, however, folks collect them and pass them along—even reread them like a good novel. So it's important to reflect that mood with your writing.

Because magazines aren't bound by strict time constraints like newspapers are and readers peruse them much more leisurely, a magazine article is going to feel more relaxed.

Breaking News
Average magazine articles range from about 1,000 to 5,000 words.

A newspaper lead goes right to the point of the story: who, what, when, where, and why—all in the first 10 words. The magazine lead might be 6, 7, or 10 paragraphs later. The article might lead with a good quote, a flashback to an event, the start of the day, or the setting of the stage. Whatever the technique, the tone is set before the actual meat and potatoes of the story.

A travel piece on back-country skiing in British Columbia will magically transport you to a pristine place of blue mountains with the scent of pine and the rush of the cold Canadian air stinging your face, where the only sound you hear is the schuss of your skis as you glide through 40 inches of fresh, crystal-white snow.

As a reader—and as a skier—you've been there and long to go back or you've been close and you want to get there. And for the next half-hour, you *are* there through a good writer's words and a good photographer's pictures.

Tips for Good Writing

There are several techniques that will ensure a more successful magazine piece, and they have everything to do with your writing. What voice and verb tense you should use as well as how descriptive you should be are some of the keys. Round it out with good transitions, quotes and a strong ending, and you're on to something.

Extra! Extra!

Magazine writing is less strict than newspaper journalism, but that's not to say it doesn't follow specific guidelines (which are important to know when soliciting a magazine).

Use Active Voice

One sure way to bring the reader with you to that gentle mountain slope—or anywhere else, for that matter—is to write in the *active voice*. Active voice draws the reader into the story, whereas *passive voice* tends to lull readers to sleep.

Write in Present Tense

Keeping verb tenses and attributions in the *present tense* also is key to making the reader feel like he or she is standing right there beside you. For instance, think of a story about a young Marine preparing for his first battle.

> Private Joby Hawkins gently tugs at the bright silver crucifix dangling from a thin chain through his sweat-soaked T-shirt. Closing his eyes, he pulls the cold steel cross to his lips and kisses it as the first bullets ring over his head. He hears nothing; he's deep in prayer. "Our Father …" his voice trembles.

Sure, you can be as descriptive as you want in past or present tense. But it's harder to set the mood—draw the reader in—in the past tense.

Color Your Story with Vivid Descriptions

It's also important to include vivid descriptions in your article—and that's going to take a good deal of reporting, more than most other forms of journalism. Suppose you're writing a story about the economic and social effects that foreign timber companies are having on the Patagonian culture. To be serious about getting the good piece—one that's going to inform and entertain—you'll probably need to be fully immersed in that Patagonian culture for some time. Writers have lived among their subjects, shadowed them, learned foreign languages, and suffered or witnessed first-hand their hardships and joys. It brings to the piece an authoritative and accurate account but also captures the very essence and mood of their subjects.

def•i•ni•tion

Active voice refers to sentence construction in which the subject is the agent of the verb: *The farmer milked the cow.* When the subject is the target of the action, then it becomes **passive voice:** *The cow was milked by the farmer.*

Present tense is the tense or form of a verb expressing action, activity, state, or being in the present time.

Research is essential for a good piece. Not everyone can travel to Patagonia and live among the native ranchers and woodsmen, but maybe we can take a week-long visit to the Wasatch mountain range and bring back that ski story. The more reporting you've done, the easier it will be to write a solid, long piece packed with color and detail.

Organize into Smaller Sections and Use Transitions

Maintain and establish a cadence, a flow that keeps the reader engaged in your story. The mood needs to be consistent, with transitions gently easing the reader between passages. In other words, don't simply ramble on and on about the subject: "… and then this happened, and next this happened, and then this happened …" No, the story must be divided into chunks of information that gently flow together. Just as a good lead draws the reader into the story, the transition moves the story from one passage to the next—piquing the reader's curiosity so they want to read on.

Cap Off with a Good Ending

Finally, make sure that your story ends on an unforgettable note. Consider a sports feature that describes the long, hard comeback of a much-adored Argentinean soccer player who one year ago was lying on his home field with his leg snapped in two after a hard tackle. The piece will show the reader flashbacks to the injury, the progress he's made in rehab, and how his life and love for the game have profoundly changed in that year without soccer. But instead of a "happily ever after" ending, we finish the story with the soccer player praying in the locker room before his first game back.

Coming *full circle* is an easy trick that will leave readers (and editors) with a good feeling. They'll nod their heads in approval and read you again.

Another ending technique is to sum up the piece. This method works especially well for analytical pieces—stories on government, politics, war, crime … tougher subjects that carry a lot of weight and a serious tone.

def•i•ni•tion

Coming **full circle** simply means taking an interesting item or subject from the beginning of the story and bringing that item or character back at the end for closure.

A piece on a three-year conflict in a Third World country might end with the number of war dead as the writer presents a clear picture of the next generation of warriors— the little boys, not quite 10 years old, playing baseball in the sandlot behind the school as bombs go off in the distance.

A third option is ending the story with a strong quote—a few sentences that succinctly sum up the story as well as bring an emotional closure. In a story about a Midwest farmer who's about to face foreclosure of the land that his family has worked for generations, he might take his cowhide gloves off, slap the dust from his sleeves, and say, "I've poured my lifeblood into these fields. I don't know where we'll go now."

The Power of Voice

The New Yorker magazine has built an empire with using an academic voice. The pronoun of choice is the academic "we"—as if *The New Yorker* was an institution. For example: "We believe the film was among the most important of our time …." Sounds stuffy, doesn't it? Relax; it's supposed to.

The stuffiness is simply part of a tone that the magazine wants to establish. It would sound silly in most magazines. Imagine such stuffiness from a dirt bike magazine. It wouldn't work.

If you're writing a how-to piece for an ultra-niche publication—say, a woodworking magazine—the last thing you'll want to do is use the academic voice. That will just spook your readers. If you're instructing them, talk directly to them. Talking conversationally to your reader works wonders because they can identify with you and feel more confident in what they are reading.

Breaking News

Most magazines avoid writing in an academic voice, but a select few demand it.

It's very important to find out how the magazine you are soliciting or writing for handles its voice. The style of the stories in the current edition is a dead giveaway. That's the style you'll want to employ when writing your piece.

Generally, the larger and more successful the publication, the more selective the editors. We'll talk at length in Chapter 10 about obtaining the submission and style guidelines from the publisher, but the best rule for now is to simply grab a copy of your target magazine and emulate its voice.

The Least You Need to Know

- ◆ Be familiar with the magazine you are writing for and its audience.

- ◆ Setting the scene for your reader means a lot of research and experience. Be prepared to spend a long time reporting on a subject before putting pen to paper.

- ◆ Attention to detail means that the tone, voice, and construction of your story must be perfectly balanced and in line with what the magazine editors mandate.

- ◆ Generally, speak conversationally to your readers unless the magazine calls for a different voice.

Chapter 9

Variety of Style

In This Chapter

- ◆ Penning the perfect news piece
- ◆ Crafting compelling feature stories
- ◆ Composing an informative "how-to" article
- ◆ Writing for trade magazines

It can be dizzying trying to find the copy of your favorite magazine at the newsstand—there are literally thousands of glossy covers competing for your attention and money. But just as there are countless magazine titles, there are also many different styles of magazines—and as a journalist, you'll have to decide which style of magazine fits your style of writing. In this chapter, we'll look at what type of magazine suits your writing style and how your writing style can suit the magazine.

Crafting a Magazine News Story

When writing news articles, it's important that your reporting and researching is accurate and extensive. It's best if the subject you're covering is something in which you have some degree of expertise. For instance, if you are an admissions counselor at a private university, you might be able to offer some insight into higher education and what private institutions are looking for in a prospective student. Simply put, you're an expert. That gives you some clout when it comes to soliciting your piece.

That's not all it takes, though. You'll need to prove that the analysis you're writing is timely, relevant to readers' lives, and—let's not forget—interesting.

Extra! Extra! _____

Keep your subject narrow when soliciting a story. Vague stories about general subjects won't interest anybody.

How do you accomplish that? Well, assuming you have a background or experience in the subject, you'll need to narrow the topic. As an admissions expert, you know what qualifications your students will need for admission to your university. You've researched what other private universities require as well, with extensive reporting and interviewing.

Pitching a story on how to get into a private college is a yawner—it's too broad. But one aspect that you've stumbled upon in your research is that most of these universities offer admissions into some programs requiring lower grade-point averages—because the programs aren't very popular and the university is having a hard time filling classes. In short, the programs aren't very competitive. You've also found that a student who doesn't have the grades to get into a mainstream program can enter the less-popular program—and after a year at the school can automatically transfer into the more competitive major.

You've narrowed your topic, and it's the kind of information that might be interesting to readers. Your reporting will back up your writing because you've spent three months interviewing admissions officers and reviewing academic policies. Sounds convincing.

Now, you're putting pen to paper: you'll need to come strong . You have a lot of supporting data, and numbers are good. For example, you note that out of 100 American private universities, 86 percent of them offer easier enrollment into less-popular programs. Instead of a B-plus average, in most some cases, B-minus averages are being allowed. In about a third of the schools, C averages are seriously considered.

Of course, you could spew out numbers all day—and only statisticians are going to give a hoot. Data-driven stories are dark, boggy places where readers often don't want to get stuck. So keep the stats relevant, but don't go overboard.

You're a writer, so don't forget to write well. Outline the piece in an order that's both easy and interesting to read. Your road map—that outline—must be dynamic. It can change depending on the data you collect, so don't be afraid to wander a bit to get to that final destination.

Be sure to build strong transitions, leads, and endings into the template for a solid news story—as we discussed earlier in the book. Keep the tone serious and authoritative. In some cases, the academic voice may be the way to go. Again, remember your audience.

Composing a Feature Story

Magazine *features* are the bread and butter of the magazine industry as well as the type of story most reporters aspire to writing. Why is that? Well, whereas a good hard-news story provides insight into a timely subject, feature writing puts emotion at the forefront. And as we all know, emotions are a powerful thing.

After spending many years writing and editing hard news, I always got a kick out of readers—even editors—who praise and reward feature writers but largely snub the backbone of the newsroom … its news writers. That's not to say their work isn't appreciated; it's just not as noticeable. Let's face it, a story about a new tax bill in Congress just doesn't have the same appeal as a piece on the 16-year-old soccer player who battles through leukemia and chemotherapy to play in the state finals and score the winning goal. Everyone will read that story, and if written halfway decently, the piece will be a smash.

def•i•ni•tion

A **feature**, unlike a news story, doesn't have to be tied to a current event; it can stem from a news event, such as the plight of Iraqi farmers after bombs destroyed their homes and fields. The story isn't about the bombing, but the effects of rebuilding.

Why? Well, writing about bills in Congress reaches a very select group of readers. Ask yourself about the last time you read to the end of a story about a bill—even an important one? And did you recommend it to a friend or even clip or save the article to read again later?

But the entrepreneur who gave up his Wall Street career after September 11, 2001, to dedicate his life to helping victims of tragedy? Yeah, that one's hanging on the fridge.

Feel the Feature

Emotional pieces are the cornerstone of feature writing. But not all feature pieces have to be mushy—they can be about, well, anything under the sun. They simply are a little less fact-intensive, more enterprising, more relaxed, and less formal.

So what makes a good feature story? Whereas in real estate it's all about location, location, location, in feature writing it's all about subject, subject, subject. Readers must feel compelled by, relate to, engage in, or even get lost in the subject. The story needs to speak to the reader's senses, and readers need to feel like the author is talking directly to them.

A good feature writer will find a way to further elevate an already good topic with his or her writing. But it's important not to overwrite the piece.

"You have to be very careful with your tone," says Robyn Passante, features editor of The Island Packet newspaper on Hilton Head Island, S.C. "You need to be very careful to not overwrite it, and a bad feature writer will do that."

"You have to keep stripping away as much emotion as you can," Passante says. "I constantly remind myself what I want the reader to feel ... I don't want to tell the reader what to feel; the reader's going to feel it ... The readers are going to get it. The less you say, the more impact you're going to have. Too much detail is going to take away from the story."

There are a gazillion adjectives out there just waiting to be overused. And just because a thesaurus is available doesn't mean you have to plunder it for more expensive words. A good writer relies on those rhythmic and understandable words to convey a thought. Readers will catch on quickly if you're trying to impress them with language that sends them scurrying to the dictionary every fifth word. And too many adjectives will cloud each sentence.

Not every piece has to feature a kid battling a terminal disease, nor does it have to be about the family pooch that gets lost at the Grand Canyon during a family summer vacation and finds its way back to Erie, Pennsylvania, just in time for Christmas. No, there are many types of feature stories—from humor pieces on the best canned clam chowder, to buying the perfect engagement ring, to a review of an off-off-off-Broadway play. The ingredients remain the same: a casual voice, attention to detail, and a more colorful presentation.

You've chosen a subject that has a good deal of emotional value, and you know you're not going to overwrite it. Now what? It's time to decide on a structure for your feature story.

> **Extra! Extra!**
>
> While creative writing is an important aspect of feature writing, let the story tell itself. If you have a good subject, you won't need to "overwrite."

Structure the Path

Once you know where you're going with your story, figure out the path of how you're going to get there. As with any story, your feature needs a beginning, middle, and an end to give structure to all that style, substance, reporting, and technique.

Think of yourself as the storyteller around the campfire. You're at center stage, and boy, do you have a story to tell. Your voice is clear and strong with all the right intonations. You set the scene, introduce the characters, create the mood, and get into the story. You move from point to point with authority; you speed it up and slow it down in the right places. You end it wisely. They applaud you. It's no different in feature writing, because that's exactly what you're doing: telling a story. If you can remember that you are a storyteller, your writing will be comfortable and casual and your readers will identify with it.

Extra! Extra! _____

Most good writers use some sort of an outline when crafting a story, and many editors demand it.

Create an Outline

Begin by outlining your story on paper: where do you want to take the reader first, second, third, and so on? Where do you want to introduce your characters? What do you hope to accomplish at the end? Set all that up on paper and let it be your road map. Remember, keep in mind what your overall goal is for writing the feature. That will help you map out a good story.

Start with the lead, just as in newspaper reporting, to establish what the story is about, except when you write it, it will likely be much longer and with more color and tone.

Second, establish some history and context to let the reader know what events surround the story. This helps readers become acquainted with the story, previewing what's to come.

Next, go more in-depth with the characters and the subject matter, adding more context, facts and relevant issues. This may be broken into three parts in the main body, such as example 1, 2, and 3.

Finally, conclude your story by tying up loose ends and leaving the reader with closure and satisfaction. To determine what facts and sources to use in your story, diagram where you need to do research and who you might use as sources. In a feature story about students commemorating three of their peers who were killed in a gang fight a year ago, one section of your outline might contain the following notes:

- Talk to the deceased teens' friends, families, and teachers.

- Find experts to talk about gang violence in schools.

- Talk to police and get stats on how common these gangs are.

- Talk to witnesses who were there when the shootings occurred.

- Find out what dreams and aspirations these kids had.

You might not use every person on your list or cover every point in your diagram, but it will help focus your story and keep it on track.

Once you have all the elements in place—all of the reporting and research is done— you can begin writing the story by following your outline and tweaking it as necessary along the way.

Revise, Revise, Revise

Once you write your first draft, it's all about editing and revising. And revising. And revising. Don't be afraid to completely rewrite entire passages or scrap your lead for one that does a better job of drawing in the reader or that encompasses more of what your story is about. Remember, you have a compelling story to tell. Be sure that it moves smoothly between points, which will take a little remolding and reshaping of sections. Your editor probably will help you, whether you want assistance or not. But remember that if you're soliciting a magazine as a contributing writer, then right away you'll need to show that you have a good command of how to write a magazine feature.

Writing a "How-To" Article

Probably the most lenient of all magazine writing genres is the *instructional*, or *how-to*, genre. These articles are just as important as news or features, and an enormous number of magazine titles have blossomed in this category alone.

Think about auto mechanics, decorating, fishing, woodworking—these are common themes among how-to publications. But what about dieting, fitness, scrapbooking, and child care? These topics, too, are just as important to readers—remember it's all about the niche.

Of course, many of these themes also show up in the form of how-to articles in larger-circulation magazines. The how-to format is ripe for use by writers who have specific knowledge and expertise and may want to reach beyond just niche magazines. In instructional writing, be sure that you "test drive" what it is you are writing about.

The how-to writing style is paramount in computer programming and gaming magazines. These subjects continuously change and grow in leaps and bounds, generating a constant need for how-to articles. Millions of readers snap up magazines to learn about new software and hardware, how to add and modify programs, or get that high score in a video or computer game. New technology is sprouting up every year, and magazine publishers are looking for experts to decipher that new technology every day.

def•i•ni•tion

The **instructional**, or **how-to** genre is just that: publications that instruct readers on how to do something, such as building a birdhouse, programming a computer, or writing prose like Truman Capote.

Breaking News

Instructional magazines continue to flourish for do-it-yourselfers and hobbyists. They are a great market for those who have expertise in a subject.

A good how-to piece must command respect. That is, the author had better know what he or she is talking about if the piece is going to sell. Therefore, the articles are often penned by pros in their respective fields. On the other hand, computer programmers might be great at their jobs—but that doesn't necessarily make them writers. And the same is true for experts in any field. Writing skills must accompany the expertise if getting published is a goal.

Don't try to be too cute or clever when writing a how-to piece, though. The goal is to accurately move from point A to point B. Again, outline your piece—which should be easier because you're explaining a process step by step—and follow that order as you clearly and authoritatively detail the subject. Your opinion, however, counts. You're an expert, and folks generally want to know why you would squeeze a lemon onto sliced apples before putting them into a pie (it keeps them from turning too brown). Just don't go into long diatribes about your personal preferences. Try to balance them with a counterpoint—an opposing opinion—from time to time—which will show that you are well-rounded and knowledgeable.

Jack of All Trades

Most writers get their start in trade publications. Why? Because most trade publications are so niche, so narrow, that there isn't a lot of advertising or money. And, well, you might not get paid much at all.

But hey, you'll get into print—and being published builds clout on your step up to the next level of magazines.

What is a trade publication? Well, any trade, such as writing, practicing law, banking, medicine, horse-trading … if there's an occupation, chances are there's a trade journal to represent it. Sometimes there are quite a few.

> **Extra! Extra!**
>
> With thousands of trade magazines to choose from and not a lot of competition to get your pieces published, this genre may be a good start for unpublished writers looking for a break.

How about *Cosmetics and Toiletries* magazine? It's a publication for folks in the cosmetics and fragrance world. *PT World?* It's for physical therapists, of course. And what about *Nebraska Lawyer Magazine?* Yup, you got it. It's for lawyers in the Cornhusker State.

You'll find all sorts of writing in trade publications, but the slant will be, obviously, toward the title of the magazine. If you want to write for *Alpaca World* magazine, for example, the word *alpaca* better come up at least a half-dozen times in your query letter (more on that in Chapter 10).

Most of these trade publications won't be as picky about your background; you might not have to breed alpacas to actually write for an alpaca trade magazine (although it would help). Many journalists freelance in trade publications to pay the bills. A couple hundred bucks for a 2,000-word piece on preparing your alpaca for shearing might not be all that sexy, but it's a start.

The Least You Need to Know

- News stories have their place in magazines as more in-depth and focused pieces.

- Magazine feature writing is more casual and relaxed and should evoke more feeling than news writing.

- Writing instructional and how-to articles takes a great deal of research and expertise in the subject.

- Trade publications are a great way to get a start in magazine writing.

Chapter 10

Getting Started in Magazines

In This Chapter

- Knowing if you're cut out for magazines
- Learning the ropes
- Understanding the costs
- Putting your best foot forward

If you think that getting published in a magazine takes a good amount of skill, just wait until you try to actually get on staff. I won't kid you: it takes a Herculean effort. There are many ways to break into the magazine world, but how you go about doing it could make all the difference.

That is, if you want to write for a big, successful magazine. Working your way up the ladder is generally the standard operating procedure, but it's going to take a lot of climbing to carve out a good living and get noticed. In this chapter, you'll find out whether you have what it takes to be a magazine journalist and what you'll need to know and learn to start your climb.

You Know You're a Magazine Journalist If ...

Many of my newspaper colleagues double as freelancers for magazines or have aspirations of doing so. Some even gravitate toward a full-time career in magazines.

Why? Well, for one, the pace is a bit more relaxed and casual. Unlike newspaper reports, magazine stories are longer—which means there's more room for colorful details, in-depth analysis, and coverage of different perspectives. In short, magazine writing allows you to be more creative. For journalists who want fewer writing constraints—time, length, or style—then magazine writing is where it's at.

Magazine journalists tend to be more free-form writers whose idea of reporting for a story means traveling to faraway places, experiencing interesting cultures, getting behind the scenes, researching, interviewing many people, and going deeper.

So, what does it take to be a good magazine journalist? A penchant for good sentence structure, a desire to not just write a story, but convey the facts in a meaningful and interesting way, and a knack for choosing the exact word for the job.

Extra! Extra!

Generally, magazine articles range from 500 words to 3,500 words—and sometimes beyond.

Good magazine journalists are good storytellers—they want to draw the reader into the story to teach, compel, and enlighten. They may be experts in a single field, such as computer science or cooking, or they may be versed in a variety of different fields. But they are relentless in pursuing the perfect story. And they often enjoy writing long, complex pieces—some even up to 3,500 words!

But it takes time and hard work. Editorial staffs, even at major magazines, are small—so the jobs aren't readily available. Also, despite hundreds of fine magazines to aspire to, a whole lot of other folks have the same idea. When a vacant writer's, editor's, or photographer's post is filled, it stays filled for a long time. Some people get to the magazine where they want to work and hang out for life. So your competition will be tight, and expect that you'll move a half-dozen times to get to where you want to be. Still, who wouldn't want their name atop a super-glossy, five-page spread in the center of *National Geographic* or *Sports Illustrated*?

So if you want to reach that peak, start querying for contributed submissions and trying for positions on editorial staffs at any magazine. Remember, just as in newspapers, experience and clips matter. You can't just say that you want to write for a magazine; you'll need to prove that you actually can write well.

What type of magazine are you after? Breaking in, as we know, is tough—but not impossible. Literary magazines are great places to start, even though the pay stinks. Still, they pack a lot of prestige and allow you to really show your writing style.

While many believe a literary magazine is fiction, there is room for literary criticism and other nonfiction topics. *The New York Review of Books,* for instance, publishes critical pieces written by literary contributors.

Trade journals pay well, but the content is generally pretty dry. If you have expertise in the area that you're writing about; however, it's an opportunity to write with authority—and authoritative pieces make good clips.

Consumer magazines pay the best. And once you get published in a decent magazine, you'll be well on your way.

Oh, and don't discount Internet-exclusive magazines (known as zines). The pay is wildly inconsistent, but hey … a clip's a clip!

What You Need to Learn

So you've decided creativity and the enterprising style of magazines are what you're all about and you want to head in this direction … great! Let's talk now about a few things that will help you on this path.

Education and Clips

Many journalism schools and continuing education programs offer an array of classes about working in magazines—and some even offer entire majors. Taking these types of classes is a sure-fire way to cut your teeth in the biz. You'll gain practical education and will hopefully land an internship at a magazine where you'll get hands-on experience—and that means clips!

Creative writing classes mixed with standard journalism, copy editing, and even design classes will help round out your education. Expect to spend your semesters reading an array of essays and magazine stories—probably even subscribing to a few—and writing, writing, writing.

Writing short features and news stories will be much like writing for newspapers. You'll need strong leads, solid nutgrafs, smooth transitions, and solid endings.

Reading great writers is critical to learning how to write, and emulating the techniques that good writers use will help you go far. So, in addition to lots of writing, be sure that you also read, read, read!

If you choose not to go the journalism school route, you'll probably have to contribute more pieces than you might want. While it never hurts to query giant magazines for your stories, chances are that getting those almighty clips is the ticket to getting your foot in the door.

As we've learned, journalism is formulaic. That is, readers expect how an article should feel, what it should communicate, and what they will learn by reading it.

Most new writers get their start by writing the short pieces, even some of the compilation pieces (or brights), in the magazine. So you'll need to practice that style of writing.

The writing must be crisp, punchy, accurate, and compelling. Your sentences shouldn't be overly wordy, and your lead will be right there at the top where it belongs in short pieces. Sure, the writing should be clever (never cute), and you'll enjoy a bit of freedom in choosing your adjectives and adverbs to color the story—but in general, you won't have room to overwrite. So, get to the point.

Longer pieces take even more discipline than writing shorter ones. The tendency is to empty your notebook when given the green light to write a 5,000-word feature piece, but that's not how you should do it.

An old professor of mine used to mockingly say, "I didn't have time to write it tight." Perhaps no truer words were spoken. A disciplined writer is not lazy, doesn't write simply to hear his or her own voice, and understands that too much information can actually be a bad thing.

Find a good magazine, and identify a long piece in it. It can be on any subject—news, features, sports, analysis, whatever suits you. The headline or summary surely will tell you about the story you're about to embark on, but notice that reading the first few paragraphs may not do much more than set the tone or the mood of the story—maybe just introduce some characters or subjects. The lead will then gently draw in the readers and get them acquainted with the atmosphere and cadence of the story—the "feel" of the piece. Then, you'll come to that peg or nutgraf that tells you what you're reading and in what context.

Extra! Extra!

Be prepared to rewrite a piece several times until it's deemed perfect by you and your editor.

The writing flows and takes the reader right inside the story, and a good writer holds his or her audience with that subject. Readers simply won't want to put the piece down. Writing strong leads—ones that grip the reader—takes a whole lot of practice and rewrites.

Know Who You Are

There are all different types of writers out there, and it takes a good deal of time to develop your own voice. Fortunately, magazine editors will allow the writer to keep that voice—but remember from earlier in this section that magazines themselves have their own voice.

So, if you're a stuffy, intellectual-type writer, you're probably not going to be incredibly successful writing for a NASCAR publication. Your writing style must fit your audience, plain and simple. Developing your voice is great; knowing when to ratchet it up or tone it down is priceless in writing for an array of magazines.

The Price of Clips

Many magazines accept unpaid contributions. State-funded recreation, tourism promotion, and environmental conservation publications seem to always be looking for submissions. Their budgets are super-low to nil, but they're not always so fussy about their authors. They need to fill up a monthly or quarterly magazine, and you need clips. It's a symbiotic relationship.

Once you have a few of those clips, you might move on to trade or instructional publications. Some of these magazines pay rather well—a few-hundred dollars for a single medium-sized piece—especially trade publications for large industries such as oil, nuclear power, automotive, and agriculture, and the clips will add to your resume.

Once you get that big story queued up in your mind, you can then query the big magazine, let them know who you are and what you've written, and who knows? Maybe you'll score a writing contract!

> **Extra! Extra!**
>
> Generally, your first published piece might garner a few hundred bucks—if you're lucky. Some magazines don't pay at all, but remember that clips are priceless.

Tools for the Trade

Are you planning to make a living from selling magazine pieces? Well, don't sign that beach house lease just yet. While a good piece in a major publication could potentially garner you thousands of dollars, the flow of pay isn't always so dependable—especially when you're just starting out.

Going Solo

Remember, magazines generally pay their writers based on their circulation. The larger the circulation, the more they can pay. For trade publications, you might earn $500 for a 1,500-word piece—for instance, in a Florida citrus producers or hotel management industry magazine. As for niche publications such as computer programming, gaming, or woodworking, the pay also depends on the circulation of the magazine—but you can probably make your car payment with a check for a published magazine piece.

Remember, too, that if you are contributing pieces, you generally get paid when the pieces are published—and in some cases that can take some time. In other words, you might write a piece on spring fly fishing in the French Broad River in Asheville, North Carolina. But as you're experiencing the abundance of mayflies skittering about from the river's edge, by the time you've queried, written, and sold the piece, it could be late summer or even early fall! That means the piece probably won't publish until the following spring. If that's the case, then don't count on that check for your Christmas presents … it won't arrive until April!

The idea, however, is to keep a good flow of stories going and solicit magazines—a variety of them—in order to guarantee that a few pieces will be published and to keep a steady flow of income. Also, if your goal is to join the staff of a magazine, you'd better be contributing strong stories regularly.

Extra! Extra! _____

Most magazines' pay scales are listed in *Writer's Market*, found in the periodical section of your local library.

Most magazines' pay ranges for contributed pieces are listed in *Writer's Market* in the periodical section of your local library. This guide will give you an indication of what to expect as well as let you know whether there are any binder fees—small deposits that the publisher forwards you to retain your writing services.

Starting Out on Staff

If, however, you are bound and determined to get on a magazine staff, be prepared to start out like the rest: entry-level with a small-circulation publication (unless you have some strong connections or a great deal of name recognition).

Plan on a starting salary in the mid-$20,000 range and probably living in an expensive city, such as New York. That's where a lot of publishers are located.

For the first few years, the publications you work for and the pieces you write probably won't be your dream stories—but they will accumulate. You might even win some local awards, and they'll help you get to the next step up.

Remember, too, that there are countless magazines in all parts of the country that focus on regional cultures, lifestyles, commerce, sports, and news. Again, while they may rely mostly on contributions, they may be a good place to start as a staff writer or editor.

Getting Your Foot in the Door

There's a process for selling a piece to a magazine. The wrong way to do it is to write a piece then try to sell it. The right way is to sell the idea, then write it.

Querying Magazines

Without a doubt, breaking into the magazine business is tough—but there's one way to help dissolve that barrier: queries. That is, get an idea together of something you want to sell to a magazine and submit that idea to the editor.

Sounds easy, right? Unfortunately, it's not. There are several steps you have to take before you even consider putting that stamp on the envelope.

Get to Know the Magazine

It's important to understand the magazine's target market. As we mentioned earlier, get to know the magazine inside and out—and don't forget the ads. Those advertisements are dead giveaways as to the magazine's demographics.

Next, become familiar with the writing style and try to emulate it without copying it. If the tone of the magazine is light and casual, don't try to sell something dark and serious. Look at the length of most of the articles. If the magazine is big on short pieces, then don't propose a 7,000-word epic.

Okay, so you have your idea. You know the magazine intimately. You've identified your audience, and you've looked at all the ads. Time to write, right? Wrong.

def•i•ni•tion

Author guidelines are exact specifications of how a magazine wants its stories written and are available by calling or e-mailing the magazine. Some are even posted online.

Extra! Extra!

Don't write the article before it's been accepted by a magazine. It would be a waste of time if it isn't sold or if an editor proposes a different angle.

The next step is to ask for the magazine's *author guidelines*. These are very specific rules governing how the editors want to see the stories, from the kind of voice and mood to the length and content. Don't for a second think that you can submit a piece written any differently just because you think they would want to see it that way. They don't. It's safe to say that 10 out of 10 times, the piece will go straight to the recycle bin if it doesn't heed the author guidelines.

Okay, so write the piece now? No. Don't be silly. The next piece of this puzzle is to submit a query letter to the magazine's editor. Call or go online and find out your contact person. Don't send it to the wrong person, and for the love of Pete, spell that person's name correctly and get his or her title right. Too many queries have landed in the scrap heap because of careless errors like these.

In your query letter, you'll want to include a brief description of what you're proposing. Don't give the whole thing away; reveal just enough to pique the editor's interest and assure him or her that you've done a good deal of research (and mean it). Tell the editor a bit about yourself, what you've published, and what makes you an expert in this subject. If you have some examples of your writing, include them. Give an outline of the story you're proposing, but again, you don't need to outline the entire story— just a few levels that convey the heart and direction of the story.

Gaining Acceptance

Now begin writing the story? Still no. The magazine isn't going to pay you a dime until it has accepted the piece, so there's no use in wasting your time writing it if the editors aren't going to buy it. Plus, they might like just a part of the idea and want to change the direction a bit. And that would take a whole rewrite if you've already penned the entire piece. Don't start writing until they tell you, "Go."

Now, you think you want to increase your odds by querying a bunch of magazines at once, right? Wrong. Don't do it. It's very bad manners to ask more than one magazine at a time. I know what you're thinking: "Well, how will they know?"

They probably won't (unless maybe they're part of a conglomerate and communicate about story submissions, who knows?). But what happens if three editors say, "Okay." You won't be able to write and sell that same piece for three separate magazines, so you'll have to call them and say, "Ah, never mind ..."

It's a bad idea, legally and morally. And legal aspects aside, the next time you'd have a story idea and want to submit it to a publication you turned down previously, they're going to say—wait for it—"Ah, never mind." Ouch.

Extra! Extra! _____

Query only one magazine with a particular story idea at a time. Anything more is considered in poor taste, and you run the risk of putting yourself in a compromising situation.

Some magazines may also pay for full rights to a story that you write—that means it can't be published in any way, shape, or form in any other magazine. And if it is, legal ramifications could result. If a magazine wants exclusivity rights, and you're in a bargaining position, they may pay more for those rights.

Be Flexible

Don't get too anxious, either. Editors, as we've mentioned, have a lot going on. They are busy folks, so cut them a little slack. Plan on hearing something back from them in about a month and a half, and if you don't hear from them in six weeks, then it's acceptable to move on to the next magazine with your query. In the meantime, a letter or e-mail to ensure that they've received your piece is acceptable.

If an editor says yes to your idea, it's probably going to come with a few strings attached in the form of modifications and edits. Be agreeable to what the editor wants, and ask him or her when you need to turn in the revised piece. Then, get busy on it.

Once you turn the revised idea back in, they'll either accept or decline it. If it's the former, you'll get a contract to fully write the piece. If it's the latter, move on—but not before asking them for advice. It's important to know what it was they didn't like about the piece or your writing so that you'll know next time how to better present your idea. Ask them to be brutally honest; you'll get over it. And your work will become stronger. Remember, these guys are experts—and you'll learn from their input.

Sometimes a piece may be perfectly good but the timing is just off for the publication. Maybe another story came in that was more timely and immediate in the community. Sometimes these things just happen, and it's no fault of your own. Either way, don't get discouraged. Just chalk it all up to experience.

Be professional. Thank them for the opportunity, and let them know that you hope to one day work together. That might go a long way toward getting future work published with them.

If you do get the gig, then get to work. Be sure you can deliver what you promised, and if possible, go above and beyond. It's always a great feeling for an editor to receive a piece that's accurate, well-written, and copy-edited. Attention to detail shows respect for your writing and for the editor's time.

The Least You Need to Know

- Magazine journalists need to be more creative and think in-depth to a greater extent than newspaper journalists.

- Classes, clips, and experience will get you where you want to go in the magazine world.

- Analyze the magazines you query. Not knowing the magazine's target audience is a rookie mistake.

- Be sure to obtain and adhere to a magazine's author guidelines before submitting a query.

Part 3

Radio

Radio first gave a voice to the newspaper and from there blossomed into its own institution of journalism. Carving its own niche, radio continues to be a dominant player in the media world through continuous evolution of its medium.

In this part, we'll explore the strength of radio in its access and portability, the components of radio reports and how to create them, the variety of radio programming in existence today, and how to get where you want to go with a radio career.

Chapter 11

Move Over, Marconi

In This Chapter

- ◆ Tuning in to early radio
- ◆ Listening to radio's Golden Age
- ◆ Staving threats from a new medium
- ◆ Understanding key moments in radio
- ◆ Keeping radio relevant today

As if sending a signal over an electronic wavelength isn't mind-blowing enough, look at the forum that Guglielmo Marconi started way back in 1895 when he gave us what is known today as the radio. More than a century ago in the countryside of northern Italy, Marconi sent the first radio signals across a distance of just one-and-a-half miles—creating an entirely new medium of mass communication.

We've come a long way since that first short transmission. Today, there are more than 14,000 radio stations in the United States alone that can be reached from distances a whole lot longer than that of a 10-minute jog. And what you hear is everything from music to talk shows to news.

This incredible medium is still running strong today and offers some pretty good careers in broadcast journalism. In this chapter, we'll look at the significance of the first wireless broadcast and how it set the course to change the world of communications.

Riding the Radio Waves

Long before TV existed and almost a century before the Internet, the most profound communications breakthrough to reach such a wide audience was the radio. In the early 1900s, that little box transformed life as we knew it. The world began turning on the spoken word rather than solely on the written word. Families could tune in to early radio programs—variety shows and "soaps"—so-called for their detergent company sponsors—as well as news programming several times a day. And audio broadcast news became an integral part of that daily life.

> **Breaking News**
>
> Guglielmo Marconi was a mere 23 years old when he began lining up investors for his Marconi Wireless Telegraph company.

Early Radio

The first radio station to begin airing regular programming was Pittsburgh's KDKA on November 2, 1920. It started with live coverage of that year's presidential election between Warren G. Harding and James M. Cox. The person who read those returns over the air was Leo Rosenberg, believed to be the first radio announcer.

The programming was actually broadcast from a shack on top of the Westinghouse "K" building in east Pittsburgh. Ironically, the results were fed to KDKA by the local newspaper, *The Pittsburgh Post*, which helped the radio station get its start and ultimately became its competitor. Today, competition between radio stations and newspapers remains strong as they compete heavily with one another for audiences and advertising.

def•i•ni•tion

The term **broadcast** was actually coined by early Midwestern radio engineers. It means to reach a large segment of the population. Narrowcast means reaching a narrower range of audience.

Despite competition from TV, Internet, and print journalism, radio is a dominant force in the world of *broadcast* news—with more than 600 million radios in the United States and 5.6 radios in every household.

What that means is folks can walk into the kitchen and listen to the radio, or into the living room, the basement, the garage, or even listen to it in the mini-van on the way to the office (and in the office …).

Portability is a big plus for radio, and radio producers and reporters know that well. More on that point in a minute.

Radio Today

Today when we think about radio, what more than likely comes to mind is music— DJs spinning discs so that we can all have tunes in the car or on the beach. But radio is much more than music; it's still strongly tied to its roots in news and talk. Look at NPR—National Public Radio. This network reaches 26 million Americans each week and has more than 800 independently operated noncommercial affiliates. That's an enormous market share, with programs such as *Morning Edition* and *All Things Considered* leading the way.

WNBC, WCBS, and WABC—the radio versions of the "Big Three" TV networks— also dominate in the radio broadcast journalism spectrum. And networks such as CNN and ESPN are making their mark in radio, as well.

Just as we discovered with TV, there are major networks and local affiliates. So, your little hometown AM radio station or that big city station on the FM dial may align themselves with big networks to bring all or part of their programming onto the airwaves. There also are pure news stations—meaning no music, no entertainment; just 24/7 news programming, such as KCBS in San Francisco, WCBS in New York, and WBZ in Boston.

> **Breaking News**
>
> There are 14,411 radio stations in the United States, with 950 in Texas alone!

Defining Times for Radio

The period between the 1920s and 1950s was really what established radio as a top medium. As programming broadened and radio sets were becoming more affordable and available, families would gather around the radio to listen to their favorite programs. This was the Golden Age of radio.

The Golden Age

We often hear of radio's "Golden Age," when radio had the run of the communications world. TV really didn't kick in until the '50s or become super popular until the '60s. So, once radio established its stronghold and began to flourish, it looked like the

Breaking News
More than 20 million homes received broadcasts from about 600 radio stations in the United States by 1934.

1940s were just the tip of the iceberg—with variety shows, music, and reporters scattered throughout the day and evening.

When TV came onto the scene, however, radio began to fade. It had to switch gears, so to speak. And radio found its strength during World War II.

World War II

The 1940s was a time of war, and radio had a strength that other media did not: timeliness. It was the only medium that could provide news right from the war front. Newspapers were a day old, and there was no audio. TV cameras weren't going to travel into war zones to transmit. Instead, reels were sent to the United States for viewing in movie theaters or as taped segments on TV. So, radio was dominant due to its ability to deliver war news as it was happening.

But radio didn't simply report news on the war. Folks were interested in diversions from all the war talk, so evening thrillers, variety shows, and dramas on radio grew nearly tenfold.

Radio was doing quite well and holding its own during this time. Some of the hot programs included music regulars such as the A&P Gypsies and the music variety show *National Barn Dance*, both in the early to mid-'20s. Grand Ol' Opry began broadcasting in 1925 and continues today! Other programming, such as the *Betty Crocker Show* followed as did the famous *Amos and Andy* show in 1928.

But as time went on, it became a losing battle for radio to try and compete with TV for programming. TV was becoming all the rage by the 1950s and '60s, with a quickly expanding program menu to choose from and the availability of television sets. Radio had to carve a niche and do it fast if it wanted to survive.

It did so in news, sports, and weather, as well as continuing to broadcast music—just not the variety shows of old. The move kept radio a vibrant medium that remains strong today.

The FCC

Another defining event in radio—and in all journalism, for that matter—was the formation of the FCC, or Federal Communications Commission. Most folks believe that the FCC is akin to the schoolteacher who slams the ruler down onto the knuckles of those students who misbehave. Well, sort of. But it wasn't always so cut-and-dried.

Back in 1934 when radio was becoming red hot, the big networks were plodding the airwaves like bullies, using the most powerful and clearest frequencies and edging out the little guys. A commission—the FCC—sprouted to help smaller affiliates with their rights to broadcast when and what they wanted, instead of the affiliate being told what would be broadcast and when.

The bigger radio networks, specifically NBC, were running monopolies, snapping up all the little companies and literally running the show. The bloated networks also would demand of their affiliates any airtime they wanted—usually during the prime listening hours. The FCC set up ground rules to protect the little guys and broke up the large monopolies. Congress passed a law in 1934 to make it so.

For the most part, radio went along swimmingly with the FCC as it listened carefully to radio stations' needs and protected their licenses. That's until 1981, however, when regulations over monopolies and consolidations were relaxed to the point of being nonexistent. Laws that once governed the radio waves began loosening, and the FCC was little more than a licensing agent.

But by the '50s, the priorities began shifting for the FCC and words such as "censorship" and "indecency" began cropping up in both radio and TV. Soon, what could be said—or rather, what *couldn't* be said—over the airwaves was getting a lot of attention. Freedom of speech advocates began chastising the FCC for its newfound goal of wiping out smut on the airwaves, alleging the measures were politically motivated.

> **Breaking News**
>
> The FCC was created in 1934 primarily to thwart off network monopolies.

The FCC, however, stands by its goal:

> The determination as to whether certain programming is patently offensive is not a local one and does not encompass any particular geographic area. Rather, the standard is that of an average broadcast viewer or listener and not the sensibilities of any individual complainant.

In other words, the majority rules.

Radio has certainly evolved since its early days, and through regulation and good practices, its signal remains strong today.

Radio Relevance

With the advent of radio and the subsequent regular programming that went onto the air, more and more radio stations were not just reading the local news but began writing it, too.

It's not odd today to hear radio broadcasters reading the news from newspapers or other sources, providing they give proper credit. But the large news networks employ their own crews of writers, reporters, producers, and editors, and their reports are fed to their radio affiliates for broadcast.

Turn on the radio, scan for a station, and … bam! There's the news. Or the weather. Or sports. These are all examples of *radio formats*. And radio has lots of formats to suit all ages, interests, tastes, and ethnicities.

def•i•ni•tion

Radio format is the primary content broadcast by a radio station and can be used as a marketing tool.

One reason why so many people believe that radio is here to stay for good, despite threats from TV and the Internet, is its portability. Stop and think about it. Most folks who own televisions have the kinds that plug into the wall for electricity. Sure, portable TVs exist—but not too many folks carry those around or install them in their cars to get their news. Plus, TV signals aren't all that reliable if you can't get cable.

Ditto for the Internet. Sure, you can listen to a whole lot of radio stations on the Internet, but your laptop isn't what you'll want to take to the beach or use while driving around in your car.

Portability is a major factor for radio, which makes it more effective than any other medium. And it's cheap, too, for the consumer, the operator, and advertisers.

Breaking News

Radio reaches 96 percent of Americans 12 years and older each week, and they listen 3.2 hours each day.

All these features lead to radio as a necessity and not merely a nicety. When a storm erupts and power goes down, where else are you going to find out what's going on or whether it's safe to come out of that tornado bunker?

Or what about when school is closing early because of that snowstorm, but you're on Interstate 88 heading to the office? The radio takes care of that.

Listening In

Just like we discussed in the TV sections, radio, too, has different ways of reaching you. TV had broadcast, which comes over a wavelength or signal, a cable, or by a satellite feed. Well, radio works in much the same way—either over the air or skipping along a satellite to your receiver. And, just like TV, radio is on the World Wide Web (more on that later).

Network

As we mentioned briefly earlier, there are several networks that produce all or most of their own programming on their stations. These networks distribute their programming to many stations at the same time or on a delay, and do so in syndication or *simulcast*—or both.

def•i•ni•tion

A **simulcast**, short for "simultaneous broadcast," is a program or event broadcast at the same time on more than one medium.

In the early days of radio, these networks produced all the content for the several stations, or affiliates, that they owned. But today, networks don't always necessarily own their affiliates yet still produce content for them. One station, for example, may be an affiliate of a few different networks to get all the programming its market wants.

In 2006, there were 106 radio networks in the United States alone—mostly commercial, such as ESPN, CBS, and ABC—but many public, such as NPR and Public Radio International, and religious networks, such as EWTN, Three Angels Broadcasting Network, or Family Radio. There are even very niche radio stations, such as First Amendment Radio, The 1920s Radio Network, and even a Chinese Radio Network!

Stations and Affiliates

If you're a radio station owner, you don't have to be an affiliate of a bigger network; you can run programming you create or desire so long as it's not pirated and is otherwise acceptable to the FCC. Remember, the FCC is the watchdog of the content that is broadcast. But most stations are affiliated with a network in order to have access to and provide quality programming. An example of a station that isn't affiliated might be a college radio station, which produces its own news programming and plays its own music.

By June 2004, the FCC had licensed 4,771 AM stations, 6,218 commercial FM stations, and 2,497 educational FM stations. Now, that's a whole lot of choices!

Of course, you can't get all these stations on your receiver, but you can get a lot of them. As a matter of fact, on a clear night you can listen to the BBC out of England thousands of miles away on an AM radio.

What's AM, you say? Well, it was merely a matter of time before we got to AM and FM differences. AM, which stands for *amplitude modulation*, was the forerunner of radio. In simple terms, the waves are broadcast by varying the amplitude, or strength, of the signal.

AM radio, which at first was more popular than FM, uses frequencies between 520 Kilohertz (KHz) and 1610 KHz. So, if you're listening to Radio 610 AM, you're tuned in to the 610 KHz frequency. FM, on the other hand, is more powerful, operating in the United States at 87.9 megahertz, or MHz to 107.9.

FM, which stands for *frequency modulation*, operates at a lower frequency and cannot carry signals as far. However, the signal is almost always clear and free of static interference. The sound quality and signal consistency of FM is leagues better. That's why by the 1960s, FM was fast outpacing AM as the frequency of choice for quality sound.

Satellite

Also on the airwaves is satellite radio. Though still in its infancy, small, and generally expensive, satellite radio is making its mark in the world of radio.

What satellite is to TV, satellite is to radio, too. Satellite radio owners choose what stations they want to hear, from hundreds of different types of programming, when they want to hear it, and where.

It takes a small powered satellite antenna to pick up the signal, and a receiver to amplify that signal. Satellite radio has its own programming independent of AM or FM radio.

Satellite radio made its initial mark as an option (or even the standard-equipped radio) in luxury cars, but it has since trickled down into less-expensive models and can even be purchased separately and installed in any vehicle.

Only two satellite networks exist in the United States at this time: Sirius Satellite Radio and XM Satellite Radio. Both have their own programming—and lots of it. From sports, to music, to news, to commentary, satellite offers much more than traditional radio.

Internet-Based Radio

As if the Internet hasn't changed every major form of media communication, you can bet your mouse pad that you can hear just about any radio station that you want on your computer with a good Internet connection.

In fact, many radio stations and networks offer their programs on the Internet, which opens a whole new world of radio. Want to hear a program from Russia? You can on the Internet. What about a program that aired last week on NPR? Yup. It's there, too.

Breaking News
Internet and satellite radio are considered strong competitors of AM and FM radio.

What about listening to a radio show that aired in 1920? Yes. And the game that's on tonight but isn't on TV or your local radio station? You got it. Just find the station's call letters and you're in business.

Some computers come with their own Internet audio players, such as Apple's iTunes, but there are several to download—even free ones—available at the click of a mouse, including RealPlayer and Windows Media Player 10.

Needless to say, radio has come a long way—and it remains a competitive force in the realm of broadcast journalism.

The Least You Need to Know

- The first radio station, KDKA, began in Pittsburgh in 1920.
- The advent of TV took a large bite out of radio but certainly hasn't killed it.
- Radio signals can reach farther than any other free electronic medium.
- You can hear radio from a network, on a station, piped in through cable, over a satellite signal, or even on the Internet.

Chapter 12

Creating a Radio Report

In This Chapter

- ◆ Coloring the story
- ◆ Piecing together the story
- ◆ Avoiding bias and maintaining balance
- ◆ Hearing voices and the use of quotes
- ◆ Matching tone and delivery with content

A lot of skill goes into writing, reporting, and producing for the radio. Just as with TV broadcasting, getting the story is half of the equation; the presentation of the story counts for that all-important other half.

From getting the story right to taping it to finding the right voice intonation, in this chapter we'll look at how to put your best ear forward.

Color in Radio

It's no surprise that some of the most well-known journalists got their start in radio. Famous news reporters and anchors such as Bill Bradley, Peter Jennings, Dan Rather, and Walter Cronkite (more on these folks later) had their early roots in radio.

Radio reporting is not all that different from TV or even print reporting. A reporter reports by collecting information about a given subject and interviews people in the know.

The obvious differences are that there are no cameras and the stories don't run in a print edition or on TV. So more imagination is needed for reporting for radio than TV. Although the audio is there, there is nothing visual.

Reporters and producers use a few techniques in radio reports to help give them color. Ever listen to *Morning Edition* on NPR? While the traditional reporting format of the news anchor reading the report dominates the program, occasionally a reporter or producer will capture the sounds surrounding the interview.

For instance, for a story on the dangers of long-line fishing off the treacherous waters of Newfoundland, audio clips of the ship's bell clanging, the deckhands yelling to each other over the din of an angry sea, the rattle of crab traps, and the grinding of the gears that hold the reels for the miles of line that are put out to catch fish are recorded and played in the background as the anchor reads the report.

You will hear the interviews of the crew and captain with the background sounds in full. Rather than just painting a picture for the listener with the reporter's words, the report will instead allow the listener to be right there, experiencing more of the story.

Researching an Enterprise Story

What makes a good news reporter? We've learned early on in this book that asking the right questions—the five Ws (who, what, when, why, and where)—are key to a good story, and for radio it's certainly no different.

Whether you're writing a colorful, in-depth story on the effects of a new immigration law that's meant to air next weekend or you're spot-reporting a deadly single-engine plane crash, your writing must be rock-solid for you to be credible and trustworthy.

Of course, you'll have a whole lot more time for the writing and reporting of that immigration piece. You can spend hours fine-tuning your writing, keeping your writing voice clear, and painting an accurate picture of what you have witnessed.

Extra! Extra!

The five Ws—who, what, when, why, and where—still count in radio reporting.

On the fly for a breaking news piece, however, it's a whole different monster. Yet the end result in each case needs to be identical: accurate reporting. Let's look at the immigration piece, which would likely be an *enterprise story*. The reporter will make a long list of subjects whom he or she needs to interview and begin researching the topic.

def•i•ni•tion _____

An **enterprise story** isn't necessarily a breaking news story but is more in-depth and requires a good deal of investigation and research into a broader topic.

Research will most likely include a lot of time on the Internet learning who the key players are in this corner of the world, looking at past stories, court cases, legislation, and situations that have affected or have been affected by immigration laws or a lack thereof.

Once the research is done, the story should be outlined. Think of this outline as your road map to how the story will progress. You still haven't interviewed much up to this point, so keep immigration knowledge at the top of your mind and have questions ready for your list of subjects. Then, you'll be ready to get out there to do interviews and get those quotes. Now's when the radio reporting can become dicey.

You head down to a construction site and begin interviewing immigrant workers. You find that many of them don't want to talk to you, so you say you'll protect them by using first names only or aliases—which should be your last resort. This situation is referred to as a *condition of anonymity*.

def•i•ni•tion _____

Reporters might agree to use a source's information but not his or her identity because naming the source might have consequences. This agreement is called a **condition of anonymity**.

They agree, and you begin asking them your questions. They tell you about the unfairness of a system that doesn't allow them to easily become naturalized citizens so they can legally work here and how the only way they can get across the border is by sneaking in illegally. And they tell you that they've been coming here for years because they need money. Next, you interview a foreman—also under the condition of anonymity—who says that at least a third of his crew aren't on the books, that they are day laborers who come looking for temporary work to earn cash. Some of them have been coming here for years. And without them, he says, there's no way these projects would get finished. The foreman also says not only are immigrant laborers cheap, but they are also among the few skilled laborers in the region who are willing to work extra hours and days to get the projects done on time.

Juicy stuff, right?

Keeping the Information Balanced

In this example, you think your report has some really good stuff—so you take the quotes back to the station, make copies of the tapes, and write the material into your story. You think you have a winner. But wait: reporters must remember that there are two sides to every story. What about the small subcontractors in town who are being undercut by these illegal immigrants? Interviews with the subcontractors show that their businesses are being hurt because they can't bid on projects low enough to compete with those that use immigrants. They've asked their local legislators and law enforcement officials for help, but to no avail. The legislators say it's a national issue, and until it trickles down to a state level, their hands are tied. The police chief tows the same line, adding that he doesn't have the manpower to chase down illegal immigrant workers.

> **Extra! Extra!**
>
> There are always two sides to every story, and good reporting means always getting both sides.

> **Breaking News**
>
> Most news stories run between 25–30 seconds, with tape pieces at about 45 seconds.

Now, you have both sides of that story. And you report and research more on how many cases regionally have made it to court, how many law enforcement officials have heard complaints, how many deportations and fines have been doled out over the years, what the estimated population of illegal immigrants is in your region, and so on.

So you begin writing your story, which will loosely serve as your script. But keep in mind two things: unlike that 20-minute read that a print journalist will produce, your story is probably going to run under a minute on the air—maybe slightly longer depending on your format. That is a short time, so you're going to have to write tight. NPR runs many long stories in its programming, some in the five-minute range. But this story length is not the norm in commercial radio.

Getting It on Tape

If you remember, writing that script is only half of a radio report. You also have to tape it using those taped segments from your interviews, those live voices and sounds you heard at the construction sites, at the police department, and wherever your interviews took you. There are a few things to consider, though, before you go shoving your tape recorder in someone's face to get a quote.

First, be sure you've identified yourself properly as a reporter and explained who you work for. Also, tell them what you are writing a story about and that you'd like to ask them questions for your story. That's an important part of the equation. First, it's the ethical thing to do; and second, it's illegal in some states to tape folks for broadcast or publication without their consent.

Extra! Extra!

Before taping a subject for broadcast, be sure you've identified yourself as a reporter and notified them that they are being taped.

The second-to-last thing you want is someone screaming at you after they've just heard their voice on the radio; the last thing you'll want to hear is a judge telling you to pay the fine for not disclosing who you were or your boss telling you he's now your ex-boss.

Don't be too obtrusive, either. The idea is to be casual and respectful with those you are taping. However, you could be at the courthouse where an ax murderer is walking into the federal courthouse in shackles to find out whether the jury has convicted him to death or not. In this case, you're probably not going to casually say, "Hey, man. How's it goin'?" You'll need to be completely direct and say, "Did you do it?"

With the immigration piece—as with many of the pieces you will tape in your career—you're going to need to build a rapport with your sources. Talk to them about the story, saying you understand the situation, that you're getting a lot of sides to this story, and that you want to be certain the story is balanced. Tell them you'd like to get their take on it and you'd like to use that information in the story. Take a few notes. Then, turn on the microphone. If they become uncomfortable—and that's a bit normal—turn off the mic and explain to them the importance of having their voice in the story to get all sides.

It's easy when you're taping the mayor. Heck, he or she might even grab the mic out of your hand and talk until the tape runs out. Folks who aren't usually in the spotlight can tend to get shy. You might have to coax them out of their shells.

If you're up front about your intentions, chances are people will be cooperative. But there's no need to badger people to the point of them lodging a complaint against you.

It's also important to note here that the way you use your quotes will have a large effect on keeping the story balanced. Taking the quotes out of context is a good example. If the town's mayor has a plan to allow the clear-cutting of trees in trade for allowing affordable houses to be built on the plot, his quote might be:

"We think that in this case, trading trees for homes for the poor is a positive step. We can always replant the trees."

But your story script merely leads into the quote, and only uses half of it:

"We can always replant the trees."

That takes away the full breadth of what the mayor is saying.

But what about a story involving a jealous husband who comes home in a blind rage and beats to death his two kids in front of his own wife? Reporting at the scene, you're collecting information and details—and what you see is absolutely horrific. You see the bodies of two little children shrouded in white sheets; you see the suspect hand-cuffed and being led out of the house by police; you see the wife crying hysterically in the back of an ambulance. It's natural for your heart to both hurt for the victims and feel rage against the suspect. Your report, however, needs to be fair and unbiased.

You interview police, neighbors, relatives, emergency workers, and the guy who called the police after hearing the children's screams. You get as much as you can on tape so you can create a report that captures the scenes and situation. As a reporter, you begin your report:

What neighbors describe as a quiet, friendly neighborhood on Carson's east side turned into a grisly double-murder scene Tuesday when the screams of two children rang out in the early morning as they were beaten to death by whom police believe to be their own father.

Police say John J. Apple of 324 Apple Street came home from working the night shift at the Fort Star Mill, picked up a baseball bat, and began beating his children in front of their mother.

Apple is being charged with homicide, police said.

It's a tough story to write—and a tougher one to read live on the air, projecting an objective viewpoint. You're going to use the tape of the interviews from those on the scene: the police, the neighbor …. Chances are you won't get an interview with the mother or suspect, though. Your recorder, however, captures the mother's wails, which continue as they load her into the ambulance.

Is that tape usable? Yes. But that's not something you need in your lead. Maybe as you transition into a sentence or two about her, you can use it.

The mother, described by police as 24-year-old Susan K. Apple, was believed to be physically unharmed, although EMS crews were tending to a cut over her left eye. As she sat wrapped in a blanket in the back of an ambulance, police and a city counselor and family tried to calm her down.

(Sound of sobs, emergency workers, the muffled voices of police and counselor, the din of neighbors gathered curbside.)

Then, you can use an interview from medical staff or police to sum up her condition. Think of the sounds much the same as the quotes in your story. There should be an order to them to maintain a balanced report. Once you piece the sounds you gathered together with your script, your report is ready to air with you—the reporter—reading the story.

Finding Your Voice

Okay, so you have your story in hand, your tapes are all set, and you're ready to head into the broadcast booth to unleash that story on America. Again, not so fast.

Before you go on the air, you have to put on your best broadcaster's voice—an entirely different way of talking than your typical casual conversation. You're not going to simply read that story; you're going to voice it. On TV, the viewer will see the reporter's facial expression and see the situations of those contractors and cops. The viewer will understand by visual cues what he or she is looking at, how it's being said, and what the emotions are.

On radio, that's mostly up to you. Think about it. In the homicide story example earlier, you're not going to launch into your story with a happy voice. At the same time, you don't want to sound like Perry Mason, either. A reporter's voice on the radio has everything to do with setting the tone. It needs to be fair and straightforward but not boring or monotonous. There are a few different vocal styles in radio reporting—different schools of thought, if you will. Choose the voice that's best for the story: a light approach for a light story, a serious tone for a serious subject, and so on.

> **Breaking News**
>
> There are three widely accepted styles or formats for broadcast news, each with its own voice: in-depth, network, and vivid.

In-Depth

Our immigration story is a good example of the in-depth style of reporting for radio. The tone is conversational, yet the reporter has some authority in his or her presentation. The report is longer and has more color and quotes, and the intonations of the reporter's voice reflect the weight of the subject.

NPR perhaps best executes the in-depth style of radio, with its long morning or afternoon reports—usually at times when listeners have more time on their hands, such as the morning commute, lunchtime, and in the evening.

Network

Another vocal style is the network style—those reports that you will find on most commercial newscasts. Generally, they are short, 13- to 20-second reports running one after another in a 90-second broadcast. The piece on immigration won't fit into this broadcast, but the double murder certainly will.

Tune into any commercial radio station at the top of the hour and network style is what you'll hear. Even smaller radio stations use this type of reporting.

Again, the tone and voice will be punchy—right to the point. There will be no drawn-out background audio, and quotes from sources will be very short—maybe limited to just one.

Here's an example:

> Bonetown officials say a 3 percent tax hike this summer will help thousands of its residents afford heat this winter. The measure will collect the tax and distribute the collections as needed to the poor and elderly who need it to pay for heat. Last winter, 38 Bonetown residents froze to death in their homes, most elderly. Mayor Mary Emory said the tax was necessary. "We just think it's a prudent step to protect our citizens." The tax goes into effect June 1.

And that's about 13 seconds.

Vivid

Last, a lot of radio stations are going to what's called a vivid style of newscast to attract younger listeners.

The note here is that many would argue that this style of broadcast is not quite journalism but more entertainment—or even "shock" radio.

Chances are you won't hear straight, serious newscasts in the vivid style. Those morning shows for commuters are notorious for this style of radio banter, and it's hard to imagine that you're getting a fair news report rather than a report for pure shock value.

An example:

> Ever have one of those days when everything seems to go wrong?
>
> John Visadams did. On Monday, Visadams showed up to work at the GE plant only to receive a pink slip. On his way driving home, he stopped at his neighborhood liquor store to get something to ease the pain. Instead, what he got was more. Visadams walked straight into a robbery scene. A man in a black mask was holding a gun to the clerk's head and demanding cash. Visadams tried to run from the store, but was shot in the back. The robber made off with not only the cash and a bottle of scotch, he also took Visadams' car!
>
> Police say they're looking for a 1998 Chevy Lumina.
>
> Good luck!

The Least You Need to Know

- ◆ Radio reports can vary from 13 seconds up to 5 minutes long.
- ◆ Playing fair means getting the whole story and reporting it without bias.
- ◆ Quotes and background sounds provide color and imagery to radio reports.
- ◆ Vocal style is a key component in shaping a radio news story.

Chapter 13

Spinning More Than Records

In This Chapter

- ◆ The roots of talk radio
- ◆ The journalistic spectrum of talk radio programs
- ◆ Sports reporting: in a league of its own
- ◆ Weather: a cornerstone of radio reporting

There's more to radio than just spinning records and reporting news. For journalists, it's a big forum. From talk radio to sports talk to calling games to weather forecasts, radio goes far beyond "news at the top of the hour." In this chapter, we'll look at programming on the radio that's all talk and how journalists fit into this format and its various forms.

The Rise of Talk Radio

It is widely accepted that disc jockey Barry Gray is the father of talk radio. As the story goes, Gray got bored with spinning records in 1945 at WMCA in New York and called conductor Woody Herman, interviewing him over the phone by placing the phone's receiver next to the station's microphone. Hence, talk radio was born.

His audience raved about the interview, and he began interviewing more celebrities, authors, and controversial people. The more he broadcast, the more people began tuning in. Soon, other stations, such as New York's famous WOR began programming for talk. Gray even moved to WOR for a few years before coming back to WMCA.

But what really is talk radio? Listener participation is the prime ingredient. The other part is an on-air host talking about a subject or issue at hand, be it sports, weather, people, or something in the news.

Also, an on-air host takes calls from listeners and puts them on the air during a program so they can voice their viewpoints. In general, a producer will weed out the more meaningful calls, and those callers who have more insight or opinions on the subject will make the cut. And the hotter the topic, the better the chances more people will call in. Journalism on the radio can be found as far back as the 1920s, when evangelist Aimee Semple McPherson traded political opinions on air, as did Charles Coughlin (one of the first political leaders to use radio to reach a mass audience) a decade later.

In the 1960s, talk radio reached a higher plane with two stations going to a full-time talk radio format. KMOX in St. Louis, Missouri, and KABC in Los Angeles, California, each claim to be the first to go with the all-talk format—meaning they had no other programming on their stations than talk radio. And they did so with some degree of success.

AM radio continued to be the mainstay of talk radio throughout much of the '60s and '70s, but as FM radio began its massive proliferation over the airwaves in the '70s and offered a wider selection of listening choices, talk radio took a hit on the AM dial.

More AM stations began switching formats to keep up with FM. Conversely, FM stations that were predominantly music—WRKO in Boston, WABC in New York, and WLS in Chicago—were finding audiences in talk radio.

Talk radio today is still found more on AM than FM. With AM's broad signal and no need for stereo for talk programs, AM is largely home to all-talk formats. FM listeners, however, want the clearer, stereo signal to listen to music. So, although some markets may offer all-talk formats on FM, they are rare.

But talk radio remains solid. From sports shows to political punditry, to religious topics, talk rules the AM roost. And it has even spread to Internet and satellite media. Longtime shock-jock Howard Stern's *Howard 100* show is broadcast exclusively on Sirius Satellite Radio.

Talk Soup

Radio has varying degrees of journalism in its spectrum of programming, just like in other media. But one question comes to mind when we talk about talk radio: is it all considered journalism?

Well, that answer is open to some degree of interpretation. You see, to call Howard Stern a journalist would be a huge misnomer. The fact is, many call-in shows have very little to do with journalism at all.

But some do. Take *Talk of the Nation* on NPR, for instance. Neal Conan, a trained journalist and veteran anchor and reporter for NPR, hosts the program. He generally takes an issue that's in the news, reports on it, and then opens the phone lines to callers who want to discuss the topic.

Sure, callers aren't necessarily journalists or even experts, but they are members of the public and have opinions—and this format allows for often intelligent dialog among the host and his callers. Many times, however, the callers are politicians, journalists, authors, scholars, and public figures who want to lend their opinions on various subjects. The result is very journalistic in nature.

But even those who were around during the "Golden Age" of radio couldn't look into the future to see what radio would be like at the turn of the twenty-first century. In 1990, with the help of more lax FCC rules, an entire genre of talk radio programs sprouted and became wildly popular. Talk radio hosts Rush Limbaugh, Sean Hannity, Michael Savage, Neal Boortz, and Glenn Beck became household names. These talk-show hosts trade barbs in politics, culture, and celebrity on the AM dial.

Journalists? No. But they discussed many of the issues that were in the news, albeit very one-sided. Conservative politics became a theme of talk radio in the 1990s, and it remains today. The programs catered to those masses.

A Pew Center for Civic Journalism report in 2004 showed that 45 percent of radio listeners described themselves as conservatives while 18 percent said they were liberal, which explains the popularity of right-oriented radio talk shows! But the interesting statistic is that 17 percent of the American public claimed that they listened to talk radio.

> **Extra! Extra!**
>
> In 2004, 45 percent of radio listeners were conservatives while 18 percent were liberal. And 17 percent of Americans listened to talk radio in 2004.

So is there a market for talk radio? You bet. How much of it is actually journalism, though, needs to be carefully weeded out when spinning that dial.

The Wide World of Sports Radio

Talk radio isn't just all politics. Some of the best journalists on the planet might not even subscribe to a political point of view or care whether the House of Representatives is controlled by Republicans or Democrats. Instead, their lives revolve more around the earned run average of an outfielder, the pass rating of a quarterback, or the free-throw percentage of a point guard.

Welcome to sports radio, one of the most popular and successful radio formats around the world. When we think of sports coverage, a network such as ESPN comes to mind (and rightfully so). ESPN is enormously successful not only on TV and in print but also on the radio.

Breaking News
There are 463 sports radio sta-tions in the United States, most with Internet sites and streaming capability.

So what is ESPN Radio? Sometimes it's talk shows, sometimes it's journalistic reporting and features, and other times it's the standard play-by-play action. Most sports radio involves these elements, so let's break them down.

Sports Talk

If you hit a couple of radio buttons—especially on the AM dial—while driving to work in the morning, chances are you won't go too far without landing on a station that has a couple of hosts spewing out archaic batting averages of ball players from the dark ages. Statistics are everything when it comes to sports knowledge. You'll hear call-in guests trying to stump the hosts; you'll even hear some arguments over who's better in the pocket or why a certain player needs to pass the ball more on the court.

But make no mistake: the majority of these sports talk hosts are journalists or have communications backgrounds. Unlike other forms of talk radio, sports radio hosts are very niche—that is, they must be experts. Generally, sports journalists—writers and editors—host their own shows on the radio, so it's a safe bet they know the material and cover more than most others. Among some of the most widely recognized names in sports talk radio are Dan Patrick, Keith Olbermann, and Jim Rome. And just like other radio programming, sports talk radio can either be syndicated or local.

Reporting a Game

Sports reporting differs from the call-in talk show format. We're talking about pure journalism in sports, where a reporter interviews players, coaches, league officials, and so on to get a story to air on the radio.

A good example of sports reporting is the 2005 steroid doping controversy in baseball. These stories were printed and broadcast around the globe, but they were primarily handled in the sports sections of newspapers or on the sports segments of TV and radio broadcasts. Even for the Senate hearings, where players testified in front of a panel to get to the bottom of the doping deal, sports reporters were there to cover those hearings, interview subjects, analyze the information, and produce a top-notch story, and air it, too. In radio, it's no different than TV. Reporters air their reports.

Nowhere in sports radio does journalism take center stage more than in sports reporting. And the subjects are as big as the games themselves.

In essence, when you listen to a game on the radio, you'll hear a reporter getting the story while the game is happening—whether it be in the dugout, on the sidelines, or at center ice—and you'll receive the reporter's analysis of the game. The reporter also collects pertinent data and pulls everything together in a report to read as soon as the game is through.

The Play-By-Play

The play-by-play is an aspect of sports reporting that shuffles between journalism (reporting) and game analysis. It's live, so there's little room for interviews; all the prep—stats and figures—are on "cheat sheets" or the computer as the game is being called.

In its very basic sense, play-calling is on-scene reporting—breaking news with every tick of the clock. During downtime, when action isn't happening on the field or on the court, there might be some analysis and even some color commentary—but for the most part, it's unscripted, in-the-moment, as-it's-happening reporting.

Some of the most notable names in game announcing are Brent Musburger, Bob Costas, and Al Michaels. These men have covered practically every major sport and many major sporting events through some pretty long careers. And they all studied journalism, and they all worked in radio early in their careers.

> ### Breaking News
>
> Many of the most prominent sports radio announcers got their start as journalists.

Let's Talk About the Weather

Earlier in this book, we mentioned how vital radio is for weather reporting. Weather reporting goes far beyond simply "rip and reads" from the newspaper reports or the latest National Weather Service (NWS) information.

Nowadays, syndicated weather on the radio is fairly common, and weather radio fills a very important niche for listeners. Take, for instance, weather alerts. When a major storm is bearing down—say, a tornado, hurricane, or blizzard—reports are updated or run constantly on radio stations.

And that's important, because radio is the only medium that is 100 percent portable. It doesn't rely on cable—it has batteries—or an Internet connection in order to be heard. All you need is a battery and an antenna to receive a radio transmission.

That comes in handy when power and phone lines go down in a storm or when you're driving in your car and a storm is approaching. Meteorologists can warn listeners via radio.

> **Breaking News**
>
> During severe weather, NOAA's Weather Radio All Hazards broadcasts continuously on many radio stations.

In cases of extremely severe weather, radio stations can go into National Oceanic and Atmospheric Administration (NOAA) Weather Radio All Hazards mode to broadcast continuously and for as long as needed. This service consists of a network of radio stations that broadcast continuous weather information directly from a nearby NWS office. These updates also include alerts pertaining to national security and natural, environmental, and public safety.

Some radio stations even carry "talk weather," where listeners can call in and chat about local weather, weather history, or the science of forecasting. So—similar to sports on the radio—weather also can be talk, reporting, or play-by-play!

The Least You Need to Know

- Talk radio's roots date back to the 1920s.
- Talk radio runs the gamut from strictly news to weather and sports and from political commentary to sensational shock-jocks.
- Sports talk radio is among the most popular radio formats in the United States.
- Radio is a key medium for weather reporting.

Chapter 14

Getting Started in Radio Journalism

In This Chapter

- ◆ A bit about the biz
- ◆ Learning the ropes
- ◆ Getting skills for the airwaves
- ◆ Landing that job

Luckily, with more than 14,000 radio stations in the United States alone and many offering entry-level opportunities, you can probably land a job at a local radio station and get on the air relatively quickly.

A good college education and practical training might get you there faster, but keep in mind that starting low on the totem pole is a given if you want to get into prime time.

In this chapter, we'll see whether you have what it takes to work as a radio journalist—and then we'll describe how to get you on the air.

You Know You're a Radio Journalist If ...

There might not be a clear-cut path to deciding whether radio journalism is your bag. When we think about our youthful dreams of what we thought our occupation would be, radio journalist probably wasn't side by side with firefighter, astronaut, actress, or professional football player. But as the journalist inside you grew, you probably realized that writing was cool—and you wanted more than just your writing voice to be heard. You wanted the words to come out of your mouth, too.

Extra! Extra!

Studying broadcast journalism in college will put you on the fast-track toward getting a job in radio.

Many radio journalists aspire to be on TV, too. Let's face it: radio is a good stepping stone to broadcast TV, but not everyone who can report on the radio can or would even want to stand in front of a camera. So if you like the thought of people hearing you but not necessarily seeing you, radio would be a good way to go.

Radio broadcasters must have a good, clear voice and like to use that voice in reading or reporting on-air. Because you might not have the chance to script your stories— you will be going live on the air—you also have to be a quick thinker. That's the mark of a good reporter in any medium, but it's critical to reporting live.

Working at a radio station as a journalist might conjure up images from hard-nosed news reporter Edward E. Murrow to sports talk king Dan Patrick, but remember that it takes years of putting in your time and earning golden opportunities to get to this league.

Plan on driving a used car and living in a modest home, because it takes time to work your way up. You'll need to be willing to hang in there for the long haul and live a little lean if you want to make a name for yourself in radio.

If you have the drive to work hard for a modest paycheck, you want to be on the air, you have the voice that people want to hear, and the nerves to report live, then radio may be your ticket.

What You Need to Learn

Outside of the basics we've discussed for all budding journalists—good writing, interviewing, and reporting skills—you'll need to learn about the radio business and how to use your voice and announce on the air. You will, and should, dabble in weather, sports, news, and talk to find your niche. You'll need to learn about all the various production aspects, such as:

◆ **Format clock:** A clocklike unit divided like a pie, where each "slice" represents a programming event and its length of budgeted air time.

◆ **Digital audio production:** Producing radio programming digitally rather than analog or on tape.

◆ **Phonetics:** Linguistic sounds of speech and their production, combination, and description in written symbols.

◆ **Diacritics:** Accent marks added to letters to alter their sounds and differentiate among similar words.

◆ **Show preparations:** Getting prepared for shows or programs.

◆ **On-air features:** Understanding the blocks of time that programming runs in on schedules.

You'll also learn how to interview and promote. It's also important to learn about FCC licensing and regulations.

Finally, you'll need a lot of practice—both in the field and in the studio—to understand the medium, how it works, and how to work well in it. Whether it's through J-school or hands-on experience (or hopefully both), getting plenty of practice time in the studio and out in the field reporting will serve you very well.

Internships at radio stations will not only provide you with the proper skill sets but also will give you a leg up when interviewing with a prospective employer. They show that you have real-world experience with broadcasting and reporting. The combination of a good education and strong internships will make you much more marketable than those without.

Extra! Extra!

Being able to write and report is only one side of the radio broadcast journalism equation. Voice and production is the second half.

But you can choose to go without formal schooling. Some of the biggest names in radio started at the bottom working as a production assistant (or even lower) before they got their big breaks. But waiting on luck can be fruitless if that position never opens up or the opportunity is missed.

There are several different jobs for radio journalists, including reporter, broadcaster or anchor, producer, production assistants, and clerk. If you want the most direct path into radio, an associate's or bachelor's degree—or even a vocational training school—can help you reach your goal.

Sometimes, journalists in other media are compelled to cross over to radio. Sports-writers are common examples. After writing sports stories and columns, they might want to branch out on the airwaves. Same goes for political writers, or just about anyone with a knack to try something new. Many times, producers will ask for print journalists to either jump ship or guest host radio shows. Other times, TV broadcast-ers, such as meteorologists, might moonlight on the radio. With the experience from another field, the switch shouldn't be terribly difficult; just don't expect to land a morning personality spot if you don't have a good radio voice.

Tools for the Trade

Salary and skill expectations in radio are important to understand. As in all forms of journalism, working in radio takes dedication to the craft.

Willing to Live Lean

Out of all journalism careers, radio on average pays the lowest. In 2006, the median TV news reporter or producer earned $46,000 a year, followed by newspaper journalists at $35,000, then radio journalists at $28,000 a year.

Why the low pay? Well, for one, radio is free. No one pays to listen to the radio—that is, unless you're buying a satellite radio package such as Sirius or XM. So the radio stations aren't making money on listeners; instead, they make money from advertisers.

Basically, advertisers buy "spots" or ad space on the radio station, and those ads trans-late into your salary. The more ads, the better your salary. So it would behoove you to work for the biggest, richest, fattest, and most popular radio station or network to earn a higher salary.

Chances are, however, you're just starting out or are thinking about a career in radio news. So brace yourself: it's a long, steep climb to get work at a bigger station and earn bigger money. But you can do it.

Skill Sets

And just as in other media jobs, reporting for the radio requires honed and specific skills. Being able to report on a subject and write a compelling, fair, and accurate story is one part of the job, but being able to produce the report and voice it on the air is the other—and potentially most critical—part.

It's important, of course, to study journalism and understand ethics, good composition, interviewing techniques, and creative writing. It's critical to read through the print journalism portion of this book to see what those writing skills are and how you can learn to write well.

Assembling a report for the radio is a much trickier job than simply writing it. You'll need to know how to produce it, too, which brings the whole thing together: your recorded interviews, quotes, sounds, and script. You'll need practice and experience in producing your own stories if you want to be a radio journalist.

Breaking News
Producing your own reports is a big part of being a radio journalist.

Don't forget that if you're the one reading the report on the air, you'll need to be versed in how to change the intonations of your voice to sound appealing to your audience. You'll need to sound compelling and intelligent. Voice is a key tool in radio.

Good radio reporters also know how to handle breaking news and think well on their feet. Heading out to a breaking news scene with a mic in hand leaves you no time to prepare.

Whether you're broadcasting what you're seeing or reading a report that you spent days or weeks crafting, creating a visual for the listeners and telling a good story is the very root of radio news—and you need all tools possible to do it

Getting Your Foot in the Door

So you have the skills, the knowledge, and the tools to walk into that radio station office and proclaim, "Look no further: I'm the person for the job." Well, that's the spirit. But talk is cheap, and producers and station owners know that. Also, so is good help, unfortunately. Although there are a whole lot of radio stations and networks out there, there aren't a whole lot of positions at each radio station. Most stations operate on skin-and-bones budgets and try to get the most work out of each person in a day.

Stiff Competition in a Radio Newsroom

Unlike newspaper newsrooms that employ dozens (even hundreds) of editors, reporters, and artists, radio is a tight operation of producers, assistants, and reporters/anchors. If radio is where you want or need to get your start, then you can't be choosy. Jobs are few and far between, and the competition is stiff. If you live in Manchester, Vermont, and there's a job in Flagstaff, Arizona, be ready to pack your bags. Large radio networks, however, might employ scores of workers. But the offices are generally located in large cities that can be expensive to live in—so be sure you take the cost of living into consideration when applying for positions.

How to Apply for a Radio Job

And speaking of applying, there are a few steps to follow. First, not every radio station is going to advertise its openings. Remember, competition is tough, so chances are there will be some resumés on hand of candidates who came close for the last open position but didn't make the final cut—and they are likely still waiting in the wings.

As with getting a job in any field of journalism, arm yourself with your current, well-written, error-free resumé. Tailor your cover letter to the station and market you're trying to become employed in, and spell the name of the contact person correctly. Details are extremely important. Promote yourself in your brief cover letter, clearly stating what skills and experience you have. State why you'd be the best candidate for this job. Education and internships are a must here, as is any other experience working in radio. A willingness to relocate will also win some points.

def•i•ni•tion

An **audition tape**, CD, or DVD includes audio samples of your on-air work, such as broadcasts and reports you did while working at your college radio station, internship, or a former job.

As we've covered already, you'll need a strong list of references—preferably including names from the stations where you worked or interned, not just names of college professors or personal acquaintances. Also have your *audition tape* ready to go and include it with your resumé and cover letter. If it's too cost-prohibitive to send a tape, compact disc, or DVD to every place that you're applying to, then let them know you will provide one upon request.

Nowadays, CDs are cheap and go a long way toward promoting yourself. Remember, any advantage that you can use to separate you from your competition will be way worth the effort and costs. You can also ask for the materials to be returned to you, but you must provide a self-addressed, stamped envelope.

Now that you have sent in your resumé package, let a solid work week go by before making contact. Radio directors are very busy. But call and ask whether they have received your materials—and if so, what did they think?

This call is very important toward your next step. At this point, if they are not interested, they'll tell you. As we've mentioned earlier in this book, ask them specifically what skills they are looking for and which ones you lack. Ask them to make suggestions as to what you could do to have a better shot in the future. Ask them to be honest; this type of criticism is invaluable and will help you hone your skills so you can land a job somewhere else (or even at the same place down the line). Thank them for their time, ask them to please keep your resumé on file, and say goodbye politely.

On the other hand, if they're interested, ask what the next steps are, what else you can provide, and when you can meet with them for an interview. If they're serious about you (and you about them), it would be a good idea to let them know that you are willing and able to meet with them at their convenience, regardless of the distance.

> **Extra! Extra!**
>
> Many radio stations are low-budget operations, so don't plan on them flying you out to an interview or wining and dining you. Offer to come out on your own dime if they don't.

When you do get the interview, be sure to show up prepared. Know about the station, what network(s) it is affiliated with, and who some of the on-air personalities are. Be sure to know about the market and the region, too, such as what the state capital is, who the lawmakers are, and what issues are critical to its audience. It might be good to know a bit about the history of the station and the background of the person who will be interviewing you. A quick Google search might do the trick. Candidates who are the most prepared make very strong impressions, so do your homework.

Also, dress for the part. Chances are, radio stations are relatively casual-attire places to work; however, you want to show respect and that you're serious about the job, so get the suit dry-cleaned and those shoes polished.

If the station is teetering on a decision, tell them you can start immediately and that you won't need much training—that you're ready to plug in and go to work today.

Remember, the important thing is to get your foot in the door with a polished resumé package first so that you can impress them with your skills when you meet in person.

The Least You Need to Know

♦ Historically, radio is the lowest-paid field of journalism.

♦ Studying broadcast journalism and getting hands-on radio training will give you the best shot at finding a decent job.

♦ Producing skills are essential for radio journalists.

♦ Be prepared to not only work hard but also to interview a lot and perhaps travel to get that first job.

Part 4

Television

Television permanently changed the face of mass communication and the field of journalism. From its humble beginnings on fuzzy black-and-white screens to the high-definition, full-color, worldwide broadcasts of today, television continues to evolve—reaching millions of people every minute of every day.

In this part, we'll cover the colorful spectrum of broadcast journalism that's so much more than just the news, the ethical issues that challenge broadcasting, and what it takes to be a television journalist and land a job.

Lights, Camera, Action!

In This Chapter

- ◆ Understanding the medium and magnitude of TV
- ◆ "The Big Three" and the rise of competition
- ◆ The roles and relevancies of national and local programming
- ◆ How cable networks redefined the world of broadcast news

When Philio Farnsworth patented the first complete television system in 1927, he probably wasn't thinking that years later we'd be bouncing TV signals off satellites orbiting miles above the earth. And when journalist Edward R. Murrow was breaking news about Senator Joe McCarthy's communist witch hunts, he probably wouldn't have ever imagined that someday someone like Jon Stewart would be blurring the lines between satire and news to millions of viewers each night.

But TV created the capacity for an enormous spectrum of broadcast news to spread over airwaves and through cables at a pace previously unmatched in the world of journalism. In this chapter, we'll look at what the world of TV is all about … who it is, where it is, and how it continues to change and evolve.

Getting the Picture

The reach of TV is phenomenal in the United States, with about 99 percent of more than 300 million Americans having at least one TV set in their homes—and most of those homes having more. It stands to reason that no single medium can reach more people simultaneously than TV.

Broadcast TV

Broadcast TV—which comes over the airwaves free—is far and away the most-watched type of TV, and its news programming is among the most accurate and wide-reaching. Broadcast TV stations are available for viewing to anyone who has a TV and an antenna. Remember rabbit ears? A TV antenna will pick up the signal of stations broadcasting over the airwaves in a general vicinity.

> **Extra! Extra!**
>
> Ninety-nine percent of Americans have at least one television in their homes.

> **def•i•ni•tion**
>
> A **network** is a broadcasting group that sells its programming to affiliates.

We're talking ABC, CBS, NBC, or "The Big Three," and FOX—which has made a significant impact in the broadcast *network* world since beginning its broadcasting in 1987. Public stations such as PBS (Public Broadcasting System) and the Spanish-language Univision also have a wide reach. As a matter of fact, Univision is the fifth-largest broadcast television network in the world.

There are more than 20 broadcast television networks in the United States alone, and they are generally divided into one of four categories: commercial, educational, religious, and Spanish-language.

Commercial networks are the mainstays of television. NBC, for example, offers a multitude of mainstream programming, from news to sports to sitcoms and drama—even Saturday morning cartoons.

Educational networks are those, such as PBS, which have much programming geared toward viewers who want to learn from TV. The programming includes everything from learning about culture, history, and science to painting a picture or hanging a door.

Religious networks are devoted to faith and spiritual programming. A good example is Eternal Word Television Network (EWTN), which offers programming from actual church services to devotional prayer shows.

Spanish-language networks, such as Univision, are just that: Networks that offer programs in Spanish. Most of these networks provide programming similar to American commercial networks—news, sports, shows, soaps ... but some may be religious in nature or even educational.

Cable Guys

Cable networks require a subscription to receive stations on your TV and have proliferated since the 1970s. Some of the cable journalism heavyweights include CNN, FOX News, and MSNBC. But, as we've learned, journalism goes far beyond hard news. Cable networks such as ESPN, Discovery, and even MTV have varying degrees of journalistic programming. We'll get to those later.

Whereas broadcast TV is limited in its reach—simply put, you need a signal to receive the program—cable can reach where no network antennas are. The signal is much stronger, too, meaning that the programs aren't "fuzzy" due to lack of a strong signal or atmospheric factors, such as electrical storms.

Satellite networks, such as Dish Network and DirectTV, are still in their infancy. But they offer some news programming as well.

What Is Broadcast Journalism?

For now, let's get a clearer picture of what we're talking about when we say *broadcast journalism*. We mean journalism in all television forms—broadcast, cable, and satellite. As it stands, there are nearly 60 networks—national and regional—that broadcast primarily news, weather, or information, such as business news or government happenings. That doesn't include sports networks such as ESPN or FSN, entertainment news networks such as Entertainment TV, or many other specialty cable networks that have some degree of news programming, such as National Geographic, Discovery, HBO, or MTV.

Certainly, the advantages of such an expansive medium are that news and information programming can reach large numbers of people at any time, day or night. The "Big Three" networks reach more than 96 percent of American viewers, and PBS reaches 99 percent.

That's a lot of people tuning in, but it certainly doesn't mean that they are all watching the news every day. However catastrophic and historic world events such as the September 11, 2001, terrorist attacks; Hurricane Katrina in 2005; and Pope John Paul II's passing in 2005 attracted millions of viewers around the globe at all times of the day and night. Normally, on a daily basis, those numbers are a mere fraction.

Extra! Extra!

Video actually never "killed the radio star," as the British rock group The Buggles, as well as doomsayers, proclaimed, but it did change the way media did business as it cut into their audience. Folks want to know what's going on, and even with the advent of the Internet and the consequential explosion of free media online, each medium has maintained a strong pulse. When new communication technology emerges, media displacement often occurs.

Still, television news—from the half-hour local news broadcast to 24-hour cable news programming—remains king when it comes to where people get their news.

More news programming is running through cables and bouncing through broadcast and satellite airwaves than ever before—from Sunday morning talk shows, to local news, to regional 24-hour cable news networks, to every sort of talking (and often screaming) heads news programming on the cable news giants.

The medium has proliferated in leaps and bounds, and isn't stopping any time soon. Despite more competition from Internet and other traditional media who are dabbling in multimedia online, television remains strong.

"I don't think that TV news will go away," says Julie Bologna, morning meteorologist at KTVT-TV, CBS 11 in Dallas/Fort Worth, Texas, and TXA 21 News. "It will just continue to alter its format. You will see more local news stations adding newscasts trying to compete with 24-hour news channels … You may notice more 24-hour weather channels popping up, too."

"Trying to compete with national weather venues like The Weather Channel or the Internet is becoming more difficult," she adds. "Local news is responding by giving viewers more weather updates during severe weather, more information on their station's website and additional weather forecasts on your phone, etc. Whatever new technology is invented, TV news will try to adapt."

TV's Benefits

The advantage of TV journalism is its availability. Viewers have all types of news at their disposal, at all hours of the day. Unlike a print product, where you have to physically run to the newsstand to feed your need, a television set already is in the home—and all that programming is a click of the remote away. Therefore, if there's a big news event—like a tornado blitzing through Midwest cornfields en route to a city—the TV stations can begin airing live broadcasts immediately.

Its reach is vast and its timeliness makes it an extremely relevant medium. Imagine a breaking news event such as the suicide attacks on the World Trade Center towers without having access to television. To get the breaking news, you would have had to listen to the radio—but there are no pictures. So you would have waited for the newspaper to churn out an extra edition. In a few hours, you could see the still images in the paper. On the Internet, of course, the sky's the limit: video and audio abound. But the images might be hit-or-miss. There might not be a professional film crew and reporters at the scene as there are with television.

Yet another advantage that television news has over newspapers is that it can break into regular programming if something big is happening. For instance, a chemical tanker overturns on the highway and leaks hazardous fluid, causing the interstate to close down during morning rush hour. The TV news station might go live with a report, letting people know to take alternate routes on their way to work or school. Generally, however, the local news program will follow the breaking news report with more information.

Local News

Television's reach is enormous and constant. But is it always relevant? Networks like CNN or The Weather Channel have been known for airing the big news stories. But no way, no how, is MSNBC going to cover the local city council meeting or tell you where to drop off your Christmas tree for recycling after the holidays. And even if little Billy runs for 100 yards and throws seven touchdown passes in the high school football game on Friday, it's not likely that ESPN will be there to interview that champ after the big game. So there are benefits to having a local news channel, and the bulk of these stations are *affiliates* of a larger network.

def•i•ni•tion

A television **affiliate** is a local TV station that runs national programming from a larger network, such as NBC or The CW Television Network.

Breaking News

Television and radio stations' call letters begin with "W" east of the Mississippi River and with "K" west of it.

Local TV is where most broadcast journalists cut their teeth in the biz. Just like with newspapers and magazines, the bigger the market the more experience that will be required—so that first job out of college will more than likely be somewhere like ABC-affiliate WAOW-TV in Wausau, Wisconsin.

Public access channels on cable also have increasingly sprung up in the last decade. Dedicated "space" on these channels has allowed communities to generate their own programming—even news programming—for a very specific audience. These markets are tiny, but they may be a good place for a young journalist to get their first taste of the business.

And there are hundreds of affiliates in the United States alone. Basically, every major market will have local affiliates representing the major networks. Savannah, Georgia, for instance, has stations affiliated with NBC, CBS, ABC, FOX, and PBS.

Being Relevant

What makes local television relevant is that it covers local events and issues—just as a local newspaper would. In fact, many newspapers and TV news channels compete not only for breaking news but also for the audience in the same market. So while the newspaper is out covering that big city council meeting for the next day's edition, TV stations can air a report—sometimes even live—by the 11 P.M. news broadcast.

The ability to provide news coverage that is relevant to the immediate community is what gives local news channels their niche and strength. Their broadcasts include news regarding high school sports, local weather, town hall meetings concerning local taxes, and all different kinds of shorts on items relevant to viewers' lives—like where to take that Christmas tree for recycling.

Generally, the news is mixed with live or previously taped reporting. For instance, a reporter might do a live feed from the local "Grinding of the Greens" recycling effort the day after Christmas. The camera crew is set up, and the reporter grabs the microphone and begins interviewing folks in line to have their trees mulched. The reporter interviews the recycling program coordinator, asking questions like how many trees were mulched last year, how long the program has been in operation, what was the impetus for the program, where does the mulch go, and so on. It's all information that affects an immediate community, and it's a level of coverage that only a local station can provide.

Small-Scale Operations

Local TV newsrooms are generally pretty small operations, with just a handful of writers and news producers. Most local TV stations run their news programs three to four times a day—a daybreak report, maybe a lunchtime show, the 5 P.M. or 6 P.M. news, and a late report at 10 or 11 P.M. Many local TV stations have even branched into morning talk shows, simulating *The Today Show* or *Good Morning America*, only with a focus on local issues and events. While most of these shows might not qualify as news broadcasts simply because of their entertainment value over actual news reporting, they might have news updates throughout the show.

Of course, depending on the market and advertising, the news budget at a local TV station may vary wildly. A public TV station with a small budget might merely read stories from the local newspaper mixed in with a local report or two. But most newsrooms employ writers and staff who write and assemble (produce) their news programs for the day.

Network News

Network news is news programming generated from the main news station. ABC, CBS, NBC, and FOX all are national networks and send their programming to affiliates—the local news channels. The networks not only produce shows and sports programming, but they also produce their own news programs that generally air after the local news stations' news shows. *NBC Nightly News*, for instance, comes on live at 6:30 P.M. across America. The same goes for *CBS Evening News*, and *ABC World News*, and the *"Fox Report"* comes on at 7 p.m.

The national news shows provide coverage and analysis on a national and international scale—politics, foreign affairs, the stock market, widespread health- and consumer-oriented reports, and may also cover entertainment, sports, and weather news of national interest. A large and generally well-paid crew assembles the news, with expert interviews from around the world and top-notch reporting. Network news is at the top of the broadcast news world, and these stations compete hard for viewers (and journalists for the jobs, I might add.)

These major networks also produce alternative news shows, from morning talk shows such as *Good Morning America* to evening news shows such as *60 Minutes* and Sunday morning interview talk shows such as *Meet the Press*. All combined, these newsrooms run 24 hours a day, seven days a week, with large newsrooms and crews of writers, editors, producers, and video journalists.

The goal is to break all important national and world news, whenever and wherever it happens. In fact, you'll often see these networks interrupting or preempting normal programming for breaking news—a speech by the president, an update about a plane crash, a tumultuous election, a nasty weather event …

If the story is large enough, the network news station might go around the clock with the programming, as was the case when Hurricane Katrina slammed the Gulf Coast in 2005. Normally scheduled programming remained interrupted by networks for several days when the storm hit. And even while the storm was being covered live with film crews and reporters riding it out to get the story, reporters back in the newsroom were piecing together related stories and features to run with the coverage, while others still were keeping track of the rest of the country and world. Network news is a non-stop operation, but they're not the only ones.

Cable News

For years, "The Big Three" networks—ABC, CBS, and NBC—dominated the world of broadcast news. FOX News came along in the late 1980s and began competing immediately. Although it has never obtained the reach that the "Big Three" have in viewership and ratings, the move showed that another network could contend. Then, along came cable news networks.

Arguably, one of the biggest events to shake up this triad of networks and their news programs was the Cable News Network (CNN).

Breaking News
Headquartered in Atlanta, Georgia, CNN boasts some 1,600 employees around the world and has more than 50 million viewers in the United States alone.

Media mogul and baseball Hall of Famer Ted Turner started CNN in 1980 as a 24-hour news channel. The network began receiving major recognition when covering that year's Democratic and Republican National Conventions. By 1985, the network was reaching some 30 million homes. Today, it reaches 50 million viewers in the United States alone—and millions more around the globe.

Why wait for the 6:30 P.M. news? CNN is there every time you turn on your TV. Its success was so enormous that other 24-hour news networks formed to compete (and have done so very well)—two of the larger networks being FOX News and MSNBC.

But for those who just wanted quicker news than what CNN was providing, Turner began *Headline News* (which, in some sense, began competing with CNN). The result, however, was more of the market shares for Turner.

Interestingly, though, the 24-hour news channels didn't stop with these national and international behemoths. Regional and somewhat local 24-hour news channels began popping up in major markets.

Bay News 9, for instance, began running regional news coverage around the clock for the greater Tampa Bay, Florida area. At first, the programming was low-budget—but over time, the channel grew to be *the* place to go (especially for traffic rush-hour checks). With its helicopter and on-site reporting, TV viewers got to see what the expressway congestion was like before venturing out. The channel also aired typical news programming with local government reporting, weather, and sports. Soon, the channel gained more and more respect and a larger audience—and, although not the first regional 24-hour news channel, many metro areas followed the same course and have done so with a good degree of success.

The Least You Need to Know

- Broadcast TV is the most-watched type of TV in the world.
- "The Big Three" broadcast networks—ABC, CBS, and NBC—have been penetrated by competing networks in cable, satellite, and even locally.
- Local TV has relevance due to its ability to report on its immediate community.
- Cable news networks, namely CNN, pioneered 24-hour news programming.

Chapter 16

More Than News

In This Chapter

- ◆ The making of a good broadcast journalist
- ◆ Broadcast journalism goes far beyond news
- ◆ Sports are a TV mainstay
- ◆ Entertainment reporting is journalism, too

So far, we've tuned in to the world of broadcast news—those talking heads on the boob tube who bring the world into our living rooms. The fundamentals of broadcast news are similar to any other media; what differs is the vehicle used to transmit that news.

But what about who delivers what we see and hear? And what about specific topics such as weather or sports reporting? How about entertainment news? And where does Jon Stewart fit into the equation? In this chapter, we'll take a look at the who, the what, and just how far we can stretch the definition of broadcast journalism.

Not Just Another Pretty Face

I'll never forget the first day of my college broadcast news class. The professor looked around the room and asked, "How many of you want to be on TV?" Most of the students raised their hands in affirmation. He then said, "Well, most of you are too ugly." I decided to study print journalism instead.

The range of knowledge, skills, and training of on-air *anchors* varies wildly in TV news. Are we looking for a great reporter or someone to sell the program? Do we want a news hound on the air or someone who's easy on the eyes?

def•i•ni•tion

An **anchor** is someone who hosts a news show. He or she usually reads the news, introduces correspondents' reports, conducts interviews, and often writes and/or edits the news for the program. The word is a reference to the anchor leg of a relay race.

Most times, the answer is both. But that's not always possible. And, well, sometimes it's just not practical. The bigger the market, the smarter the reporter or personality—and generally, the more attractive the reporter. It may be a sad commentary on our society, but on-air personalities—broadcast journalists—are also selling a product, and it pays to be able to sell that product well.

Building Clout

Education and training are essential to good news reporting, both on- and off-camera. Big-name journalists such as Jim Lehrer and Christiane Amanpour have strong journalism backgrounds and years of reporting under their belts.

Amanpour, for instance, graduated from the University of Rhode Island with a journalism degree. She worked as a reporter, anchor, and producer in local radio before getting on the CNN international desk in Atlanta, Georgia, then doing stints in New York and Frankfurt, Germany, for CNN. She's covered a range of important stories, including the Gulf War and the wars in Iraq, Afghanistan, Bosnia, the Balkans, Rwanda, Darfur, Sri Lanka, Somalia, and the breakup of the Soviet Union. She's earned a host of awards and accolades through her career and is one of the most respected journalists working in news today.

We'll discuss the skills that you need to become a good TV journalist more later. But for now, let's get an idea of what constitutes TV journalists.

On a more regional level, Julie Bologna—if you remember from the previous chapter—who has worked as a reporter in print, radio and television, is the morning meteorologist at KTVT-TV, a CBS affiliate in the Dallas-Fort Worth, Texas, market and at TXA 21 News. Twelve years into the business, Bologna's work is highly regarded. But she didn't start out in a major market. Earning degrees in journalism and meteorology, she worked in both radio and TV news before moving into weather full time.

"I suggest having a degree in meteorology if you want to be a meteorologist or a degree in journalism if you want to be a reporter-anchor," says Bologna. "These days, it's getting more and more competitive, so having a degree or background in your field is highly recommended."

Extra! Extra! _____

If getting on the air is your goal, you're going to need the brains and personality to do it.

Correspondents such as Amanpour and meteorologists such as Bologna are surely journalists. They report on very different things, but each is a journalist nonetheless—bringing all the necessary qualities to the screen.

And what about the other talking heads? What about the Sunday morning pressure cookers and the prime-time anchors? Is that journalism, too?

Knowing the Difference

Just as newspapers, editorial page editors, and writers have their own opinions, so, too, does TV news. Shows such as *Crossfire* and *The News Hour with Jim Lehrer* are on opposite ends of that spectrum of journalism. But what you're looking at in a basic sense is an interviewer (reporter) asking questions of a subject for a report. The questions can be leading and opinionated, such as they were on *Crossfire*, or neutral and unbiased—as is the case with Jim Lehrer.

Crossfire, which ran from 1982 to 2005 on CNN, featured two interviewers—a liberal and a conservative—and two guests—again, a liberal and a conservative—who generally engaged in an often fiery debate of political or social issues. The idea was to flesh out what each side stood for and why, and that format was successful for many years with many respected and prominent hosts including James Carville, Robert Novak, Lynne Cheney, Pat Buchanan, Paul Begala, John Sununu, Tucker Carlson, and Mary Matalin.

Breaking News

The line between journalism and entertainment tends to blur between bona fide news programs such as the 6 P.M. news and the prime-time news talk shows.

The show was canceled shortly after TV satirist Jon Stewart's appearance on October 15, 2004, in which he harshly criticized the show. Stewart told hosts Tucker Carlson and Paul Begala, "It's not so much that it's bad as it's hurting America." We'll talk more about Stewart in a moment.

But if *Crossfire* was on one end of the spectrum, then surely Jim Lehrer is on the other. Lehrer got his start as a newspaper reporter before co-hosting a show with Robert MacNeil on PBS. The show, *The MacNeil-Lehrer Report*, was wildly successful for its straightforward journalistic approach. It was unbiased and intelligent, and Lehrer molded his trademark *fair reporter* in that show, which began way back in 1975. His balance and fairness garnered his own show, *The News Hour*. It also made him the obvious choice for moderating presidential debates—10 of them, as a matter of fact.

Not all TV anchors are trained journalists; they might be so-called "TV personalities." These anchors pretty much get paid to read the stories that reporters have written ahead of time. Sure, they can interview—they can do journalism—and the perception may be that they are journalists. However, the line becomes blurry as TV stations aren't going to promote their anchors as nonjournalists. But it might go without saying that not everyone on TV news programs is a trained journalist.

There is, on the other hand, an array of anchors with a solid background in journalism. Although famed TV reporter and anchor Tom Brokaw received his training in political science and got his start on TV by hosting a game show, his reporting experience has shaped him into one of the most prolific TV newsmen in history—having covered every major news event from Watergate to the Berlin Wall's fall to the war in Iraq.

The Forecast for Weather

When broadcast news programs, such as the 6 P.M. news, were in their heyday back in the second half of the twentieth century, their formats generally were separated into three main subjects: news, weather, and sports. For a half-hour show, news dominated the program followed by just a few minutes of weather, then ended with sports (or some corny 30-second fluff piece).

Overlooked was that most of the viewers wanted more weather—and they wanted it, in some cases, before the news segment. By the 1980s, many news programs began *teasing* to weather with a brief forecast, then following it up later in the program with the full report.

def•i•ni•tion

A **tease** used in news programs is a snippet of information that gives viewers an inkling of what's to come later in the broadcast. Its goal is to get viewers to stay tuned to the program.

Channeling in on the Weather

Just as producers began realizing that more weather meant more viewers, along came The Weather Channel. This 24-hour weather behemoth took the broadcast world news by storm in 1982 and instantly became a success. In just six years, The Weather Channel became one of the top 12 cable networks—having more than 70 million subscribers and being available to 95 percent of American households.

The Weather Channel also produces weather stories and weather packages for more than 60 newspapers, including *USA Today*, with a combined circulation of about 8 million.

This network also took to the Internet, where it receives 350 million page hits each month—leading all other online weather services.

So weather, as The Weather Channel has certainly proven, is much more to viewers than just something to stuff into a one-minute segment on the program.

Breaking News

The Weather Channel reaches 95 percent of American households with 70 million subscribers.

A Changing Landscape

Turns out that adding more weather programming was a pretty good idea. Local weather forecasts are the network's bread and butter. Also the network's reporters and crews began to jet to any region of the United States any time a major storm blew in. Americans got used to a meteorologist not simply covering the weather while standing in front of a green screen in the studio but on a beach as a hurricane bore down or in whatever apocalyptic weather phenomenon was happening. And that changed the way all those other weather forecasters did their jobs.

"Usually, meteorologists forecast for their city," says Bologna. "Viewers want to know if they should carry an umbrella to work or if they should dress the children in a jacket. Local television weather focuses on the regional area; however, when there's a big national weather story, news stations cover that, too. They can even be sent to cover the big story live for their station. You always see live hurricane coverage, blizzard stories, storm chasing, etc. More and more, viewers will see the important weather stories all across the world."

So what does it take to report the weather? To be successful, it's going to take a degree in meteorology or journalism. You need to know how to write, report, and broadcast on air plus have a thorough understanding of meteorology.

"There are exceptions though," says Bologna. "In regards to weather, there are still stations that will hire you without a weather or news background. They will train you themselves or send you off for schooling. So, you can break into weather or TV news in many different ways. However, I always suggest getting your schooling in ahead of time, because the majority of stations want someone with a background in weather—meaning you have your weather seals in either the National Weather Association or the American Meteorological Society or a degree right off the bat. There are exceptions for sure, but again, the majority do prefer to hire someone with a background in their field."

Meteorologists generally have a bachelor's degree in this scientific field and have taken additional tests or completed a series of specific courses to earn their seals from the National Weather Service, which is the foremost government weather authority in the United States, and the American Meteorological Society, which promotes education and disseminates information on weather and oceanic and hydrologic sciences.

Putting on Your Game Face

Just as sports writing for newspapers or magazines relies on solid journalism, ethics, and timeliness, it does so even more in the TV world. From live coverage of games to studio analysis and features reporting, the world of network TV sports is a place that many sportswriters hope to reach.

A Tough Audience

Sports is immediate, and its fans are passionate. Imagine writing a story to run on the air about the cost of home heating oil, but your audience has a good deal of knowledge about the industry—how oil is measured, why it has so many taxes, what the current Middle Eastern situation is and how that affects the oil prices, and so on—along with a very good knowledge of Wall Street influences. Add to that equation that many of the people whom you are addressing have worked in the oil industry, even if those jobs were very low-level—and have followed the industry very closely since they were little kids.

That's what you're up against in the world of sports journalism. Many viewers have been fans since they learned to change a channel on the remote and have played the game at least recreationally. Also they have lived and died with every Hail Mary from their team's quarterback or every sub-.500 season. So yeah, you need to really know your sports.

We'll talk more later about what you'll need in the way of a sheepskin and experience to do this job. But if you're looking to break into the world of TV sports, you'd better bring your best game.

The ESPN Zone

Just as The Weather Channel shook up the world of TV meteorology, ESPN came along with its 24-hour programming in 1979. Not only did it force the TV world to add more sports programming—but it told them how to do it: with authority.

Again, like weather, local TV sports segments were brief and jammed into the end of the news show—until ESPN came onto the scene, that is. Now, even local news channels have half-hour shows dedicated to local sports—from the area's pro team coverage right down to college and pro sports. But local sportscasters also do it with more flamboyance, more attitude, and more authority.

Breaking News
ESPN has become the authority in sports broadcasting, reaching more than 190 countries worldwide (including more than 97 million Americans).

ESPN has shown the rest of the world how seriously fans take their sports: 24 hours a day, 7 days a week, over multiple channels, with news, features, and entertainment, live games that might seem irrelevant, and covering a wide spectrum of sports. For instance, ESPN owns ESPN, ESPN2, ESPN Classic, ESPNHD, ESPNEWS, ESPN Radio, *ESPN The Magazine*, and ESPN Zone restaurants. Don't forget ESPN.com and a handful of video games. Its programs reach more than 97 million people in the United States alone, in addition to 190 countries around the world. Now that's big!

Entertaining an Argument

So we've talked about weather and sports as journalism, both in the medium of TV broadcasting. But is there any journalistic value in entertainment writing and broadcasting?

Clearly, there's a difference between, say, James Lipton on *Inside the Actor's Studio* and Melissa Rivers commenting on Angelina Jolie's dress as she's walking the red carpet at the Oscars.

E! Entertainment Television is known for its gossip-laden reporting, and a lot of what goes into producing a segment is similar to a news report. Reporters are out digging up information on movie stars and those who are in the spotlight, putting that information together for a story and fitted it with video images.

Journalistic value? Well, it's not as if they're trying to make stuff up; however, they are capitalizing on the sensational and padding the writing to be more sassy and leading than straightforward journalism.

But, just because entertainment TV isn't wholly journalistic or admittedly doesn't try to be journalism most of the time, a show or network that's predominantly entertainment only can still offer news value.

Not Just Music Television

Take MTV, for instance. The programming ranges from music videos to reality shows to spring break parties. But the network also produces *MTV News* and has programming that brought attention to some pretty large social concerns, such as AIDS, homosexuality, drug abuse, racism, and eating disorders. And they've urged people to vote.

In 1992, MTV began its Rock the Vote campaign and encouraged its target audience—18- to 24-year-olds—to vote by airing public service announcements with influential stars and offering programming that even included an interview with Bill Clinton, the young Democrat running for the White House.

MTV News has covered elections, interviewed politicians, and created programming such as *Enough is Enough*, which examined crime, drugs, and violence in America's youth. Although the format was basically question-and-answer, the writing was a bit leading. Tabitha Soren, the host, commented: "We are losing a whole generation to crime, to drugs, to lost hopes."

It would be hard to imagine that type of writing in a *New York Times* news story, but as we've discussed, journalism cuts a very wide swath—as is shown in editorial and column writing. And *MTV News* might be at the very line of that definition.

> **Breaking News**
>
> *MTV News* features more than just the latest information on musicians and stars—it also delves into heavy social issues and is directed toward the 18-to-24-year-old audience.

When Journalism Lines Become More Blurry

What has certainly crossed that line, however, is *The Daily Show with Jon Stewart*. The enormous success and ratings of this late-night spoof on evening news has spawned debate over whether what Stewart does is actually journalism.

It might be a sad commentary that people would even debate this issue, showing just how close some of the interview-type programming on the cable news networks resembles the satire that Stewart produces.

Stewart's tongue-in-cheek reporting looks at an issue that is in the news, then comments on it or twists it for a humorous reaction. For instance, he says that Donald Rumsfeld (former secretary of defense under President George W. Bush) reminds him of "Pete the crazy guy outside my apartment."

Can you learn things from Stewart about what's in the news? Sure. But as Stewart told *The Washington Post*, "It's not fake news. We are not newsmen, but it's jokes about real news. We don't make up anything other than the fact that we're not actually standing in Baghdad ..."

Calling Jon Stewart a newsman or his work journalism would be remiss; but while it should be easy to see the lines of journalism blurred between some of the evening talk-pundit shows and Stewart's spoofs, often it is not. Entertainment reporting can be good journalism, but not all entertainment reporting, or satire, is journalism.

The Least You Need to Know

◆ There's more to TV news than just another pretty face.

◆ Weather reporting has become a serious business.

◆ Sports broadcasting goes far beyond just game-calling.

◆ Entertainment news can be as serious as any form of journalism, but the lines quite often become blurred.

Chapter 17

Ethics on the Airwaves

In This Chapter

- ◆ Trading journalism for ratings
- ◆ Getting used to sensationalism
- ◆ Carefully choosing your words
- ◆ Using the camera to sell stories

We've all heard the criticism: TV news has no ethics, it blatantly violates fairness, it's all about sound bites and ratings … The list goes on, and much of the criticism is well-deserved. Case after case exists in broadcast journalism's vast archives where ethical slips and stumbles have occurred—some more frequently than others. It's no different for other media. The last quarter-century, especially, brought into the spotlight a litany of bad examples, from sound bites for shock value to flagrant unethical undercover reporting—such as the case involving Food Lion and ABC (more on that in a minute). Ethical errors and bad judgment in print journalism have only added fuel to the fire. After all, to readers and viewers a journalist is a journalist, no matter what medium. In this chapter, we'll look at some of the ethical pitfalls journalists sometimes stumble into and those who try to skirt them.

All About Ratings?

Should ethics be any different for broadcast journalism than for print journalism? No. But is there a difference? Yes, quite often.

"Chasing" Stories

Newspapers are generally metaphoric one-horse towns when it comes to print competition. Only a handful of major metro dailies directly compete with others. However, as we learned in Chapter 15, there are many TV affiliates for any given region—including some that overlap and compete fiercely.

Look at your hometown TV news options. Most viewers probably have affiliates for NBC, CBS, ABC, and FOX. Add to that the cable giants CNN and MSNBC. And then there's PBS. Sure, it's likely that you have one newspaper primarily to cover your city, but you have an array of TV affiliates from which to choose.

So just as the saying goes, "If it bleeds, it leads"—meaning there might be, and more than likely are, all sorts of sensational news stories leading off the newscasts to hook people's attentions. These aren't necessarily life-changing stories, but they have some shock value to get you to watch.

We've all seen seemingly more important news "buried" in a newspaper or newscast in trade for the brawl at the local Wal-Mart or the sensational accident on the interstate. Is that unethical? No, not really. Is it *sensationalism*? You bet. Is it wrong? Well, that one's harder to measure. If the station's goal is to remain a reputable news source and present the most important news to the viewer, then always covering sensational events or subjects first might not build clout with viewers. Building *ratings* is often what comes into play here instead.

def•i•ni•tion

Sensationalism in journalism is when news is artificially enhanced to make it seem more important than it is—in an attempt to arouse a quick, intense, and usually superficial interest or emotional reaction.

Ratings in television are measurements and estimates of how many viewers are tuning in to specific programs.

Good ratings are important because advertisers pay billions of dollars to air their commercials during top-rated shows. The higher the TV ratings, the more money to be made during that programming or on those channels. Sensationalism in TV news, then, might draw many more people to the set. Remember the expression "if it bleeds, it leads"? That means footage from an air crash or a suspect fleeing police in a high-speed car chase grabs viewers' attention. The more viewers, the higher the ratings.

Is it cheap? Sure. Is it news? Most often. Is it the most important news item? Well, not so much. After all, viewers also know that scandal and violence and other sensational news sells in terms of ratings. And that's not all that's different from print journalism. Strip headlines are often about the same topics.

The danger, however, is when journalists start manufacturing news—in other words, scouring the streets like paparazzi for sensational news or manipulating non-news to make it something more than it is.

Ever since the O. J. Simpson incident in 1994, viewers became transfixed on watching car chases. Simpson, who was believed to have been fleeing the scene of his ex-wife's and her friend's murder, led police on a three-hour chase at slow speeds on a Los Angeles Freeway. The murder trial that ensued was dubbed "The Trial of the Century." Simpson was acquitted.

For whatever reason, that became "news." TV shows spawned from helicopter footage of cops chasing fleeing cars on Los Angeles, California, freeways. Networks even began breaking into regular programming to bring us the latest car-chase news.

Many of us look back at that type of journalism and say, "So what's the big deal?" And it's true. For instance, what's the big deal about a guy who robs a liquor store, then steals a car, then jets down the shoulder of a freeway in the wrong direction at 75 miles per hour to evade police—in a city where that situation probably happens a few times a day?

Nothing. It's simply pure entertainment. So is it ethical to peddle sensationalism under the guise of news? No. But it happens all too often.

Just Another Day

And what about a slow news day, when the local news has a few lead-worthy pieces such as: a new sales tax taking effect at midnight around the state; a morning school bus wreck (only the bus was empty); the beginning of a trial of a man charged with nonfatally shooting his wife downtown; and a small, private plane crash that injured the solo pilot.

None of those items is of immediate concern to the masses, right? Well, the affiliate can lead with something from the national or international news wire, such as the war in Iraq, the peace process in the Middle East, nuclear talks in North Korea … But none of it is that captivating.

Breaking News

Credibility in TV news hit an all-time low in 2005, with public trust dropping from 36 percent in 2000 to 28 percent in 2005.

So the only choice that seems to remain is to find out more about those options and see whether there's some hook that will grab readers. That's good journalism, digging deeper to find out more in an attempt to make these stories as compelling as possible. But the ethical dangers come into play when information is contorted to seem more appealing.

For example, let's look at the following story.

Assault and Attempted Murder Trial Begins for Former Coach

The trial of a former Swampsville basketball coach accused of launching into a jealous tirade, pulling his rifle from a locked cabinet, and trying to kill his wife by shooting her in the head goes to trial tomorrow morning in front of jury and judge.

Roger Dean Doe, a 47-year-old man who has been called a fiery personality by at least one neighbor, took the gun from his locked rifle cabinet, stormed into the bedroom where his wife was sleeping, and opened fire.

Phyllis Doe wasn't killed by the gun blast but was listed as touch and go in the hospital for 17 days.

Doe is charged with aggravated assault with intent to kill and could face up to 60 years in prison.

Is any of it lies? No. But is it hyped? Absolutely. You see, normally the story might not make a brief in the paper or on air. The fact is, unless it's an actual murder trial, it's probably not going to be covered because it's not sensational enough.

So what did we do? Dug harder to find some sensational information—more interesting tidbits. And what was uncovered? Doe had been a high school coach (implication: we left our kids in his care, and how long ago was that?); the gun was in a locked cabinet (shows that he must have really wanted to kill her since he had to—gasp—unlock the cabinet); he went on a jealous tirade (did it even really happen, the police report just said it was a fight over her talking with another man?); he's got a fiery personality (one neighbor made this comment, and was that in the context of his coaching?); his wife was touch and go (what does that mean?); and he could face up to 60 years in prison (sure he could, but what are the chances of that?). Contorting news to elevate it is the journalist equal of making a mountain of a molehill.

Desensitizing Viewers

Many TV news writers and producers have failed horribly at holding the middle ground on ethical writing to the point where viewers have become desensitized to their sensational writing style. Viewers not only expect it, but the stories also barely capture their attention simply because there is so much of it. Take a look at the war in Iraq. When the United States began its campaign to liberate the people of Iraq from its dictator, it was done so with a powerful show of military might.

As in the first Gulf War, viewers were glued to the TV to watch the surgical attacks on buildings and airfields. More than 10 years later, we watched in fascination the same coverage as the city of Baghdad was pulverized by high-tech American weaponry.

The coverage went on for weeks. Some networks offered 24-hour news coverage out of the firestorm. Others interrupted regular programming or updated throughout the day. But within a few weeks, something happened: folks stopped watching it, and coverage ratings declined.

The headlines began blurring together. "Four Americans Killed By Roadside Bomb," "U.S. Helicopter Crashes in Desert," "Iraq's No. 5 Caught"… and on and on it went. Three years and about 3,000 U.S. servicemen and women later, readers might not see a front-page headline—and viewers will have even less of a chance seeing the war lead off the newscast.

 Extra! Extra! _____

By repeatedly airing a story with only incremental updates, a viewer will become bored, desensitized, and even apathetic toward the news event.

Is the war important and newsworthy? Yes. But after three years and counting, will people still gravitate toward repetitious coverage? Hardly. So unless the story has some sort of angle to hook the viewers—one of the soldiers was from nearby, some sort of freak accident or instance occurred, or there was some sort of measurable landmark (3,000th U.S. soldier killed, anniversary of a specific attack, Associated Press poll on those who believe we should continue, and so on)—the report probably won't make the first 10 minutes of a newscast and probably won't make the evening or nighttime talk shows.

That doesn't mean that the news is unimportant. But it can mean the viewers are just used to it and unmoved by it—even though they do care about what is happening with the war. And the media have a role in that desensitization because they keep hammering the audience with the same story, so eventually, it's bound to happen.

Therefore, a balance should be reached. Sure, we lead with the most important and relevant news of the day, but we don't lead with it because we want to squeeze every last drop of ratings out of it.

The Language of the Misleading

Loaded words are the tools of irresponsible journalists, and their use has eroded the ethical foundation of reporting. Listen closely to news broadcasts and see how the language runs the gamut of the sensational—starting with PBS, then local affiliate news, the national network news, and ending on the political punditry of the evening's talking heads. As the evening grows, so too does the leading language.

Loaded Words

We briefly mentioned above an example of using sensational language to doll up a story when we talked about the former basketball coach who shot his wife. Using adjectives and adverbs is one way to show your journalistic colors, but when using those techniques, you must be sure they aren't misleading.

Check out this sentence about a developer who destroyed three acres of wetlands while building a new shopping mall:

> To make way for the new shopping mall, only three acres of city wetlands were drained by the developers.

def•i•ni•tion

Loaded words can mislead a viewer by their connotations, such as "only," "claimed," and "hopefully."

What is "only" telling us? It's a loaded word. It says that three acres is a small number. That point might be debatable, and it sounds like we're downplaying the incident.

What if we found out the city had four acres of wetlands total, meaning that three-fourths was now gone? From the way it's written above, though, it doesn't seem like three acres is a big deal, does it?

So with a different bent, another broadcaster makes the following statement:

> An astonishing 75 percent of the city's critical wetlands were destroyed by overzealous developers in order to make way for the new mega-shopping mall.

Whoa, Nellie! Not only do we have an immeasurable 75 percent (sure it's a big number, but 75 percent of what—four acres or four million acres?), but we now also have the loaded modifiers "astonishing," "critical," "overzealous," and "mega." We're on the other side of the debate. With words expressed in this way, the viewers will likely be calling for the developers' heads.

The facts, however, may simply be that the developer is going to mitigate those lost acres—and maybe even go beyond by building a 10-acre wetland area just south of the new mall. Maybe the Army Corps of Engineers is helping ensure that the move is conducted properly and that any wildlife (assuming it exists—we don't know that, either) won't be harmed. For a journalist, it's a better bet to rely on full reporting and play it straight. The facts will speak for themselves.

Claiming Bias?

There are many pitfalls to avoid in the language of journalism. Keep in mind that some we might just take for granted because we are simply so used to hearing and seeing them said and written. But there are dangers in journalism, and avoiding them will not only save your reputation for being fair but might even keep your name off a libel lawsuit.

Claim and *admit* are two words that are overused in attributions and carry a lot of weight. Take the following sentence, for instance:

> The mayor claimed that the measure would save taxpayers money.

What we're really saying is that we don't necessarily believe the mayor. The mayor's statement is not straightforward—it's his defense that the measure would save dollars. If the writer used the attribution "said" instead, there would be no bias:

> The mayor said the measure would save taxpayers money.

Extra! Extra! _____

Bias creeps into writing in many ways. Be careful of the adjectives, adverbs, and attributes that you use (and read!).

"Admitted" is another dangerous word in an attribution. In fact, it's even more dangerous than "claimed." It strongly suggests that there is something to defend, that there was some wrongdoing. The point is, you admit to doing something—and the connotation is usually negative.

The mayor admitted he knew how much the contract would cost the taxpayers.

This example implies some wrongdoing, doesn't it? As if to say the contract was faulty or overly expensive. But the fact is, the mayor's job is to know how much the contracts will cost the taxpayers, right? Go ahead and sign a contract and not know what the cost is and see how long you last in office.

Consider the following rewrite:

The mayor said he knew how much the contract would cost the taxpayers.

Duh, right?

Making a Comment

Journalists keep another evil little tool in their top drawers, ready at hand. It's the no-comment technique.

Far too often, we hear this statement:

The mayor refused to comment on whether the mall project would cripple local businesses.

Heck, I wouldn't answer that question, either. First, it's extremely speculative—but even more, maybe what he told the reporter was that he "didn't know" or "couldn't say" whether the mall would affect local businesses.

The two are not interchangeable, and this sentence makes the mayor sound shifty. So did he "refuse" to comment or wouldn't comment on the specific question?

When we use the word "refused," we are telling the viewer that this person, the mayor, has an obligation to comment to us. Private citizens surely have no obligation, and depending on the instance, even public officials aren't obligated, either. The better word choice here is "declined."

What about when you're on deadline and you need that one comment for your story? So you pick up the phone and call your subject—only to find that she's not home.

You write:

City Councilwoman Jane Baar could not be reached for comment.

That's true; you called her, and she couldn't be reached for your comment. But how hard did you try? This statement could also imply that Ms. Baar is hiding from the press. Now, the ethical burden is squarely on your shoulders to give the councilwoman the chance to comment. Without her response, you're allowing a bias into your story.

Imagine this scenario: the councilwoman's position was attacked by an opposing candidate running for her seat. During the interview, the candidate alleges that Councilwoman Baar voted against every measure to help the city's poorer residents improve their homes. The obvious question now is whether she did vote against these measures—all of them. So you call her, but she's not home. She might be at a function downtown, maybe out having dinner, maybe she's at a benefit for the homeless … You write that "she couldn't be reached for comment." That's not fair.

Reporters must make every effort within reason to contact the subject. One, even two phone calls are not even close to enough. I've sent many a reporter to subjects' homes, jobs, meetings, and anywhere else I think they might be. In extreme cases, I've left very pointed messages with their family members or on their answering machine, sent them e-mails, and even faxed them. I called a friend of the person they were believed to be with, and I've even called the hotel or restaurant where they were believed to be.

If the source is critical to the reporting, I'd hold the story for 24 hours. Once, I even sent the subject questions via overnight mail. You do what it takes to play fair. They will appreciate the consideration, and so will your readers. Then, if they can't be reached, then they *truly* can't be reached.

Extra! Extra!

Using "could not be reached for comment" better mean that you tried more than once to contact him or her.

Pushing Video to the Limits

There are several techniques that, when misused, can lead to unethical reporting in broadcast news. We're talking about undercover reporting, hiding the camera while reporting, and using camera angles to manipulate an emotion or dupe the viewer. When and how this technique is used can be the difference between legitimate reporting and a hack job.

Going Undercover

Perhaps no greater example of undercover reporting for broadcast news—and a question of ethics—exists than the famous Food Lion case of 1992. Claims that the supermarket chain was selling old food, including spoiled meat bleached to kill the odor and rat-gnawed cheese, hit the news desk at ABC's *Prime Time Live*. To report the story, the staff went undercover—a technique that means subjects of a report are being taped without their knowledge or consent.

Two ABC producers lied on applications to get jobs at two Food Lion supermarkets in North Carolina. With tiny cameras and microphones tucked into their wigs, they showed up for their jobs and began taping. They assembled a report using footage obtained while working at Food Lion.

> **Breaking News**
>
> ABC was sued by Food Lion for more than $5 million for fraudulent reporting tactics in 1992.

When the supermarket was finally notified of the reporting, the company sued ABC. The program ran November 5, 1992, and Food Lion didn't deny the undercover report's allegations. Instead, it charged ABC with fraud, trespassing, and deception. A judge ruled in favor of the supermarket chain.

Where are the ethical boundaries here? Obviously, a reporter can't walk into a supermarket and accuse the store's manager of selling rotten food. I'm fairly certain the manager is either not going to comment or will flat-out deny the allegation. Then, quite possibly, the spoiled meat would continue to be sold.

The press does have an ethical duty to shed light on any wrongdoing, but are there limits? Certainly. Privacy rights are strengthening each year, protecting innocent people from being taped without their knowledge. But what about when wrongdoing harms people's health?

The justification was that in order to get this story, ABC had to go undercover—even lie to get the jobs. The problem was that ABC waited six months to air the program, and the criticism was that if people were eating spoiled meat and ABC felt it had an ethical responsibility to let people know, they didn't do a very good job of getting that information to people in a timely manner.

But we all love hidden camera reports, don't we? Let's be honest—as a viewer, when you hear the words, "We go undercover to shed light on a government scandal …" your heart beats a few times faster, doesn't it? Well, news folks know that, and that's why we now have undercover reports on everything from a celebrity marriage to the investigation about whether low-fat donuts are really low in fat.

When we go undercover for any random story and do it too frequently, the effect lessens and people become desensitized. Take a look at your favorite cable news network. I'd be willing to bet that if you tuned in right now, there would be a breaking news banner scrolling across the screen. We, as viewers, have become trained to virtually ignore breaking news. More often than not, it's not really breaking—it's just news, maybe.

The same goes for undercover reporting. If you air an undercover report every day, the technique will lessen the actual impact. Sure, you might have actually gone undercover, but why? To unearth the lies of low-fat donuts?

Extra! Extra! _____

Hidden camera techniques should only be used for stories of public interest involving wrongdoing that is causing great harm to people.

All About the Angle

Entire volumes have been written to describe the right and wrong use of cameras. As we discussed earlier, hiding them is deceptive but needed occasionally.

So can lighting and camera angles mislead a viewer? Sure. For example, how many news segments have you seen where an accused murderer is coming out of a courtroom in super slow motion?

What are we saying with that technique? Maybe nothing, or maybe we simply want to stretch out the few seconds of video we have (heck, we'll even run it over and over!). Or maybe the accused is making a sour face. Maybe we zoom in on his eyes—they look a little shifty, don't they? And we accentuate all that by running the film even slower. You will certainly notice that the more sensational the news show, the more these cheap camera techniques are used.

Extra! Extra! _____

Lighting and camera angles can skew a story. Play it straight when possible.

Camera angles don't just affect their subjects. One technique often seen is that famous back-of-the-reporter's-head shot while they sit and interview someone as if to say, "Look here—this event is really happening. I'm actually sitting across from Jimmy Carter." You see the reporter's head nod as if he's speaking and his hand with the pen in it, gesturing as if he's talking—because, after all, we can hear his voice. But he isn't talking. Most often than not, the interviewer is going through that little skit on camera after the show was taped, just for effect.

You'll also see the subjects of the interview looking as if they are listening intently. But that reaction might have been edited out of a previous shot and used for a later one—again, for effect (as if to say, "Yeah, I'm listening. Good point.").

It's best to just play it straight. If you have a good interview and you are doing good reporting, then let that reporting speak for itself. Smoke and mirrors are, well, just that: cheap tricks.

The Least You Need to Know

♦ Inflating stories for ratings walks an ethical line of journalism.

♦ Language can greatly lean a story and mislead viewers.

♦ "No comment" doesn't always mean there isn't a comment.

♦ Undercover reporting can be deceptive journalism.

Chapter 18

Getting Started in Television Journalism

In This Chapter

- Choosing the right path for you
- Getting a proper education
- Getting the skills
- Breaking into the business

By now, you might be convinced of one or two things: you want to work in broadcast news no matter what it takes, or you want to know why anyone would torture themselves for years to get a shot at television success.

We're hoping it's the former. And if so, the reality—as we've discussed in other mediums as well—is that it most likely will take some time to get a job in a good market. That means a decent-sized city and decent pay. In this chapter, we'll create a road map of how to get exactly where you want to go in television journalism.

You Know You're a TV Journalist If ...

What do you hope to achieve as a TV journalist? Are you the anchor type who wants to read the news each night or the investigative journalist who has a panache for the live interview or going undercover to get the real story? Or are you the person behind the scenes—the one who edits the story, putting it together with film and audio to create a good story?

If your answer is yes to any of these questions, then you're heading in the right direction. So let's narrow it further.

Whether it's network news or local TV news, reporter and producer jobs are more numerous and available than anchor positions. A reporter collects information and data—in other words, gets the story—and writes it. That's not a whole lot different than what a print journalist does. Each follows specific rules for the industry. But most TV reporters also do their jobs in front of a camera—many times, unscripted. Take a spin of the TV channels during the 6 P.M. news. What you'll see are reporters with microphones in their hands, standing in front of scenes where some action is happening or has happened, either reading a report they and their assistant writers just wrote or doing an interview for tape or live broadcast.

> **Breaking News**
>
> A reporter researches and writes a story, a producer assembles it, and an anchor reads it on camera.

The reporter spends much time researching or poring over research that others have helped piece together to create a workable report and broadcast it. It takes nerves of steel and the ability to think on your feet to do this job well. Being prepared and knowing what you're talking about is the key.

If you're more of the editor type, then your job track will be more in line with what a producer does. Producers are charged with assembling the coverage and crafting it into a story. They need to know what the news is, where to get it, and how to get it on video—all while making it look swell and ensuring its accuracy. It may be simply for a segment, a taped piece that a reporter narrates, or an entire show start to finish.

"It's a tough gig to break into," says Sheila Conolly, promotion producer for WNYT 13 in Albany, New York, whose work has included producing shows and segments for some of the biggest names in TV: ESPN, NBC, HBO, CBS, ABC, OLN, and USA Network.

"If anyone asks me what it's like to work in this field, I just let them in on my schedule once I graduated from NYU," she says. "I worked seven days a week for crappy pay with no benefits for a number of years: Mondays, Tuesdays, and Wednesdays I would work as a freelance research assistant for a documentary at HBO Sports, and on Thursdays and Fridays I was a tape PA (production assistant) for a kids' tennis show for CBS. On Saturday afternoons, I worked as a logger for ABC college football and at night I would take a cab down to Madison Square Garden to do graphics for their live news show, which I also did all day on Sundays. It all sounds very glamorous ('Holy cow, you work at the Garden?'), but the reality of it isn't glamorous at all. I worked in sports television, which meant I worked weekends and holidays. I'm on the road a lot. The majority of the people I work with are either single or divorced a number of times over. Family and friends take a huge backseat to late-night edit sessions and cross-country flights."

J-school professors will be the first to tell you: if you plan on working in your home-town while raising a family and having most nights and weekends off, forget about it. Many of your hours will be spent working, and the phone always rings most during those few hours that you are off work. But what about the benefits?

"There are perks, you betcha," Conolly adds. "I got to meet and hang out with Cal Ripken in Cooperstown! But the reality is that it's a job. Ever stand outside in minus 10-degree weather on the top of a mountain in the middle of nowhere, waiting to get an interview with an Italian luge athlete who barely speaks English but who needs to make this show that I have to edit by midnight or the International Luge Federation will have my tail? I have, and I'm here to tell ya, it ain't so much fun."

Sure, some of the most recognizable people in the world are TV journalists—Tom Brokaw, Katie Couric, Wolf Blitzer … but there aren't all that many of that stature. You could be a news hero in your town, though. TV reporters are a very recognizable lot, and there is a bit of celebrity status in being even a local on-air journalist. So if long hours for little pay early on for a shot at the big leagues—or just making a good living for a noble cause—is your bag, producing and reporting for TV might be a good fit for you.

> **Breaking News**
>
> Broadcast journalism isn't all glitz and glamour; it involves years of hard work and many sacrifices.

What You Need to Learn

There are a couple of different approaches to becoming a broadcast journalist. Whether you want to be a reporter or a producer, you will need to choose between going the traditional journalism school route or learning it all along the way with job experience.

Going to School

The more sure-fire approach is to study broadcast journalism at a university. A bachelor's degree in journalism will get you hired, but it will also better prepare you for your job. You'll learn technical skills, ethics, and how to think on your feet. You'll also learn how to write and how to write for a specific audience. Those who want to major in the production aspect of broadcast journalism will learn even more technical skills, from video and camera operation to assembling a segment and an entire show.

> ### Breaking News
>
> There are many specialties, or niches, in broadcast journalism. News, sports, business, lifestyles, and weather are among some of the more popular.

There are niches as well. Do you want to do video photography or purely sports? And don't forget weather, business, lifestyles, and documentary. It's all there to learn for the cost of tuition. Many schools offer full broadcast journalism programs, from affordable state schools to Ivy League universities.

Remember our old friend Julie Bologna from early chapters? She has worked for many years in many different areas of journalism to get to the top. Her resumé contains an impressive list of positions that include working as a production assistant for a public TV station, writing for a magazine, and recording commercials for radio.

"It can be very hard to break into TV news and weather," Bologna says. "There just aren't as many jobs as there are students graduating in the communications field. Therefore, recent college graduates end up taking a job in an unrelated field. They soon find out that they are making much more money at their current job. To take the TV job would require a pay cut, working weekends and holidays, having no moving expenses, etc. So, they stay in their other jobs."

"If you have a passion for the news business, then just prepare to make very little money at the station, to work weekends and holidays, and to move around the country," she says.

"If you are serious about it though, here is my best advice," Bologna adds. "You should prepare by doing as many internships as you can before you graduate to see if you really want to be in the field. When looking for your first full-time job, you should think small: small pay, small market, and small title … I suggest starting in a small city to learn your craft. Make as many mistakes as possible there. Once you get a few years under your belt, then try to move up to a larger market where you can make more money and gain more experience. You should continue working your way up to a larger market or to some place that you will enjoy living. People often end up staying in a medium-sized market because they enjoy the area or have family there. That is a wonderful choice. Sometimes, journalists and meteorologists want to continue climbing up the ladder to a top-five market or to the national arena. No matter what route interests you, you should be prepared to move often and to make friends quickly! You may stay at a station two years then move across country to your next job, leaving behind friends and family. So, you must be a person that can adapt well to change."

As Bologna mentioned, journalism schools are great places to get into great internships. The more real-life experience you have, the better off you will be. But continuing education classes in your community and technical trade schools are other avenues available for gaining knowledge and hands-on experience.

Extra! Extra! _____

Journalism school is practically mandatory if you want to break into the business, but internships are just as important to get real-life experience.

Finding Alternative Paths

Many experts note that J-school isn't a prerequisite, but with the competition out there and so few jobs per graduate, you should use every advantage that you can get.

Some experts even argue that the internship should come before making the decision to enter—and spending thousands of dollars on—journalism school. This way, you will get a taste of what the work is like and can decide whether it's up your alley or not. But take caution! Many of the internships out there may not be attached to universities and can be unpaid. That means living with Mom and Pop for a while longer and having a part-time job schlepping pizzas or slinging burgers while learning the journalism ropes at the internship. But at least you'll have that line of experience on your resumé.

Pay Expectations

Whether you choose J-school or jumping straight into the fire, know that a good journalism school will probably take you farther. A *great* journalism school will take you even farther than that.

Reporters who have degrees from the top J-schools do the best. According to a study by PayScale.com, Columbia University grads earned the most in 2006 with a median income of $75,000. That ain't too shabby! Syracuse University grads earned $54,000 a year, followed by Ohio State and the University of Texas, both at $50,000 a year. Grads of the University of North Carolina earned $32,500, followed by Northwestern University at $31,500 and Ohio University at $30,000.

Just as with any journalism job, whether it's print, broadcast, or Internet, the bucks often don't come easy or quickly. They do, however, if you're patient, persistent, and good at what you do. And for those select few who have all the right stuff, the pay—and even the star power—can be awesome.

Breaking News
The median annual first-year pay for a first-year TV news reporter was $23,750 in 2006.

But first, let's plant our feet solidly in reality. Your first job will probably pay below $25,000. And the chances of it being the job you've always dreamed about ... well, maybe not so much.

But with a few years and a lot of hard work under your belt, that pay scale will increase. In fact, after that first year and within four years, you can expect to earn about $31,000 a year—which should give you a good jump on paying off those college loans. The good news is that the median income of those who stick with it between their fifth and ninth years in the biz is breaking the $50,000 mark—$55,000, to be exact, according to 2006 figures. The median income of those in the TV news reporting business for more than 20 years is $67,500. Not too shabby.

Perhaps one of the most critical elements to your success is the market in which you work. After all, money isn't everything—but it sure helps, especially because you'll be working for such a noble and worthy cause.

Los Angeles, California, by far pays journalists the most. The median salary in the "City of Angels" was $90,000 in 2006. San Francisco was second, with a median salary of $70,000, followed by Seattle ($64,500), New York ($58,000), and Denver ($56,000).

Breaking News
The median salary in Los Angeles, California was $90,000 for journalists in 2006, which is the highest in the United States.

Also, there is a difference between working for a network and working for a local station. Generally, the former pays more. The median salary for a network journalist was $52,000 in 2006, while that number at a local station was $46,000.

Still, you are aware of the obstacles standing in your way and you're going to persist through hell or high water. Good, because TV could use some good journalists.

Tools for the Trade

Okay, so your compass is set: you're going to be the next Tom Brokaw. But you're going to need a few tools in your journalism toolbox to reach that goal.

Your Thinking Cap

A good journalism school will teach you not only how to write and splice, as we mentioned earlier, but it will also equip you with the context of how some of the best in the business have performed the job through the history of broadcast journalism. Critical thinking, looking at the bigger picture, and being able to not only ask tough questions but also follow them with an intelligent line of reasoning will become your modus operandi. You will achieve this goal through a whole lot of study, examples, and practice.

Most journalists need to be experts in many different subjects. But they can't all get law, medical, and engineering degrees. They must be able to quickly comprehend complex issues, prepare for interviews, and keep focused on the information that needs to be conveyed to the viewer. Listening to arguments and debating points is good practice, and certainly watching how the pros think on their feet as they interview tough subjects can be inspiring.

A rookie journalist will make the mistake of losing focus of the point of the story—getting twisted around by a tough interview. Seasoned politicians, lawyers, and press secretaries are among the best spin-controllers out there and, unfortunately, they will be among your top sources of quotes in news reporting.

Take, for instance, a scenario where a reporter is interviewing a school board candidate. A typical question will be to ask him how he plans on bettering education in the district with the lack of funds available from state coffers.

He might answer by telling you he'll hire better teachers.

You ask how will he pay for them?

He tells you he'll do it without raising taxes.

At this point, you have to know that the current funding structure in the state doesn't allow any more allocations than the district is receiving, so raising taxes may be the only way. At this point, you have to tell him his math is fuzzy. Or yours is, so have him prove you wrong. Solid lines of questioning—even playing devil's advocate—can go a long way in fleshing out the truth.

Most J-schools will teach you how to write all types of stories—sports, weather, business, features, and news—and then how to read them on-air without looking like a stiff or a buffoon. You will gain much-needed experience in reporting for all different types of situations: politics, urban issues, the legal system, government, medicine, the environment, the arts, and so on.

You will need to know what current broadcast issues are and how they affect the world today. It's also important to know which federal regulatory bodies govern your field—the Federal Communications Commission, for instance. This sort of practice and discipline is the very stuff that composes a good journalist.

Dealing with Technical Difficulties

Learning the technical aspects of the job will be a challenge, but it's one of the most exciting—getting into the studio or cut room and learning the ropes of production. Sheila Conolly, the New York TV producer, knows the importance of good production training and the ability to think on your feet.

"You are at the mercy of your camera working; you're at the mercy of the light being right," she says. "If you're doing an interview outdoors, you better hope to God it doesn't rain. And audio—audio is always such an issue. You'll do an entire segment, umpteen takes, it took an hour longer than you had scheduled, but you got it done, just before the sun was about to set, and then your audio guy tells you, 'Um, we gotta do that again. I hear a buzzing noise when I play it back.'"

I've cursed many a production because of equipment issues. What a pain in the neck!"

Needless to say, going into this field without some real-life experience and an education to draw from can be quite daunting, but a good education and awareness of world events will go a long way in building a solid journalistic foundation.

Getting Your Foot in the Door

So you have the education and the sheepskin to prove it, you've done the internship experience with everything from making coffee to subbing for the Sunday evening newscaster who was snowed in halfway across the planet, and your snappy wool suit was just dry-cleaned. So you're ready to go and get that job, right?

Well, brace yourself: it's not that easy. As it stands, you're hoping that your top education and experience will separate you from the rest of that pack. But that's a mighty big pack. Persistence will pay off for you. That means sending out a whole lot of resumés and clips and going on a whole lot of interviews. Don't expect to land the first job you interview for, though, or even the second or third. Prepare to be on the hunt for a while, and be willing to work wherever you get hired.

But let's not get ahead of ourselves. Getting your resumé together also takes a good bit of discipline. First, you'll clearly want to list your education and experience and briefly sum up what you've learned and accomplished. If you have special awards or achievements, you'll want

> **Breaking News**
>
> For every one entry-level production hire, 60 resumés were thrown away.

to note them. For instance, if you started your internship as an assistant but within three weeks were reading on-air, that's a good thing to note. Also, if you graduated with honors or were the producer of your university's news station, those would be good to add. What you are looking to do is tout your education and your experience in a way that separates you from that pack.

Be certain that every word is correctly spelled and that your grammar is perfect. I'm here to tell you that as a guy who has thrown out more resumés than I care to remember, simply because my name or the organization's name was misspelled. Editors and producers have little time to pander to those applicants who didn't bother to take the time to get the facts right or use a spell checker. Remember, if you stick a messy resumé under the nose of an anchor or producer, the first thing he or she will think is, "Man, this person would make us look like morons." But that's if the resumé even gets that far.

> **Extra! Extra!**
>
> Nothing turns off editors more than misspellings in resumés; be sure to triple check yours and have someone else proofread it for you.

Your cover letter should be equally as perfect. Keep it brief—a half- to about three-quarters of a page is about right. Give them a bit of an appetizer (or tease!) of what they are about to read in your resumé.

Keep it tight, with not too much stuff, and just get straight to the point. Save the rhetoric about saving the world through your journalistic passion for the interview—if that. Let your accomplishments speak for themselves. Let them know you are willing to do whatever it takes to get the job—move to a different area, work a lesser job, spend long hours perfecting your craft, and so on. Assure them that you'll require little training—because you already have some—so you can plug right in and get to work.

It's also important that you have some strong references. Don't list your college buddies here. I once got a resumé with a reference from the applicant's mom. Sheesh!

College professors will likely always give glowing reviews, although that is expected and therefore somewhat discounted by a prospective employer. (Do you really expect the professor to say, "Yeah, she's a decent student, but this university didn't prepare her well enough …"?) Those internship bosses—now, that's the ticket for references. Here's where reputations are on the line and honest answers will come. So if you use those folks at the local TV station where you interned—asking them first if it's okay to list them—you're golden.

Samples of your work are also needed. Therefore, your internship will come in extremely handy. Gather all the video clips of your reporting, samples of your writing, snips of your production skills, and so on. These show what you're truly capable of.

> **Extra! Extra!** _____
>
> A resumé videotape with your clips and production snips may get you a leg up on your competition when applying for a job.

If you're at the top of your game, you will have that resumé tape ready to go—all those examples of stories you've done on one tape, compact disc, or DVD. There's nothing better for you than to give a TV producer the ability to simply download your clips or slip a disc into the hard drive in the very chair where he or she first opened your resumé package. That's pretty cool.

So if it's good and the planets are in alignment, you might actually get a phone call while your images are whirling right in front of the producer:

"May I speak with James?"

"This is James."

"Hi, this is so and so from KTYG. Your resumé is outstanding!"

Hey, if you're persistent, it will happen.

The Least You Need to Know

- Be sure you understand what avenues broadcast journalism has for you before choosing your niche.

- A solid journalism school education paired with internship experience is the best way to break into broadcasting.

- Be persistent: to get that job, you'll need to be open to relocating, working for less than you wanted, or working a lesser job to gain experience.

- Touting your achievements and education on a spotless resumé will help you get that interview.

Part 5

The Internet

The Internet, as we know it today, is seemingly the most powerful media source we have ever known. Traditional media, while slow to catch on at first, have embraced the influence that the Internet commands—catapulting journalism into an entirely new reality.

In this part, we'll talk about how the Internet affects all traditional media, Internet audiences, the significance of blogs, and how to carve a niche and solidify a future in online journalism.

Chapter 19

Brave News World

In This Chapter

- ◆ Newspapers find their extra edition online
- ◆ Magazines get more timely on the Internet
- ◆ Content that's exclusively electronic
- ◆ TV joins the online bandwagon
- ◆ Radio that reaches far beyond the car stereo

In terms of the history of the *"Fourth Estate,"* Internet journalism is just learning to crawl. But in terms of its impact on traditional news sources, it's in a world-class sprint.

Still, the journalism industry has been slow to turn the corner on using the Internet. The news outlets that consider themselves innovative and aggressive on the World Wide Web usually augment that statement by saying they are still behind the curve ... but catching up.

Why? The Internet is a big, free, limitless, and increasingly competitive medium. *The New York Times* has few advantages over Tony down the block who operates his own online newspaper from his basement in the 'burbs.

def•i•ni•tion

The **Fourth Estate**, a term coined by Thomas Carlyle in the early nineteenth century, refers to the press as advocate of the public.

This statement may be a slight exaggeration, but Internet news sites have scooped traditional media on some pretty big stories in the past couple of years. And that isn't stopping anytime soon.

In this chapter, we'll look at how traditional media are entering this new world of the Internet and how the Internet is changing them.

Online Newsprint

When the Internet really began gaining momentum—way back in the mid-1990s—the Internet was barely a blip on the screens of traditional media outlets (TV, radio, newspapers, and magazines). Either the weakest writer in the newsroom or the guy who liked video games was given the job to post online the day's edition or some of the stories it ran. Or someone was actually hired to do this job, and no one really knew what to call the new person or how much to pay him or her. At the time, posting on the web was a minor task that gave some sort of advantage over the next guy who didn't use the Internet.

Soon, whole new strains of ethics, court cases, and ways to monitor and edit stories differently cropped up, and newsrooms thought of pulling the plug on this hassle.

Nontraditional mediums such as Yahoo! sprung up and started posting the news of the day, linking to credible news sources, designing web pages with a lot of quick-hit items, and even letting readers decide what news they wanted on their screens everyday.

def•i•ni•tion

A web **hit** happens when someone visits a specific web page. In other words, one person visiting one web page is one hit.

Oh, and it was free.

Advertisers thought, "Hmm. If I can buy an ad on that website that gets a gazillion *hits* an hour, maybe my business will pick up." Therefore, Internet sites began making money from advertisers posting ads on their sites.

Expanding Readership

Once traditional media saw that they were getting scooped, that the Internet audience was potentially the entire planet, that kids (an elusive audience) were online, and that there was a virtually untapped advertising pool—well, that jump-started their engines and an entire movement. If you don't have a website, you're toast. And if you don't take the Internet seriously, you're losing an incredible audience.

Brian Dearth, digital editor at *The Desert Sun* in Palm Springs, California, knows first-hand how critical this relationship is between a newspaper and the Internet. Trained as a journalist, Dearth started his career in newspapers working specifically on the paper's Internet edition.

"There is no other medium, except perhaps cable television news, that offers such immediacy. More and more, when breaking news happens, people flick on their computers instead of cable or radio. News on the [World Wide] Web keeps people as updated as they want to be," he says.

In 2005, there were 1,452 daily newspapers in the United States with a combined circulation of more than 53 million. In the same year, online editions reached 54 million people. In fact, a study by the Newspaper Association of America (NAA) shows that 63 percent of online newspaper users check the World Wide Web to get their breaking news each day.

So it's a safe bet that this industry—the one that newspapers thought was just a big hassle—isn't going anywhere but up.

Immediate and More Extensive Content

But how do newspapers use the Internet? Well, in the early days, journalists were afraid to post their stories on the Internet before the print edition hit the doorsteps in the morning. In essence, they thought that another medium could then scoop their stories and make the newspaper insignificant. Also, it gave competitors a clear picture of what stories you were writing, and they could scramble overnight to write the same story for their print edition.

That was quickly squelched for a couple of reasons. One, competing newspapers also began posting their news first, claiming that they broke the story the earliest. Second, publishers began noticing that the more fresh stories that were added to a site earlier, the more hits that site would get. From an advertising standpoint, posting stories early was money in the bank.

But Internet newspapers go far beyond just breaking news. There is a world of opportunity for posting stories, columns, and art—all the traditional print newspaper items—onto a website. And there are many special features that can't run in a newspaper but can appear on the boundless Internet.

For instance, a newspaper runs a story on the school board's proposed budget, showing that millions of dollars will be put into a slush fund to be used at the board's own discretion. It also shows cuts in building maintenance and in teachers' salaries. In the print version, there is a complete story, a sidebar, photos, and graphics. In a typical newspaper, that's a decent package. On the Internet site, however, what also can be posted is the actual budget—the 30-page document that shows budget items line by line—and *links* to related stories and information, such as budgets from the past 10 years. The print version capitalizes on the fact that there is a web version, too, with more information—which drives more people to the online edition.

def•i•ni•tion

A web page **link** is a word on a website that, when clicked, takes you to another web page of related information.

Wait a second, you say. So why would people buy a newspaper when they can get it—and more—online, for free? Good question. While most newspaper websites are free, others will post only abbreviated stories. And still others may charge a fee if you want to access archived material.

Newsprint Hangs On

But while an increasing number of people are surfing the web for their daily news, print editions are still holding fairly steady. In 1960, newspaper circulation was a robust 58 million in the United States. It peaked in 1985 with more than 67 million and today holds at about 53 million, so circulation has suffered a steady decline since the mid-'80s. But still, the numbers—which are also affected by cable news and other mediums—remain strong. Those on both sides—print and electronic—agree that while newspaper circulations are in decline, online editions might never kill off print newspapers altogether.

> **Breaking News**
>
> Print newspapers have survived the infiltration of all other journalistic mediums, including the Internet.

"There's a lot of hand-wringing in the newspaper industry these days because of challenges from other forms of media, primarily the Internet," says our veteran sports editor Jeff Kidd from Chapter 5. "Of course, newspapers have been challenged before—by radio, broadcast television, cable television—and survived those threats. I think we'll do the same in this instance, too, for while electronic media have powerful advantages over 'old' technology, newspapers still have the advantage of portability, affordability, and the ability to satisfy readers' tactile senses. In other words, I don't think newspapers will go away any more than books have."

"That said," Kidd continues, "I think it is almost certain a great deal about our business will change before I retire. I can see, for example, the newspaper becoming a detailed index used to drive people to a website, where news receives more thorough treatment. Those who hold sentimental attachments to the medium itself—newsprint or news arranged on a printed broadsheet page—will not cope well with these changes."

Change is the keyword. More and more newsrooms are embracing, not fighting against, their online versions. Newspapers are beginning to put more journalists and editors into their online departments to write, edit, and produce better web content.

Says Dearth, "I see media websites, especially those of newspapers, continually growing in importance. With essentially an unlimited news hole and minimal daily production costs, not to mention the web's ability to use multimedia to tell the story, more and more people will log on to newspaper websites. Eventually there will be a tipping point where more people use the website than read the printed newspaper. I don't think we're at that point yet, but that day is not far off."

"I'm not saying news on the Internet definitely will kill the dead-tree version (although someday it may very well do that)," he adds. "But as time goes on, the generation that grew up reading newspapers will give way to the generation who grew up surfing the web. And by that time, news websites may be in danger from the emergence of some not-yet invented delivery mechanism."

Whatever the future holds for newspapers, journalists, editors, and publishers on both sides of the spectrum will be looking for more new ways to peddle their wares, so to speak. At the heart of the industry is the journalism, and that message has remained clear. The vehicle used to disburse it may change, but the message remains the same: reach as many people with as much relevant, balanced, and timely information as possible.

Magazine Websites

Printed magazines have many advantages over newspapers. They are glossy, colorful, extremely portable, and feel substantial when holding them. The obvious disadvantages are that they are more expensive to produce and the news isn't as timely as a newspaper.

But how does that thick, glossy publication translate onto the Internet? For that matter, what web advantage would award-winning magazines such as *Time*, *Sports Illustrated*, or *National Geographic* have over a lower-tier magazine?

Also do a quick surf of the web and you'll find much of the same financial information on *The New York Times*'s website as you would on Kiplinger.com—right down to Associated Press stories and a live stock market ticker. So what's the difference?

The Branding Differential

Well branding still has a lot to do with it. Magazines—in their quest for subscriptions and counter sales—still must establish brand loyalty. *Niche publications* are great examples. Do you subscribe to *Sports Illustrated* or to *ESPN The Magazine?* How about *Car and Driver* or *Motor Trend? Time* or *Newsweek? The Atlantic* or *The New Yorker?*

def•i•ni•tion

A **niche publication** caters to a specific audience, such as train collectors, runners, or baseball fans.

When it comes to the Internet, magazines carry brand loyalty—that recognizable name that can attract readers to their website because they're loyal subscribers of the print magazine. But for those simply surfing the Internet for information, well ... the publication's name might be random.

The first magazine website to pop up during a quick Google search of "war in Iraq" is *BusinessWeek*. Other recognizable names such as *The New York Times, The Washington Post,* CNN, MSNBC, and the BBC also show up in the search following *BusinessWeek*. Readers will more than likely go to the site with the brand name that is most recognizable and familiar to them.

Crossing Over

Ken Palmer, an editor, beat writer, columnist, and author who works in print, broadcast, and Internet sports in the New York-New Jersey market, knows that print publications such as a weekly sports newspaper or magazine have a hard time competing with the Internet in terms of timeliness. "Our paper is a weekly publication, so we have to do more timeless material. Our website is the place where we can post up-to-the-minute and breaking info," he says.

Just as newspapers struggle to break news online and keep their print publications vibrant, so do magazines. And they use many of the same tricks. Referring online viewers to the print publication is fairly successful, as is referring print readers to the publication's website. The more *crossover* readers, the more hits, the more advertisers, and so on ... hence, the more money to be made.

def•i•ni•tion

A **crossover** occurs when one medium, such as a magazine, refers its reader to another of its formats, such as its Internet site.

Online versions even refer readers to other sites, known as an affinity program, where one site sends users to another that sells related products. And that site shares the profits with the referring site.

And print versions not only send their readers to their websites but to others' websites, as well—namely advertisers. An ING financial advisement advertisement in *Runner's World* referred readers to an ING site where they could read stories of runners in the 2006 ING-sponsored New York City Marathon and find several links to the main ING website. The symbiosis between magazines and their sites and advertisers is what makes the publication more profitable and more valuable.

For journalists, a magazine with a successful online edition means greater opportunities. Competition to publish in a magazine is fierce, as many magazines tend to use time-tested writers or frequent contributors. But opportunity lies in features that run on the magazine's website and not necessarily in the print edition.

Internet Only

While online versions of print magazines have proliferated and profited, it didn't take long for folks to realize that they, too, could have their own magazines—only online.

Known as Internet newspapers and *zines*, any regular Joe can start his own online edition and publish whatever he likes. Some are as unprofessional as can be while others are well-designed and have really taken off.

Matt Drudge started the Drudge Report in 1994 as a simple e-mail to a list of subscribers interested in alternative takes on politics and society. It grew successfully into something resembling a *weblog* (often shortened to *blog*) and an Internet newspaper by 1996. How did it grow successfully without any sort of physical publication? Well, for one, atop Drudge Report were those flashy national advertisements (and more toward the bottom of the page). That's how.

def•i•ni•tion

A **weblog** (also known as a **blog**) is a website where entries are posted in journal format and often displayed in reverse chronological order. Blogs offer commentary on everything from politics and food to photography and daily life, and readers in turn can interact with the blogger by leaving blog comments.

The website has been good to Matt Drudge. *Business 2.0* magazine estimated in 2003 that his income was about $1.3 million a year, while in an interview the same year in the *Miami Herald*, Drudge estimated his income at $1.2 million yearly. What also made Drudge Report successful was its ability to break news before mainstream media—and not simply because of the Internet's timeliness. Drudge broke the news of the Monica Lewinsky-Bill Clinton sex scandal in 1998 and that Jack Kemp would run alongside presidential candidate Bob Dole in 1996. True, these rumors had been broken on his site, but whether it was actual news has been long debated. Also in 1998, a federal judge in a libel lawsuit ruled that Drudge wasn't a "reporter, journalist, or a news-gatherer."

On the other end of the Internet spectrum are *e-zines*, which mimic magazines in their frequency of publication—monthly, weekly, and so on—and their content, generally on a single topic. It's hard to say when e-zines got their start, and claims of who started the original e-zine are generally debated—but the genre got off the ground in the early 1980s, with publications such as *Cult of the Dead Cow* and the now-defunct *Phrack*.

def•i•ni•tion

A **e-zine** is an electronic magazine, or one that appears solely on the Internet, with no paper version.

Zines picked up some steam by the mid-'90s, but with the proliferation and ease of a typical blog and the programs available to create them, e-zines have taken somewhat of a backseat. But they're still relatively hot with gamers and programmers.

Other online news sites have proliferated as have e-zines or Internet newspapers. *Internet portals*, Yahoo! perhaps being the most notable, have become more than just search engines or mail hosts. Yahoo! News not only is an outlet for wire services—although the majority of the site's content is wire-driven—but it has also broken stories with its own staff, which include writers and columnists. This move made Yahoo! a true media company rather than simply a search engine or mail host. For example, journalist Kevin Sites has trotted the globe exclusively for Yahoo!, writing his *In the Hot Zone* online pieces. Most revolve around war, conflict, and human suffering but also culture and interesting places. He's even covered the war in Iraq.

def•i•ni•tion

An **Internet portal** is a site on the World Wide Web that offers a starting point for users to get to other points on the web.

Electronic Boob Tube

It's somewhat funny to think that a medium such as television, which is around-the-clock and instant, would even need the Internet to break its news. But if television news has one downside, it's that once it's said, it's basically done. That's why when a big story breaks, regular television programming gets bumped for live coverage of that news event.

We talked about continuous news mode, where news events such as the war in Iraq, Hurricane Katrina, the September 11th attacks, or the 2004 presidential election bumped regular programming. But not every news story is worth interrupting or bumping even *Happy Days* reruns. An election in Afghanistan, a tornado in Kansas, a high-speed chase in Los Angeles …. While these stories might break into regular programming, they're generally very brief updates.

Here, constant updating on the Internet can help. A TV station's website can post bulletins in the same manner as a newspaper's can. At this point, the TV station and the newspaper are competing for a breaking news audience. Reporters, photographers, and video staff—from both TV and newspapers—are on the scene feeding the information electronically to the online departments in a rush to post the latest and most relevant news. Some newspapers and TV stations have even joined together to broadcast each other's news on the Internet—or even in their main mediums.

> **Breaking News**
>
> With TV film footage being broadcast on its Internet site, a television station or news network virtually has a worldwide audience.

Remember Julie Bologna, our meteorologist from Dallas-Fort Worth? She has seen the Internet's role in broadcast journalism change during her 12 years in the business.

"The television news industry continues to change and evolve," says Bologna. "You will notice stations continuing to push viewers to their websites for more stories or additional information. You will see more TV stations doing separate newscasts designed specifically for the website."

The main format of television news, though, has an advantage over newspapers or other journalism mediums on the web because the majority of what it does is taped. Therefore, all of its programming can be put onto its website for anyone to watch whenever they want.

> **Breaking News**
>
> Viewers of Internet news sites can tailor the news they want to their own needs by setting up their own preferences on the site. Local news, sports scores, or the latest weather are examples.

On CNN.com, for instance, viewers can watch interviews from earlier in the day—or maybe even see previews of an upcoming taped interview. Sports fans can watch highlights on ESPN.com. Weather junkies can watch complete programs on The Weather Channel's online version. Even better, national television programming, such as The Weather Channel, can allow viewers to tailor their weather preferences to their own region. In fact, many news and weather channels have built live radar or weather maps on their websites—enabling viewers to zoom in on the weather that's happening right in their own back yard, live.

Local or national? Weather or sports? Crisis or peace? It doesn't matter. When a big or interesting story breaks, Internet viewers on TV websites can check out footage from any part of the world. It doesn't simply have to be the big story.

Streaming Radio and Podcasts

The World Wide Web also has been both a boon and burden to the radio medium. Already suffering from oversaturation and satellite radio, add to the mix Internet radio. Just as satellite radio further tailors its programming (and does so largely commercial-free), so, too, does Internet radio.

Let's say you've recently moved to Miami, Florida, but want to listen to your favorite old radio station in Cleveland, Ohio. No problem: find that radio station's website online and voilà! You're back in Cleveland.

Huge radio stations have been able to tap into the online listener demographic by putting their programming on their own website. And just as any other medium has produced and profited on the web, so, too, has radio by drawing readers to its website and selling ads on its web pages.

Just as any Joe in his garage could start an Internet newspaper or blog, you could—with the right equipment—open your own Internet radio station (so to speak). The FCC, as we've said earlier in this book, governs radio. But simply spinning your own discs or commenting on the world offers no real glitch to that system. Of course, there are copyright infringements on music, but your own or public-domain music or commentary is fair game. One way of hosting your own forum is by operating a so-called *podcast*. Podcasts are similar to radio broadcasts but are Internet-exclusive.

def•i•ni•tion

A **podcast** takes its name from the MP3 player made by Apple, called an iPod, and the word "broadcast." It's a downloadable format that allows listeners to hear their favorite radio or Internet programs when they want on their computers or handheld players.

Podcasts are a whole new genre of Internet broadcasting and have proliferated in recent years. Podcast programming includes everything from sports talk shows to political commentary to music concerts to how to scale a fish. You can download podcasts and listen to them whenever you want.

The technology is boundless, and anyone with a podcast program—such as iTunes— can get access to podcast content on the Internet.

Podcasts can be free or paid downloads. Former Penn State University's football player Tony Pittman and Phil Collins offer a free weekly podcast to gab about the gridiron during the football season. Producers of the hit ABC TV show *Lost*, Damon Lindelof and Carlton Cuse, talk about plots and answer submitted reader questions on their podcast.

All in all, the technology of the Internet means the ability to put newscasts, music, and podcasts in the palm of your hand in a personal digital assistant (PDA) such as a PalmPilot or onto your cell phone. This technology is here now, not just the wave of the future. The Internet makes it possible to take the world with you just about any-where you go.

The Least You Need to Know

♦ Newspapers aren't cowering from the Internet; rather, they are embracing it.

♦ The Internet opened up a whole new world of jobs for journalists.

♦ Breaking news is an even playing field now across all media, thanks to the Internet.

♦ The world, be it local or global, is just a few clicks away on the World Wide Web.

Chapter 20

Branching Out

In This Chapter

- Targeting the Internet audience
- Ethics on the Internet
- Consistency of design and philosophy
- The benefits of web hosting

A saying from an old college journalism professor of mine should always ring sharply in your ears: "Know your reader."

This truth hasn't changed much since the early days of newspapers and broadcasting, but it's never been more important or prevalent now with every traditional medium hawking its wares on the World Wide Web. In this chapter, we'll show you how to keep your audience in mind (and, well, keep your audience on your website), focusing on the journalism, the visuals, and—let's not forget—those all-important Internet ethics.

"Sticking" the Audience

Internet audiences are even more particular than those watching or reading traditional media. They are becoming generally more tech-savvy, are viewing content at their convenience, and have other places to be online.

Think of the differences in your audiences now. Writing and editing for an Internet crowd is a bit different than for a print or broadcast crowd. Also, getting them to hang around on your site and not jump somewhere else is key, and that takes its own set of skills and tricks.

Who's Who

Let's take it point by point. Just like a business journal or political round-table TV show has a niche or target audience, Internet viewers are also a certain type of audience—one that is broadening each day. Generally, Internet users are more tech-savvy than traditional media users, so it's important to cater to this characteristic.

The situation of ol' Granddad not understanding how to program the VCR, let alone change the flashing clock, doesn't really exist on the Internet. Using the Internet is a whole lot easier than programming a VCR. You can surf to your heart's content by just clicking where you want to go.

def•i•ni•tion

Broadband is high-speed Internet access as much as 50 times faster than a dial-up Internet provider (such as America Online, or AOL). It can come through a cable or via a digital or satellite feed.

Statistics vary on Internet usage, but the Pew Charitable Trust in March 2006 counted 84 million Americans on *broadband* alone and 47 percent of all Americans with some sort of high-speed Internet connection at home. That's up 30 percent from the prior year.

And that's only at home. So while you may think that the Internet is simply for the young, chances are your grandma is talking with her friends in a chat room or shopping for Christmas presents on eBay. Who knows? Maybe she's downloading the latest Pink album …

Still, whether your audience is grandma, her kids, her kids' kids, or some combination, it's important to keep in mind exactly who your readers are. For instance, while early newspaper websites were basically copies of the front page with links to the stories of the day—or simple headlines with links to the corresponding stories—newspaper websites now offer more than just this bread and butter. They provide links to related material and buttons and pull-downs to access commentary, sports, lifestyles, and other features. There are polls and surveys, video and audio streams, blog posts, and lots of flashy advertising. The idea is to keep the reader on their site (or one of their other sites).

In this regard, a viewer might click on a story, read it head to tail, find a related story, look at a photo gallery that goes with the story, and join a discussion in the blog—all while watching the streaming ads. That's a far cry from reading a story in a newspaper. Your reader online is much more interactive.

> **Breaking News**
>
> 47 percent of all Americans in March 2006 had some sort of high-speed Internet connection at home.

Consider, too, that the reader can read the story on his or her own time. Sure, he or she can grab the morning coffee in one hand and a copy of the *Daily Bugle* in the other and head out the door to read the story on the train or at the office. But the Internet audience will use a PDA or laptop on the train, or a computer at work, to access the news of the day at a newspaper or TV website or listen to their favorite news radio stations on the Internet. They will find the coverage they want how and when they want it.

Stick Around

Know, too, that once the viewer locks onto a site, that doesn't mean he or she won't jump ship to another site. And why wouldn't they? Say the *Daily Bugle* has a story about President Bush's speech on the immigration bill. Sure, the *Bugle* had the story—maybe even a sidebar. But for your viewer, well ... he or she might be a rabid right-winger. So off to FoxNews.com he or she goes. After absorbing the video stream, it may be on to Drudge Report. The story for them might end on RushLimbaugh.com for the radio show. That's three more venues than the *Daily Bugle*, so Bugle.com had better have something to offer that will keep the viewer glued. Sticky content keeps viewers coming back.

Our friend Brian Dearth at *The Desert Sun* knows firsthand about trying to keep his readers from drifting.

"The migration of web users to broadband has given news sites the opportunity to exploit the web's possibilities with audio, video, podcasts, Flash, and more and still be reasonably certain most of our audience has the ability to utilize these technologies," he says. "And there are always cell phones, BlackBerries, iPods, etc. Increasingly, people want to get their news wherever they are, and sites need to be able to satisfy those needs or readers will go somewhere else for their fix."

Simply put, the more you can offer, the better off you'll be. That certainly doesn't mean the viewer won't want to get that fix somewhere else, but your odds are greatly enhanced if you can offer sidebars and related topics, blog discussions, and even sound or video clips.

My newspaper's sports department will cover the local high school game, same as always. Staff the game with a reporter and photographer. The reporter will come to the game loaded with stats and contacts, then file a good report on deadline. The action photos will accompany the piece in the next day's edition.

On the website, though, that story might be accompanied by links to past stories, stats, rosters, and schedules. It also might have a photo gallery of other photos that were shot but couldn't fit into the print edition. Last but not least, we might even have video footage of the game, shot by someone in the Internet department who toted a video camera out to the game and got some highlights.

> **Breaking News**
>
> User-generated material or content contributed from readers—such as blog entries, photos, or even video and audio clips—has greatly changed the way viewers use the Internet.

It's neat to be able to offer video of little Billy breaking three tackles en route to the end zone. That's something that the local news channel might not have because its coverage area is larger and they didn't have anyone at the game shooting video. That TV station, however, might have a site similar to ours with all the same capabilities—and another newspaper in town might have the same offerings on its website, too (and so on). The moral: lots of competition exists, so you'd better put your best foot forward.

But even traditional media with limited resources can look professional online. We'll talk more about design and formats later in this chapter, but for now let's take a trip down to the local ballpark on a Saturday afternoon.

Chances are that besides the kids, you'll see the parents. And in the parents' hands will be cameras and video cameras. Placing a quick *beggar box* on your website asking parents to send in their best clips to be posted on the website is an easy way to get more bang online for very little buck! Heck, they might even write some content. And, if you're living right, you can have them do it all themselves on your blog. If you keep it fresh, interesting, and easy to navigate, your site is bound to be a hit.

def•i•ni•tion

A **beggar box** is a graphic element that ask viewers to respond about a specific topic.

Internet Ethics

Just as every medium has its own set of ethics to follow, Internet news sites can either contain a culmination of those ethics or be tailored to the traditional medium's set that it follows, such as a newspaper's website following the print version's ethics.

But all too often, ethics are an afterthought on the Internet. After all, there's not usually a crusty old editor making the rounds on the newsroom floor, rolling his eyes and poking reporters in the chest. Rather, news websites have largely been run by techno-geeks—not journalists—and if the latter has been the majority, chances are a code of ethics has been made up as they've gone along.

 Extra! Extra! _____

Ethics on the Internet cannot be a second thought. They are as important to your viewers and product as in any traditional media.

Separate but Very Much Together

Why? Well, consider again the venues that Internet sites have. Sure, a story taken from the newspaper and reprinted on its website will have followed the same ethical recipe—say, a balanced, fair, timely, and nonsensational story. If we're living right, the headline will be the same as in the print version—and if there's art, it will be somewhat played the same way.

According to Dearth, the ethics of the traditional medium and its Internet counterpart should remain the same.

"The ethics of a website need to be as stringent as that of the (traditional) product. After all, it's the same journalism, just displayed on a computer screen instead of on paper."

So if the strip lead in a newspaper is, "Mayor Passes Tax Break to City Residents" with a small mug shot of the mayor, then you shouldn't wake up the next day and see that page 3A story of the semi that rolled over on the interstate as the lead on the website with an enormous photo and beefed-up headline: "Driver Flips Rig After Dodging Runaway School Bus!"

Right? Well, not exactly. You see, the Internet is a 24-hour-a-day, seven-day-a-week operation and is going to have—and possibly break—more stories than its traditional counterpart. Also, as we've said, there are whole sites independent of any traditional format, and they are operating under their own ethical standards.

But in our semi-versus-mayor example, is it wrong to run one story over the other? We've discussed that there are different audiences for each medium and that a breaking story will usurp the last big story.

"The Internet is tough when it comes to ethics," says Miranda Bender, corporate project coordinator and web developer for Morris DigitalWorks in Augusta, Georgia. "I have seen too many publications sacrifice their ethical beliefs for the sake of advertising, and unfortunately, since the advertising pays the salary of those in new media, there's a new generation of webmasters who have adopted a nonchalant attitude about the content for which the site was built. Even national news websites will throw a political story on the altar for a Britney Spears belching video."

"And since the Internet is considered the future," Bender adds, "it does not paint a bright picture of the ethical beliefs or the quality of the content that will accompany the news in the future."

It's important to note that not all media websites are part of their respective advertising departments' payrolls, but a good portion of them are (or are on some other payroll altogether, independent of the news products). Is that a bad thing? It can be, as Bender points out. Regardless, a website—whether a new media version or a traditional product—must have a code of ethics and remain consistent with following them. Conversations must be at the forefront of establishing that code before the website is launched, and if that train has already left the station, that discussion needs to be held today.

Extra! Extra!

Being consistent with your message between your traditional and online products will maintain credibility.

A newspaper's website, for instance, can do a lot of damage to the reputation of its print product if it compromises its ethics. Too often we hear, "Well, the newspaper said …" when in fact, the "newspaper" to which they are referring is the online edition. It's important to note that the right hand had better know what the left hand is doing.

For this reason, web personnel are slowly transitioning into newsrooms and away from their independent offices and wings (or worse, ad departments). Ethics, as we mentioned in the first part of this book, have taken a dip in the world of journalism. And they need to be shored up before the product can regain public trust. If your audience hears two completely different messages, although the *Daily Bugle* is atop both of them—print and web, for instance—you might have a problem maintaining credibility.

So we're cool with ethics, right? We know to have a dialog between editor and web-master before posting something that's out of line with the traditional form. We make our decision for what's best for all venues. We've established a good code of ethics. It's hanging on the wall right over the coffeemaker. It's all good, right?

Voice of the People

Wait a second. What about the *vox populi?* The Internet has that little something that most traditional media doesn't: an instant voice of the people.

Sure, magazines and newspapers have letters to the editor; TV news personalities interview folks on camera; and radio has call-in shows—but not to the degree of the Internet. User-generated content is a big part of new media. It's what makes it exciting and fresh. Stories have links to comments and blogs, allowing folks to tell their stories, post their pictures, download their audio and video clips, and so on.

What happens when those items go unchecked? Are editors actually editing comments? Are webmasters screening for bad facts or information? Who is policing the sites?

 Extra! Extra!

Disclaimers and rules should be clearly posted on your website if user-generated material is requested.

In most cases, the answer is hardly anyone. The theory is that once you manipulate or edit user-generated content, you run the risk of being responsible for it. Put your paws on a viewer's allegation, and it might hold up in court that you willingly accepted the bulk of it as fact because you only edited out a small portion.

Disclaimer or not, a courtroom jury can be a scary place. So most user-generated portions of a website will run a disclaimer and only yank a comment if it's blatantly inaccurate or contains foul language. The rest is fair game. Again, that's a decision for the entire product's top brass to make, not just the department's.

"User-generated content comes with an asterisk," says Dearth. "How do you know some parent isn't posting inflated stats for his kid? And more seriously, when operating comment boards, how do you deal with the inevitable profanity and libel issues that crop up? And where do you draw the line of what is acceptable? There has to be some safeguards (registration, board monitors, etc.), but your posters will far outnumber your staff. At this point, I think most news websites, including my own, are still feeling their way around these issues."

If an editor, for instance, is going to police the comments and any user-generated pieces, the whole gist of the free comments area becomes compromised. Editors carry big sticks, and readers or viewers should be allowed to freely comment without fear of being corrected or embarrassed by an editor. When that happens, it kills the blog and may even discourage that viewer from returning. Of course, if that viewer is a blockhead, there's no harm done. Still, the point is for the comments to stay above the belt—something that can be established easily with a good disclaimer and a scan of the blogs for profanity and baseless allegations.

But sensational tabloids or right-leaning news shows for instance don't exactly disclaim that their content is agenda-driven. And folks might not understand that a tabloid leans one way or the other unless there's a huge picture of Elvis being spotted at a gas station outside of Reno, Nevada. At this point, you know something's amok. And not everyone is politically savvy to know, for instance, that a certain radio program is leftist. It sounds like news …

Well, we don't have to go crazy with disclaimers, but our viewers should know that someone is watching. Some readers must register on websites; that is, provide information about themselves in order for the web master to be able to track where a comment came from. They should have to register in order to leave a comment, and they should realize that a blatant disregard for such policy will get them banned from commenting. In the end, most folks play fairly, but there will always be a few blockheads.

Good Design

We've talked about the principles and importance of good design throughout this book. Newspapers and magazines have done endless studies over the many, many years of their existence to overhaul the look and content of their product to maintain good design. Broadcast has changed formats in much the similar way. But what does any of that have to do with an Internet website, and is website design even journalism? A lot and yes, respectively.

No Mixed Messages

If a newspaper's design is conservative—not in the least bit gaudy or sensational—should it's World Wide Web counterpart reflect that philosophy? There are a couple of ways to look at this argument. The first is a bit more purist. It would answer that question with a resounding yes.

The product, let's not forget, is in this case a stodgy newspaper. Going to color in the '80s was probably done so with more than a few arguments and a couple of resignations in the newsroom. That stalwart approach to change reflects a paper's philosophy: we're consistent, classic, serious, comfortable, and above market gimmicks. "The *Daily Bugle:* We're Serious About Our News."

> **Breaking News**
>
> Many traditional media send mixed messages: It's hard to tell if their websites reflect their traditional product.

And probably as reluctant as going to color, the decision to create Bugle.com was met with equal fervor. So at Bugle.com, the viewer expects the same approach: "Gee, will this thing even have pictures on it? Will it be all words, all black and white?" The last thing those viewers will expect to see is a Flash presentation, ads in neon colors, an array of icons, entry points, pictures, and—gasp!—colored headlines. And if this design is what they find, they might ask themselves if they clicked the wrong link.

Product is product: there are no two ways about it. What exudes from the newspaper ("We're Serious About Our News") probably should exude from its Internet counterpart if branding is any part of the game plan.

That is, when the audience thinks *Daily Bugle*, it thinks serious business. Going to its website shouldn't be such a different experience.

Often, though, the relationship between traditional media and their online product is disjointed because no plan has been laid out for what that relationship should be. Much of the time, their philosophy is lost or completely left out. Again, that approach started a decade ago when traditional media began incorporating an Internet site into their product line and the only thought was, "Put this stuff on that site."

> **Extra! Extra!**
>
> Design your website for different types of web browsers to capture access to the widest possible audience. Various browsers—such as Firefox, Internet Explorer, and Safari—often handle and display web pages somewhat differently.

Programmers weren't exactly journalists, and only recently have publishers, editors, and directors taken seriously the online product—no longer the little cousin of the big product.

But then some in new media began realizing that the audience they were capturing was more diverse than the traditionalists. Again, they were more tech-savvy, younger, more educated, had more disposable income, had different reading patterns, and were not loyal to one product only.

So is it right for the *Daily Bugle* to simply reach out electronically to the readership it already has, or should it find all those others out there who might like the news but want more from the Internet site? An interesting debate, to be sure. In the end, it has just taken some time for traditional media to step out of the stodgy gray and into a more colorful, engaging, and interactive online forum.

Does an online product change the philosophy of the traditional product? Not really; the *Daily Bugle* can still maintain an approach that's consistent, classic, serious, comfortable, above market gimmicks … well, maybe use a few, but that's OK. If the overall feel of the site achieves that strong belief, then the online site could be a bit more playful without going overboard. The "TomKat" wedding in Italy would not be the lead story in either product …

Looks Are Everything

Take a look at *The New York Times* and NYTimes.com. *The Times*'s print edition has been made a bit more contemporary over the years, including the controversial move to using color photos on page one in 1997. The site pretty much follows the print mold, although there are ads, Flash presentations, plenty of links, more color, and fun diversions. You can even find the "TomKat" story there if you do some searching.

So deciding what your website looks like takes some degree of thought (and not so much afterthought). You take into account who you are, how serious you want to be taken, and who you're trying to attract to the site—and whether a design is sensational or even unethical, you are making journalistic decisions. So the answer to the second part of the question is not just yes, it's a resounding yes. Online design is, in fact, journalism and should be treated as such.

> **Extra! Extra!**
>
> It's important to spend equal resources on your new media department as it is in your traditional newsroom. Nothing is worse than looking at a news site that doesn't feel like journalism.

So is a web designer a journalist? Well, hold your horses. Just as the press guys who spool up the paper on the presses aren't journalists, web designers aren't so much journalists, either. Again, however, most online sites have been treated like distant cousins and weren't given the same resources as their traditional counterparts. If 100 people were working for the print or broadcast product, there were perhaps two or three in the online end.

Although those folks who are now online editors may have had a degree in journalism then had to scurry to learn how to program (or vice-versa). So things are certainly changing. Many mediums have begun to take seriously the need for bona fide journalists running the online product, and the result is a better—and more successful—product.

What is good web design? Keeping in mind that the traditional product should be somewhat reflected—assuming there is a traditional product to reflect—the site must reach your target audience and set a tone (are we serious, sports-dominated, into features, a gay and lesbian publication, left- or right-leaning, a bit on the sensational side …). The site won't reach your desired audience if what you're going for is light, fun, interactive, and entertaining yet your design is a simple gray background with black lettering and one or two pictures with some links to stories. I'm falling asleep just thinking about that.

No, it must reach out and grab you. It must have pictures—maybe even video and audio! It should take you inside to more flashy, intelligently designed pages. It should feel like a place where you would want to spend some time. And if you've done it right, your target viewers can identify with what you're delivering to them. And that will keep them coming back.

One mistake is trying to give everyone everything all at once. You type in Bugle.com and whoa, Nellie! You're hit with several blinking ads saying, "CLICK HERE!" "CLICK HERE!" You want to read about last night's game, but you can't find it with all the different pull-down menus and buttons. If there's a blog, it can't be found for all the other distractions: "Breaking News," "Top News," "Entertainment News," "Partly Cloudy Today," "There's a Wreck on I-95," "Get Your Free Umbrella with a Paid Subscription"… the distractions go on and on.

Many viewers will grow frustrated: "All I was looking for was that obituary …"

 Extra! Extra!

Sometimes less is more when it comes to good web design. Don't overdo it.

Not a news website (but certainly offering news), search engine Google has built an empire going counter to the jam-everything-you-can-possibly-fit-and-sell-onto-the-home-page approach and put just one simple thing on that page. You open the website, and what does it say? Google. Search. Then, there's a box where you type in what you're looking for.

That overly simplified approach has made Google a household name. It's even being used as a verb: "I Googled that information yesterday."

So on the far spectrum of good web design, you have the oversimplified. On the other end, you have a gazillion words, art elements, links, and ads. Maybe we want to be somewhere in-between. But it should be clear where the reader is: Bugle.com should be somewhere prominent on the page other than just in the URL. And just as a story might have a descending order of importance, so too should the website.

Useful and Simple

What's most important to the viewers? Breaking news, perhaps? Okay, let's make that the visual point of the page. Maybe follow it with other story teasers that will bring you to another page that has the full story as the dominant item. On the home page, maybe there are links to other news and departments. Don't clog pages up with too much, though, or the viewer could become disoriented. Keep it simple.

Extra! Extra!

Be sure your site is easy to navigate. Don't try to be too cute with names of buttons and links. Confusing your viewer is the last thing you want to do.

Remember, the idea is to make the site as useful as possible. Don't get cute with names. If blogs are what they are after, you don't want to label them "Soapbox." They might never get the connection (and shouldn't have to). It's like grabbing a menu in a trendy sports bar. None of the food items say what the item really is. You want a tuna fish sandwich, but they call it the Bill Parcells.

The site must be easy to navigate. The refer points should be compelling. If a viewer is reading the latest weather story on a hurricane that's approaching the mainland, there should be links to the latest satellite images and projected path, tips on how to stay safe during a hurricane, weather in other regions, and other related stories. If the viewer is looking for his kids' little league baseball story, assuming it's not the lead sports story, it should be a click or two away under "Sports," "Local Sports," then the story.

Getting Up and Running

Assuming you want your own website for your journalist voice and you're not an ace programmer, not to worry. There are many ways to create your own spot on the World Wide Web.

Most media companies employ their own qualified web design staff or contract with a web company to do some of it for them. Still, others might need to do it all themselves, like a college newspaper or public broadcast station without a huge budget—as well as the guy in his garage with a lot to say and no venue to say it. Let's look at what it takes to get a website up and running.

So you have a little community weekly with five employees, and you can bet that they aren't all in the newsroom. In fact, it's you, the owner, a sales guy and gal, and a part-time receptionist in a transformed ranch house somewhere in central Florida or eastern Kansas. As for budgets, well … it's better if we can do this website thing on the cheap. Sure, we can sell some ads online, but we want to just get started.

Where do we begin? Well, lucky for you, there are several cheap—maybe even free—ways to get your site up and running, although the fees will come later when you need the site hosted for a larger audience (more about that later).

So little Tony down the block can have his own website for his garage band with pictures and gig dates, and he can do it with little to no investment with what's available for free on the Internet.

But when it comes to a website that needs exposure to a broader audience and more sophisticated capabilities than just posting pictures from the gig at the high school dance, it will need to be in a prominent place to give it the opportunity to be seen by many people. You need a place to put your page. That's called *web hosting*. The more visible your website is depends on how good your host is—and many times, how much you spend. And of course, you must have a good product. But even if you have a great online product, you might not get viewers to see it if it's not in a prominent, high-traffic place.

def•i•ni•tion

Web hosting is simply the allocation of your website on a web server that is connected to the Internet.

A good web host costs anywhere from a couple bucks a month for a shared site to close to $10 a month for a dedicated site. There are maintenance and additional storage fees as well as costs for e-mail addresses, and they usually also charge for database storage, blog hosting, photo galleries, and no host ads. It adds up pretty quickly. Still, for the upstart looking to start up a cheap new medium, a trip through Google for "web hosting" will get you some of the best cheap—or expensive—hosts, depending on your preferences.

These web hosts offer dozens of templates—predesigned pages that will define the look of your website. Or you can build pages yourself by using *HTML* or a program such as Microsoft FrontPage and having a host put them up on the web for you.

def•i•ni•tion

HTML—or Hypertext Markup Language—is the language or code used to structure text and multimedia documents and set up links among documents on the World Wide Web.

Of course, who has time to learn all the language and skills needed to code everything from a headline to a photo? Most large media companies have whole staffs dedicated to just this job.

So if you're short on staff and capital, you may want to go with a good web host to get yourself out there.

The Least You Need to Know

 ◆ Just like any media, you must know your audience in the online venue.

 ◆ Ethics play an enormous role in creating, maintaining, and operating your website.

 ◆ Design is a major aspect of a website and should send a good, clear, and consistent message of your product to your audience.

 ◆ A good web host will not only give you a good-looking and useful product, but more people will also be able to find you.

Chapter **21**

The Power of the Blog

In This Chapter

- ◆ What is a blog, anyway, and who uses them?
- ◆ Is blogging journalism?
- ◆ How blogs contribute to media competition?
- ◆ Using blogs to get the story

Think blogging is just for kids or folks who have tremendous amounts of time on their hands? Think again. *Blogs*, or *weblogs*, have not only become the predominant forum for sharing information on the World Wide Web—they are also affecting journalism! In this chapter, we'll show you how.

An Online Room of Your Own

The word "blog" sounds like a rash or some sort of alien space creature, but have no fear—blogs are simply webpages produced by individuals online where anyone can add their two cents, sort of like a journal or a message board. Bloggers write about anything they want to on their own personal blogs, and others who visit those sites—be it friends, family, or complete strangers—can write on those pages, as well. Bloggers can also post photos or movie and audio clips on their blogs; it's not necessarily just restricted to text.

So your 13-year-old sister has her own blog site where she talks about her life. Her friends write back to her on her blog. Others who stumble upon or are invited to her blog can do the same. And so, this little conversation becomes blogging.

To create your own blog, do a quick Google search for "blogs" and it will direct you to scores of free programs that you can download to create it. Probably the most well-known and popular blogging program is Blogger, but other services—such as Movable Type, TypePad, and WordPress—can also help you create your own site in minutes.

Millions of people are joining this world of blogs, sometimes nicknamed the "blogo-sphere." According to the Pew Internet and American Life Project in 2005, a non-profit research group studying the effects of the Internet on Americans, a new weblog is created every 5.8 seconds—meaning 15,000 new blogs each day!

And it's not just kids creating them. A year later, Pew's new data show that 12 million American adults keep a blog while 57 million adults read blogs.

> **Breaking News**
>
> In 2006, more than 12 million Americans were posting blogs while 57 million were reading them.

So it goes without saying that with so much blog traffic happening on the World Wide Web, it would only be a matter of time before everyone from businesses wanting to create a dialog about their services to politicians reaching out to their constituents to musicians wanting to entice more record sales would create their own blogs.

Look Who's Breaking the News

So what do blogs have to do with journalism? Well, a whole lot. Remember from previous chapters when we talked about storytelling, where in the early days people told stories about subjects, people, and events. This way of life began the very communal and tribal form of journalism.

In the twenty-first century, the offspring of storytelling remains journalism. The word's very root, "journal," indicates information that is gathered and collected. How it's shared is the difference in journalism as we know it today.

And what could be better than free sharing on a multimedia venue with the capability of reaching endless numbers of people? So the sharing of thoughts and information in blog form can certainly be considered journalism. Well, a five-minute video clip of your sister and her best friend dancing to a pop song is not—but under the employ of news websites, a strange thing has happened. Bloggers are tipping off media to stories. Is that really so strange?

Without the telephone, there might not have been a "Deep Throat." Much like the telephone, blogs have been freeways of communication to reporters of every medium. And they're not slowing down anytime soon.

With more and more people on the Internet each day, blogs are not just becoming popular—they are changing the way journalists gather news.

Many newspapers, television stations, and radio stations offer their own blog forums where people can speak their minds regarding information relevant to their programming—let's say daily news, for instance. In this case, a typical news blog would take an excerpt of a story from the day's newspaper and invite readers to respond—much like letters to the editor. If it's an interesting issue, bloggers will engage in the online discussion. They might praise a story or criticize it. The blog also might urge readers to share their own knowledge and add even more context to the story.

I can't tell you how many times I've posted a blog on my newspaper's site, asking how readers feel about a certain subject. In their responses, a good deal of the information is hugely useful—from what people want to see in the paper, to how they want a story to be presented, to what the story should include. And they might even do some of the work for me by giving me some history of a subject or some key players I might not know about.

The best bloggers are the ones who have a lot of experience with and knowledge of the subject matter. They may be great resources as well, whether for a news tip or as marketing subjects.

 Extra! Extra! _____

Blogging in journalism is a two-way street that provides additional content by soliciting comments from readers.

My newspaper broke a story not too long ago about a senior police investigator believed to be linked to a gambling operation. Investigating the story took weeks to uncover, but it wasn't until the blogs started lighting up that a lot of leads began opening for us. Sure, a good deal of them were bunk, but a few led to uncovering the story. In the end, the cop's resignation came just as the story got red-hot and a bust of the operation ended its run.

Would we have gotten the story without the bloggers? Sure. But the help we had received from them proved very useful.

"Some reporters, and some who have never worked at a newspaper, are turning to the Internet and creating blogs," says Christopher Zurcher, a veteran reporter and communications director of Connecticut Fund for the Environment. "And even blogs are changing on a daily basis. A blog used to be simply a record of the favorite sites someone visited on any given day. Now, they're practically becoming the grass, or technological, roots of social movements. Social movements used to be formed in streets, classrooms, and student centers. Today, they're starting on the Internet."

Truer words couldn't be said. The "grass" that Zurcher speaks of are the tips—the information—fed to reporters that ignite our curiosity and help us get a leg up on a story (and the competition).

A New Competitor?

Blogs are new and becoming a bigger competitor; right now, they're not a major competitor but are heading that way. How many news outlets are there in the world? It's impossible to say, what with the Internet breaking the mold. Just as traditional media eventually joined the ranks of Internet competition among themselves, out pops the blog empowering anyone to break their own news.

So now journalists don't only have to worry about getting scooped by competing newspapers or TV or radio stations—in their traditional mediums or on their Internet sites—but there is now a host of motivated, above-average Joes out there with the capability to break and share scoops on their own blogs, too.

But are blogs really direct competition with mainstream media? Maybe not yet. Will blogs continue to make a greater impact on how traditional media gathers and reports news in the very near future? The answer is a resounding yes. In fact, they are having a small impact now. Keep in mind that the publisher of the *Los Angeles Times* isn't going to cringe when some startup news blog out of a home office down the street begins breaking its own news of some Washington, D.C., insider with a lead on a scandal. Why not? One reason is because individual blogs are usually tough to find without significant web hosting.

Most bloggers haven't reached the point that they are institutions, such as newspapers are. Even if they're report is accurate, how would anyone know to trust them? Any Tom, Dick, or Harry could break news on a blog. To be credible, they must be established, and becoming established takes some time and a fair following.

Even with the best hosting sites that can get you out in the forefront, coupled with all the glitz you can put up on your blog, without name recognition and a proven track record of legitimacy with the information you put forth (or until you get that), an individual blog is likely not going to get much attention. At least, not right away.

The Blog Evolution

I mentioned Drudge Report earlier—Matt Drudge's D.C. insider website where he has broken a significant chunk of mainstream news. While his site is not really a blog anymore, having morphed into a conglomerate news website without blogs or commenting features, it did start out as a blog.

So who and what started this whole blog thing, and when? The first blog began way back in 1993 when the National Center for Supercomputing Applications (NCSA) at the University of Illinois at Champaign-Urbana began compiling a "What's New!" list of interesting sites on the web. The same year, Netscape began its "What's New!" site. But it wasn't until 1997 that the terms "weblog" and "blog" were coined.

The blog was significant because it was the first time information was disseminated that wasn't just techno-babble. You didn't need a degree in computer programming to understand it.

The community of blogs is now so vast and diverse that the International Academy of Digital Arts and Sciences, a 550-member body of leading web experts, business figures, luminaries, visionaries, and creative celebrities, ranks the top blogs in three categories with its annual *Webby Awards*.

For instance, The Huffington Post (huffingtonpost.com) won the 2006 Webby Award for best political blog. The Huffington Post was launched in May 2005 by Arriana Huffington and Kenneth Lerer as a left-leaning blog that contains news, business, entertainment stories, and commentary. It enables viewers to comment on individual stories and opinion pieces. And it's quite successful, at this time ranking fifth among all weblogs and first in political blogs. And The Huffington Post also started as a meager website that was snatched up by a major sponsoring site and is now enormously successful.

So if you work for a typical daily newspaper that's not the *Los Angeles Times*, are you worried about losing your readers and even your Internet audience and bloggers to blogs such as The Huffington Post? Perhaps even if you *are* the *Los Angeles Times*. But the bigger insight is realizing that your current and potential readers have additional bona fide sources of information: distractions, or more places they can spend their time and get their news.

But even if The Huffington Post presents some competition, it's nowhere near as diverse in content or as unbiased as the *Times*.

A Changing Landscape

So can Granny really scoop you? Sure, it could happen. The Huffington Times may scoop you, too. And what about readers breaking news on your blogs?

Extra! Extra! _____

If your newspaper or station doesn't have a blog reporter, ask your editors or directors if they'd be interested in you breaking news on the company's blog.

That point has led some forward-thinking editors to hire reporters to do just that—blog. These roving reporters hit the streets in search of news, and rather than simply reporting it online or in the traditional medium, they write blogs and start dialogs with other bloggers.

What's the value, the desired result? The answer is tips—sometimes major tips that can possibly lead to bigger and deeper stories. How does this work? Let's take a general assignment reporter, call her Lucy, and have her dig around town to find some news.

Lucy begins a blog at 9:45 A.M. to report that the city has put festive bags over the parking meters in the downtown shopping district for the Christmas season. She chatted with the mayor and the Chamber of Commerce folks who were adorning the meters with the gold and red bags. She even snapped a picture of them and posted it to the blog.

The officials said it's to give shoppers a "little holiday gift" by not having to pay for parking and to encourage shoppers to come downtown to shop, rather than going to the big mall just across the city's border.

At 10:10 A.M., a viewer writes in to comment on this issue. Then, more comments come in at 10:12, 10:15, and 10:21. Everyone thinks that it's great to have a reprieve from paying for parking during the few weeks before Christmas.

Then, at 10:26 A.M., another blogger writes that each year, the city budgets a certain portion of money in its general budget based on anticipated revenue from parking tickets. The blogger notes that there must be a surplus in that budget line item if they can go a few weeks with no collections from parking tickets.

At 10:32 A.M., another blogger says the real trick is that while the downtown meters are free for a few weeks, all the other meters in town have been adjusted to make up the difference. This blogger found that the meters across town used to be 25 cents for half an hour but now are 25 cents for 15 minutes. He notes that the parking lots near the hospital and health facility have done the same, as well. No, this blogger notes, the city isn't giving any such gift; it is simply catering to the downtown merchants and putting the screws to everyone else.

Now, this blog is becoming a story—and doing so pretty quickly. In fact, it's probably going to be a front-page story the next day or even on the 5 P.M. news that same day.

Lucy, being a thorough reporter, will follow the story by pulling and reviewing the city budget and parking ticket revenues for the past few years and seeing for herself what the patterns have been. In some regards, this type of reporting is similar to the old "Man on the Street" technique. But keep in mind that journalism is simply that: putting an ear to the ground in hopes of sharing news with others. And these days, putting an ear to the new ground of the blog is becoming increasingly significant in journalism.

> **Breaking News**
>
> Blogging is becoming a significant part of traditional media as more and more people flock to the Internet and begin commenting.

The Least You Need to Know

- A blog, short for weblog, is a place where bloggers can write about whatever they want and readers can respond.

- Anyone can have a blog and participate in blogging.

- News can break first in blogs.

- Blogging is becoming a larger part of journalism.

Chapter 22

Getting Started in Internet Journalism

In This Chapter

- The Internet permeation into all journalism
- Learning a more technical side of journalism
- Meeting the demands of an Internet audience
- Speed, accuracy, and technical skills will get you the job

If there's one thing journalists can count on, it's that their lives will continue to change as traditional media keep crossing over to the Internet. Some believe that the Internet may replace the entire world of print journalism, while others—most, actually—believe that print publications might slip in circulation but won't disappear anytime soon, even though Internet news sites will continue to grow and become more relevant. Remember, TV and radio were expected to kill off newspapers, and that hasn't exactly happened.

Also broadcast media are relying more and more on their Internet counterparts. The changes that are occurring are exciting for those journalists who want to use this new frontier as a career.

In this chapter, we'll look at what the different media offer for online journalism careers and how you can get a leg up.

You Know You're an Internet Journalist If ...

As we mentioned earlier in this book, change has come slowly to the newsrooms in the world of journalism. They've been slow to embrace this new technology of the Internet that's been thrust upon us. Ironically, the Internet is the polar opposite of slow. It's all about speed—the here and now—and is a symbol of the future and new frontiers, rather than what was, has been, or never will be. If the former sounds enticing to you, then working in the Internet journalism field might be a good career for you.

Working at the Speed of Life

Many journalists already are working on the Internet; they just might not realize it. At any media outlet, it takes the collective effort of journalists working together to keep up with the speed of the Internet news world.

Take, for instance, this scenario: a traditional reporter in a newsroom gets a call about a bad accident out on the interstate during morning rush hour. Three are dead, 15 are injured; there's a major pileup, and the highway's being closed for who knows how long. People need to know about this accident, and they need to know fast because it affects getting to work and maybe even coming home. The reporter and a photographer do what they do—head out to the scene to get the story firsthand.

Breaking News
While traditional media aren't going away anytime soon, the new media field of online journalism is growing rapidly.

This story in a print newspaper won't get to your doorstep until the next morning, which is way too late. A TV station will interrupt programming to report the incident and conditions, although they won't stick with a live feed all day. A radio station will update the accident periodically between other programming.

These are all traditional ways to get information to the public. But they're too slow. Today, Internet journalists can immediately get to work piecing together information coming in from the reporter and posting it on the website. Additionally, they can find maps and alternate routes, create info-boxes of the accident location, upload film clips from the scene, and update the report by the minute as conditions change.

The traditional journalist most certainly contributed to this story that got posted online. He or she was there and got the story! The Internet journalists back at the office got that story onto the website as soon as possible, with additional pertinent information and links. So Internet journalism is more often than not a collaborative effort—and journalists all over the newsroom are part of it.

Being Part of the Future

For the sake of jobs, the good news is that more and more traditional media are putting Internet news at the forefront. In other words, journalists will increasingly need to have Internet skills—and more jobs will continue to evolve in Internet journalism. You might expect only large, rich media companies to employ a full-time online news staff, right? Think again. The Internet is inexpensive; therefore, it evens the playing field somewhat.

Check out this job listing from JournalismJobs.com, one of the leading media job posts in the United States:

> The Star Press, a 32,000 Gannett daily in Muncie, IN, is looking for a reporter to cover the city's neighborhoods from a grassroots level as a roving journalist, filing stories and photos directly to the Internet throughout the day. The successful candidate will excel at covering a wide range of subject matter, from spot news to features on schools, businesses, nonprofits, and everything in between. Most of the reporter's stories will be short takes, much like a blog. Some content will also be used in print. Candidates should have a demonstrated ability to be a self-starter, innovative at developing a wide variety of story ideas and sources, comfortable with a fast, demanding reporting pace, and at ease with technology. This is an innovative approach to making our news report even more local and reaching new readers, and we are looking for a reporter excited about the potential and challenge of this opportunity.

The salary? $30,000 to $35,000.

Most online editors will earn more than this to start off. Online editors have many skills not only pertaining to journalism, but to programming and web maintenance. These positions could pay double that to start. However, a web reporter starting out working for the new media department of a traditional medium probably will earn a salary in the $30,000s.

A quick search on this job-posting site shows 124 online-specific jobs, many of them for reporters, editors, or producers—from ESPN and *The New York Times* to Stone Street Media and KLAS-TV.

So is it safe to say that Internet media careers are plentiful? Maybe not yet, but will they become more plentiful in the future? "You bet," says Miranda Bender, web editor and corporate market consultant for Morris DigitalWorks in Augusta, Georgia.

"The Internet is pretty much all the rising generations know of news," Bender says. "They have become accustomed to a real-time paced world, and sitting still for the news just doesn't hold water. The print medium is, in fact, yesterday's news, while the Internet is able to provide today's news as it happens. There is little doubt that the print product will never cease to exist, but at some point in the near future, the Internet will replace it."

More and more, newsrooms are pushing Internet reporting as well as breaking news throughout the day, adding special features and additional information to their websites and making those sites as competitive as their print publications. Again, no one is saying print publications are going the way of the dinosaur—at least, not yet. But publishers and corporate bigwigs are putting much more emphasis on this new medium than ever before.

"The Internet is considered the future of news," says Bender, who has also worked as a web editor and graphic designer for a newspaper. "It will become more important as journalists and programmers design more interactive ways to provide readers their national, community, and personal news in different mediums. Right now, the focus is providing interactive news on PDAs, but as soon as that is developed and marketed—and probably before the public has really embraced the idea—the 'next big thing' will already be in the works."

> **Breaking News**
>
> More and more Internet journalism jobs are becoming available. Whether reporting or editing, they are both journalism.

What You'll Need to Learn

In colleges and universities, curriculums for new media journalists still revolve around a core of traditional journalism. That is, the good old Journalism 101 and 102 classes aren't going away. But you'll find the Internet incorporated into all of them now—not just typing words but coding, using HTML, and learning web programs. And probably a good deal of graphics programs, too.

These technical skills are important for an Internet journalist, whether they're learned in college or otherwise. Why? Well, as we've discussed, the field is relatively new and is evolving and growing every minute. Those equipped with the fundamentals of the journalism field, coupled with the latest technological skills, will have a considerable edge in the job marketplace—not to mention be up with the times!

Also keep in mind there typically aren't as many Internet journalists or even web editors at a media outlet as there are traditional writers, reporters, editors, and copy editors … at least, not yet. So the more technical skills you have to offer, the better off you will be.

> **Breaking News**
>
> Classes in Internet journalism are becoming more available, with entire curriculums with even Master's programs being offered.

"In larger newspapers, where there are usually more than one or two positions available, it can still be difficult to 'break into' Web sites," says Bender. "The best way to prepare for a position in media websites, or *new media*, is internships and work on college publications," she adds. "Taking courses in certain subjects, depending on which technical field (design or development) you're interested in, is always advisable.

But as more and more traditional media add Internet journalists to their staffs over time—like our Muncie, Indiana, example earlier—good candidates for these jobs will be the ones who know more than a thing or two about posting stories and the inner workings of a website.

def•i•ni•tion

> **New media** is a journalism medium that combines traditional reporting for an online venue and can include print, video, and audio updated by the minute.

Tools for the Trade

As an Internet journalist, you'll need to subscribe to the philosophy that while a story might be a story, your audience might be quite different from that of the traditional medium.

For example, there are many people who don't subscribe to newspapers or magazines and won't be caught dead watching the 6 P.M. news. They will, however, open up that laptop or boot up their personal computer. They might also surf around their PDAs or their office computers while the boss isn't looking. Is it a much different reader or viewer than one of traditional media? Well, not all of them. But those who do receive the majority of their news online are generally considered more sophisticated, tech-savvy, and more engaged because they have the opportunity to, and often do, instantly comment on a story online. Knowing your market and whom you are writing to is just as important in online news reporting and editing as it is in traditional newsrooms.

Remember our friend Brian Dearth? He's the former online editor at *The Gazette*, *Island Packet*, and *The Beaufort* (all in South Carolina) and knows firsthand the benefits of being both a journalist and a tech whiz.

"My background is foremost an editorial one that also requires strong technical knowledge," says Dearth. "I was a communications major and gained experience reporting and editing for a college newspaper. As far as the technical knowledge, I'm completely self-taught. I started at a small newspaper, the *Island Packet*, which has an online staff of two, so I often experienced a trial by fire. When something had to get done and I didn't know how to do it, I had to learn awfully fast."

"That's not to say that everyone who wants to break into online journalism needs to be a code monkey," he continues. "The editorial sense is more important, and as online becomes more important to the news industry in both revenue and readership, newspapers are more willing to hire designers and developers to handle the code. But it's imperative to know at least what is possible and what's not with the resources and technology available."

For example, let's say an international business scandal has erupted and some bigwig execs are looking at subpoenas. Your boss asks you to get a story onto the website. While your readers may include the traditional types, you're going to be writing for those who actually give a hoot about the stock market and business world and specifically seek out this type of story online. They'll expect a thorough report.

> **Breaking News**
>
> The advantage of online reporting is that the stories not only will beat, or be as fresh as, other media, but they can also have endless amounts of space and be updated constantly. They can also link to other formats, such as video, audio, or even relevant archived stories.

This story will include a good history of the company, analysis of the effect on the market, links to other articles, a live ticker, and an endless array of graphics and photos. A traditional publication, even a business journal, can't put that information on the street as fast as you can post it online—and it can't be as comprehensive, either. And the Internet audience knows, so they expect online reports to be comprehensive and up-to-the-minute.

You must be prepared to work quickly. People expect your report to be the most timely, so accuracy and speed on deadline is even more critical.

Your viewer will be demanding, and you'd better be able to meet that demand if you want your website to be reputable and successful.

Internet viewers also typically are looking for quick hits on stories with the option to "go long"—that is, to read the full story and check links to other stories. The online journalist needs to understand that not every story will be a 30-incher on a single subject. Get the news in, get it fast, make it pop, and keep it smart. If the reader wants more, make available related stories—whether in-house or on another site.

Also the web reader—as we've said—is generally more tech-savvy. That means your language has to match. Writing can be a bit more edgy, fresh, and conversational than its traditional counterpart. Again, keep the report fair and not sarcastic, but speak to your audience. And most importantly, be sure you know who that audience is.

Getting Your Foot in the Door

Breaking into the online journalism world generally is going to be tougher than traditional newsroom jobs because there are simply fewer jobs, and more and more people are naturally gravitating toward the new media field because it's the next big thing.

More online journalist positions are being established at newspapers than other media, but with the field growing in leaps and bounds, more and more new media jobs are being created every day. The edge you're going to need is simple: you need to be able to write on the first line of your cover letter or speak those first words to a potential employer, "I can do exactly what you're asking for right now, and I can do it fast."

Of course, you're going to have to back it up. The best candidates who you'll be competing with know HTML and other coding languages; they'll also understand graphics, photo, and web programs such as Fetch, Illustrator, InDesign, Quark, and Photoshop. And they will be solid reporters and writers that can really hustle. They too will have internships and a file of clips and online links to websites that display their work. They'll also have solid professional references. These are all the qualities that an employer will look for.

What is your edge? "I can do exactly what you're asking for right now." That means stop the candidate search; you're ready to plug in and get to work and meet and exceed expectations.

Extra! Extra!

If online journalism is your goal, be sure you not only learn how to write and report but also how to program and understand web platforms.

Check out some of the more innovative online reporting in newspapers, TV, radio, and magazines. Emulate it. Be able to get video with a print story, add graphics or a slideshow, get it—and post it—far before the print deadline.

Coding isn't rocket science, and journalists still working their way through college should take some electives that will bolster this skill. But there are lots of classes available to nonstudents, too, that help professionals get a leg up. And get experience however possible.

When all is said and done, the candidate most qualified for the job will be able to plug right in and begin producing top-notch journalism and visuals.

The Least You Need to Know

- New media mixes every aspect of traditional media—print, video, and audio.
- Internet journalism is an innovative field, and not everyone has caught up. You may be a pacesetter.
- Deadlines are even more critical in online journalism.
- Understanding both reporting and some web programming will give you a leg up when landing a job.

Glossary

Newspaper Terms

ABC   Audit Bureau of Circulation. The preeminent advertising auditing organization that independently verifies and disseminates its member's circulation, readership, and audience data.

ad stack   The layout of ads on a news page.

advance   A preview story.

agate   Small type generally found in sports statistics or stock pages.

angle   Perspective of a news story, also called a slant.

Associated Press   A wire news service.

banner   A headline at the top of a page.

beat   A reporter's assigned area of coverage.

border   A frame around art, stories, or ads.

box   A framed image over or around a graphic element or text.

budget   A list of the day's or weekend's stories, which are ranked according to their value for that edition.

bumping heads   Headlines that run too close to each other.

byline   The author's name at the top of a story.

Caption   The identifying information for a photo.

circulation   The number of copies of a newspaper distributed in a single day.

city editor   The editor who runs the local news desk.

column   The space on a page where a story runs; also, a regular piece written by a writer (referred to as a *columnist*).

copy desk   The area of the newsroom where copy editors review written material.

copy editor   The person who edits the copy and checks it for accuracy.

copy   All written material.

correspondent   A reporter who works on a far away assignment, such as a war correspondent.

credit line   The photographer's name, which runs beneath the picture he or she took.

crop   To cut part of a photo to make it fit better or to edit out certain images within the photo.

cub   A new or young reporter.

cutline   The caption below a photo.

cutline   The caption beneath a photo.

deadline   The latest time that a story can be turned in to make the publication.

downstyle   A style in which only the first word of a sentence and proper nouns are capitalized.

dummy   The layout of a newspaper page.

ears   The far right and left spaces at the top of a newspaper's front page, flanking the newspaper's name or masthead.

edition   The publication of a newspaper off the press. Large metro dailies might have more than one edition.

editorial   An opinion piece in a newspaper.

editorialize   Opining on a subject in a news story.

exclusive   A scoop or story written by one paper before any other papers have a chance to print the story.

feature   A human interest story.

first-day story   A breaking or news story.

five W's   The questions generally answered in the story's lead: who, what, when, where, and why?

flag   A newspaper's name and logo at the top of the front page.

folio   The newspaper's name along with the date and page number and sometimes the section name at the top of each page.

font   A specific type family.

gutter   The space between pages that face each other.

headline   Large display type at the top of a story that summarizes what the story is about.

hook   A tool used to entice a reader into a story.

inverted pyramid   The most accepted structure of a story, with the most important information at the top and gradually diminishing in importance as the story progresses.

jump   A continuation of a story from one page to the next.

kicker   A smaller headline beneath the main headline.

lead   The first paragraph of a story, also sometimes spelled as *lede*.

letter to the editor   A letter written to the editorial page editor for publication.

libel   Printed injury of a person's reputation.

masthead   A box inside the newspaper that lists key personnel and the publisher of the newspaper.

morgue   A newspaper archive; where old newspapers are stored.

news hole   The remaining space on a page after the ads have been placed.

news service   News agencies, also called wires, which send stories they've collected or written to subscribing newspapers.

obituary   Biographical story of a person who recently died; often printed for public record.

off the record   Not intended for publication.

op-ed   The space opposite the editorial page, usually reserved for columns or other opinion items such as letters to the editor.

orphan   A single line separated from its related text that appears at the bottom of a page.

plagiarism   Stealing someone else's work for print.

play   How a story is placed on a page.

point   A unit of type-size measurement that equals about $\frac{1}{72}$ of an inch.

proofreader   One who checks or proofs pages or stories for spelling and accuracy.

publisher   The CEO of a newspaper.

pulled quote   An excerpt taken from the text and blown up on the page to break up text or garner attention.

Q-and-A story   A story written in a question-and-answer style.

runaround   The line of space surrounding an image to separate it from other elements; also called *keyline*.

scoop   An exclusive news item.

sectional story   A major news story with different aspects featured under two or more headlines.

series   Related stories that run on successive days.

sidebar   A related story that runs beside and supports another story.

skyline   Text above the banner that refers readers to an inside story.

slant   A story's angle.

source   A person (or a document) who provides information for your story.

spot news   Breaking news reported on the scene.

stet   Proofreader mark that means leave as is.

stringer   A correspondent.

subhead   A small headline in the body that breaks up the story.

tabloid   A small-sized newspaper, usually about half the size of a broadsheet.

typo   Spelling error in a story.

widow   A word or line separated from its related text and appearing at the top of a page or column.

wire service   A news service, such as The Associated Press, that sends stories to subscribing newspapers.

Magazine Terms

ABC   Audit Bureau of Circulation. The preeminent advertising auditing organization that independently verifies and disseminates its member's circulation, readership, and audience data.

advertorial   An ad that reads like a story.

audience duplication   Magazines that reach the same audience.

backbone   The bound edge of a magazine or book (spine).

bimonthly   A magazine that is published every other month.

biweekly   A magazine that is published every two weeks.

bleed   Printed matter that extends beyond the trimmed edge of a page.

body copy   Main text on a page.

callout   An enlarged section of text that appears in its own box to break up the text.

center spread   Middle two pages of a magazine.

circulation   The number of copies of a magazine distributed or sold.

CMYK   The four colors—cyan, magenta, yellow, and black—used in the standard color printing process.

consumer magazine   General interest magazines that cover a wide range of topics.

consumer specialist magazines   Magazines that serve a specific niche.

content   Editorial material, such as stories and art.

contributing editor   A writer or editor not on the staff but who writes for the magazine.

copy editor   Someone who edits the copy and checks it for accuracy, spelling, grammar, and so on.

copy   Editorial material, such as stories and art.

copyright   Legal ownership of a story, photograph, illustration, or other material.

cover-wrap   An additional cover over the magazine's regular cover for advertising purposes.

crop   To trim editorial material such as copy or photos to fit a certain size.

dummy   The layout of a newspaper page.

ed/ad ratio   The radio of editorial content to advertising content.

editor   One who edits, assigns, and budgets stories and otherwise directs a newsroom.

editorial assistant   A person who assists with editorial responsibilities.

editorial board   Those who advise the editorial staff in content and protocol.

editorial   Content produced by editors, writers, and artists.

extent   The number of pages in a publication.

e-zine   An electronic magazine; one that's on the Internet, for example.

face   A type's style or design.

facing matter   An ad that is opposite editorial content.

fact checker   One who verifies copy for accuracy before it goes to press.

flush   The alignment of text or art to one side of a page; flush right or flush left, for instance.

FM (facing matter)   An ad that is opposite editorial content.

folio   The publication's name, along with the date and page number and sometimes the section name, most commonly atop each page.

font   A specific type family.

footer   Text beneath the main text area on a page.

format   The size and shape of a magazine; also, the style of or slant to the magazine.

gutter   The space between text legs (columns) or around a text area.

header   Text at the top of a page, usually over the regular copy.

imprint   Information about the publisher.

justified   The alignment of text that is flush and equal on both sides of the column.

kern   The process of adjusting letter spacing in a proportional font, refering to the horizontal space between letters.

keyline   The line of space surrounding an image to separate it from other elements; also called *run-around*.

layout   The design of a page.

leading   the amount of added vertical spacing between lines of type

managing editor   The editor in charge of the newsroom below the editor or executive editor; assigns, writes, budgets, and edits stories.

masthead   A box inside the publication that identifies personnel and the publisher of the newspaper.

pass-along reader   A reader who was given the magazine by another reader who purchased it.

preferred position   The page on which an advertiser would like his copy to be placed.

production   The process of assembling a magazine.

proofreader   One who checks, or proofs, pages or stories for spelling and accuracy.

publisher   The CEO of a magazine.

publisher's statement   Unaudited sales figure by the publisher.

pulled quote   An excerpt taken from the text and enlarged.

white space   Nontext areas, or blank space, around normal text or art for effect.

Television Terms

A/D   Analog to digital conversion.

ABC   American Broadcasting Company. Formed in 1943, it operates television and radio networks in the United States and Canada and was the most-watched network in 2006 with more than 4 billion viewers. Its parent company is The Walt Disney Company.

aircheck   Recorded copy of a broadcast.

Arbitron   A company that provides the industry standard for measuring the size of an audience.

archive copy   Material that is stored in the archive.

archive   A place where old footage is stored.

artifacts   Distortions or other losses of video and audio due to low technology.

aston   A graphic, usually of the reporter or speaker, on screen.

BBC   British Broadcasting Corporation. Formed in 1922, the BBC is a public broadcasting network that has a television and radio audience around the world

billboard   A brief announcement to identify a sponsor at the beginning or end of a segment.

B-roll   Video to be used for a reporter's story.

bumper   A voice-over music recording that transitions to or from another segment.

CBS   Columbia Broadcasting System, which began in 1927 in New York as a radio network, expanded to TV and became one of the "big three" networks in America. It was the most-watched network in the United States in 2003.

closed captioning   On-screen text version of a program's dialog for the hearing impaired.

copy   The written material used to produce a public service announcement, promo, or commercial.

FCC   Federal Communications Commission, which governs U.S. TV and radio broadcasting.

format clock   Diagram that shows where each programming element appears in an hour.

HDTV   High-Definition Television.

live-on-tape   A prerecorded program produced in real time, usually with a studio audience, for later broadcast.

log   A written record of broadcasting.

NBC   Formerly known as the National Broadcasting Company, this American network was formed in 1926 by RCA. It has expanded immensely, becoming one of the "big three" broadcasters. By 2003, an estimated 100 million viewers were tuning in to NBC programming in the United States, where it reached more than 97 percent of all households.

network A broadcasting group that sells its programming to affiliates.

optical An on-screen graphic.

package A completed, taped television news story with stand-ups, narration over images, and cues.

producer One who manages the operations of a station and is responsible for a program or the station's programming.

sound bite An audio recording used to attract attention, such as a strong quote.

spot A commercial.

stand-up A reporter's image during a television news story, usually at the beginning or end of the story.

super The name of a news source over his or her image.

teaser An audio or video recording used to entice the audience to stay tuned for a future story.

UHF Ultra-High Frequency; frequencies between 300 MHz and 3.0 GHz, used for television broadcasting.

VHF Very High Frequency; frequencies from 30 MHz to 300 MHz, used for radio and television broadcasting.

Radio Terms

actives Listeners who call in to radio stations to make requests, enter contests, or speak during talk shows.

actuality A *sound bite* lasting 10 to 20 seconds.

advertorial An ad that sounds like a story.

angle The slant or emphasis of a story.

attribution The source or credit to the person who has spoken in a story.

bias An opinion or position in a story.

call letters The official name of a radio station in the United States.

clock The schedule of a broadcast hour in minutes and seconds.

copy The written copy of a public service announcement, promo, or commercial.

cut   A tape containing a voicer, wrap, actuality, or natural sound.

dateline   The date and place where a story was filed.

daypart   The broadcast day of a radio station split up by four-hour increments and starting at 6 A.M.

drive time   The time when the majority of radio listeners travel to and from work, usually 6 to 10 A.M. and 2 to 6 P.M.

FCC   Federal Communications Commission, which governs U.S. TV and radio broadcasting.

hourly   A five-minute newscast at the top of the hour, usually by a network.

human interest story   An emotional story about people or places.

IQ   Short for *in cue;* the first words recorded on a cut.

lead   First sentence of a news story; also spelled *lede.*

lockout   Last words a reporter speaks at the end of a story, which is usually the reporter's name and the station's call letters.

MOS   Abbreviation for "man on the street"; a type of interview where the reporter talks to ordinary people about a common subject.

nat   A recording of a natural or raw atmospheric sound.

network   A broadcasting group that sells its programming to affiliates.

off the record   Information not intended for publication.

OQ   Short for *out cue;* the last words recorded on a cut.

reader   Live news story script with no actualities.

script   A news story in its written form.

slug   A script's title.

sounder   Recorded tune used to introduce segments of the broadcast.

source   A person (or document) who provides information for a story.

spin   Slant of a source or writer.

spot   Recorded commercial advertisement.

target audience   Those who advertisers or producers are aiming to reach with their products.

tease   Brief promo that lets the listener know about the story to come.

UHF   Ultra-High Frequency; frequencies between 300 MHz and 3.0 GHz, used for radio and television broadcasting.

VHF   Very High Frequency; frequencies from 30 MHz to 300 MHz, used for radio and television broadcasting.

voicer   Recorded report of the journalist's voice with no actuality.

wrap   An actuality wrapped by a journalist's voice at the beginning and end of a broadcast.

Internet Terms

backbone   High-speed connection to a network.

bandwidth   How much information or data that can be sent through a connection.

binary   Information consisting entirely of ones and zeros.

blog   Short for weblog, a website that contains an online personal journal with reflections, comments, and often hyperlinks provided by the writer.

broadband   Internet connection with greater bandwidth than a modem, including digital subscriber line (DSL), cable, or satellite.

browser   A software application that allows a user to display and interact with text, images, and other information on a web page.

client   An application that communicates with a web server using HTML.

cookie   A piece of information sent by a web server to a web browser that the browser saves and sends back when a request from the server is made, such as login or registration information or data for an online shopping cart.

domain name   The name that identifies an Internet site.

download   The transfer of data from one computer to another over a network, such as the Internet.

e-mail   Electronic mail.

firewall   Computer hardware or software that prevents unauthorized access to private data by outside computer users.

hit   A single request from a web browser for a single item from a web server.

home page   The web page that your browser is set to use when it starts up.

HTML   Short for Hypertext Markup Language; the coding language used to create documents on the World Wide Web.

Internet   The worldwide, publicly accessible network of interconnected computer networks that transmit information.

intranet   A private network.

Java   A programming language written by Sun Microsystems.

JPEG or JPG   Short for Joint Photographic Experts Group; an image file format.

listserv   A trademarked e-mail list.

mode network   Two or more computers connected to each other.

PDF   Short for portable document format; a file enabling the printing and viewing of documents with all of their formatting intact.

Podcast   A form of audio broadcasting using the Internet.

posting   A written entry on an Internet page, such as a comment on a blog.

router   A computer device that handles the connection between two or more networks.

spam   Junk e-mail; also, an inappropriate attempt to use a mailing list or website, such as unsolicited information.

upload   To move files from one computer to another or onto the Internet.

web page   A site on the World Wide Web.

World Wide Web   The servers that serve web pages to web browsers.

Major U.S. Media

Top 10 U.S. Newspapers (By Daily Circulation, 2006, According to Burrelles*Luce*)

1. *USA Today:* 2,272,815
2. *The Wall Street Journal:* 2,049,786
3. *The New York Times:* 1,142,464
4. *Los Angeles Times:* 851,832
5. *Washington Post:* 724,242
6. *The Daily News*—New York, NY: 708,477
7. *New York Post:* 673,379
8. *Chicago Tribune:* 579,079
9. *Houston Chronicle:* 513,387
10. *Dallas Morning News:* 480,484

Top 10 U.S. Magazines (By Circulation, 2005, According to ABC)

1. *AARP The Magazine:* 22,673,663

2. *AARP Bulletin:* 22,075,011

3. *Reader's Digest:* 9,658,765

4. *TV Guide:* 7,8881,625

5. *Better Homes and Gardens:* 7,407,332

6. *National Geographic:* 5,237,108

7. *Time:* 3,887,480

8. *Good Housekeeping:* 3,864,089

9. *Ladies' Home Journal:* 3,832,710

10. *AAA Westways:* 3,676,058

Top 10 U.S. Broadcast Television Networks

Broadcast (Number and Percentage of Households Reached, Respectively)

1. PBS: 105,579,120 (99 percent)

2. NBC: 103,624,370 (97.17 percent)

3. CBS: 103,421,270 (96.98 percent)

4. ABC: 103,179,600 (96.75 percent)

5. FOX: 102,565,710 (96.18 percent)

6. The CW: 102,565,710 (96.18 percent)

7. MyNetworkTV: 102,565,710 (96.18 percent)

8. ION Television: 91,000,000 (83 percent)

9. gubo: 91,000,000 (83 percent)

10. NBC Weather Plus: 145,450,000 (76 percent)

Cable (Dollars in Millions, 2005)

1. The Walt Disney Co.: 6,463.2
2. Time Warner: 5,691.4
3. Viacom: 4,825.5
4. News Corp.: 3,358.0
5. NBC Universal: 2,614.0
6. Discovery Communications: 1,743.4
7. CBS Corp.: 1,213.5
8. A&E Television Networks: 1,08.2
9. Cablevision Systems Corp.: 1,085.6
10. Lifetime Entertainment Services: 926.8

Top 10 U.S. Radio Companies and Properties (Dollars in Millions, Based on 2004 Revenues)

1. Clear Channel Communications, 3,754.4 (WLTW-FM, New York)
2. Viacom, 2,096.1 (WINS-AM, New York)
3. The Walt Disney Co., 612.3 (WPLJ-FM, New York)
4. Westwood One, 562.2 (CBS Radio Network)
5. Cox Enterprises, 438.2 (WSB-AM, Atlanta)
6. Entercom Communications Corp., 423.5 (WEEI-AM, Boston)
7. Citadel Broadcasting Corp., 411.5 (WIVK-FM, Knoxville, Tenn.)
8. Univision Communications, 328.4 (KLTN-FM, Houston)
9. Cumulus Media, 320.1 (WEBE-FM, Westport, Conn.)
10. Radio One, 319.1 (KKBT-FM, Los Angeles)

Top 10 U.S. Online News Sites (By Page Views, 2005 Monthly Average, According to Nielsen/NetRatings)

1. Yahoo! News: 24,100,000

2. MSNBC: 23,400,000

3. CNN: 22,000,000

4. AOL News: 16,200,000

5. Gannett: 11,800,000

6. IBS: 11,400,000

7. NYTimes.com: 11,000,000

8. Knight Ridder: 9,900,000

8. Tribune: 9,900,000

9. USA Today: 9,400,000

10. ABC News: 8,000,000

U.S. Newspapers by State and Major City

Alabama

Birmingham	*Birmingham Business Journal*
Birmingham	*Birmingham News*
Birmingham	*The Birmingham Times*
Huntsville	*Huntsville Times*
Mobile	*Lagniappe*
Mobile	*Mobile Register*
Montgomery	*Montgomery Advertiser*
Montgomery	*Montgomery Independent*
Talladega	*The Daily Home*
Tuscaloosa	*The Tuscaloosa News*

Alaska

Anchorage	*Alaska Journal of Commerce*
Anchorage	*Anchorage Daily News*
Anchorage	*Anchorage Press*
Homer	*Homer News*
Homer	*Homer Tribune*
Juneau	*Capital City Weekly*
Valdez	*Valdez Star*

Arizona

Douglas	*The Daily Dispatch*
Flagstaff	*Arizona Daily Sun*
Flagstaff	*Navajo Hopi Observer*
Phoenix	*Arizona Business Gazette*
Phoenix	*Arizona Capitol Times*
Phoenix	*Arizona Republic*
Phoenix	*Business Journal of Phoenix*
Phoenix	*Jewish News of Greater Phoenix*
Phoenix	*Prensa Hispana*
Phoenix	*La Voz*
Phoenix	*New Times*
Phoenix	*The Tribune*
Sedona	*Sedona Red Rock News*
Sun City	*Daily News-Sun*
Tucson	*Arizona Daily Star*
Tucson	*Explorer Newspapers*
Tucson	*Inside Tucson Business*
Tucson	*Tucson Citizen*
Tucson	*Tucson Weekly*
Yuma	*Yuma Daily Sun*

Arkansas

Fayetteville	*Fayetteville Free Weekly*
Helena	*The Daily World*
Little Rock	*Arkansas Business*
Little Rock	*Arkansas Democrat-Gazette*
Little Rock	*Arkansas Times*

California

Eureka	*The Eureka Reporter*
Eureka	*Times-Standard*
Los Angeles	*Investor's Business Daily*
Los Angeles	*Jewish Observer*
Los Angeles	*L.A. Weekly*
Los Angeles	*Los Angeles Daily News*
Los Angeles	*Los Angeles Downtown News*
Los Angeles	*Los Angeles Times*
Oakland	*East Bay Express*
Oakland	*The Oakland Tribune*
Sacramento	*Sacramento Bee*
Sacramento	*Business Journal*
Sacramento	*Sacramento News & Review*
San Diego	*Community Newspaper Group*
San Diego	*La Prensa*
San Diego	*San Diego Union-Tribune*
San Diego	*San Diego Reader*
San Diego	*The Coast News*
San Francisco	*Business Times*
San Francisco	*El Mensajero*
San Francisco	*El Observador*
San Francisco	*San Francisco Chronicle*
San Francisco	*San Francisco Guardian*
San Francisco	*San Francisco Weekly*
San Jose	*San Jose Mercury News*
San Jose	*Metro*
San Jose	*San Jose Business Journal*
Tahoe	*Tahoe Daily Tribune*

Colorado

Boulder	*Boulder County Business Report*
Boulder	*Boulder Weekly*
Boulder	*Colorado Daily*
Colorado Springs	*Business Journal*
Colorado Springs	*The Gazette*
Denver	*Denver Business Journal*
Denver	*Denver Post*
Denver	*Rocky Mountain News*
Grand Junction	*GJ Free Press*
Grand Junction	*The Daily Sentinel*

Connecticut

Bridgeport	*Connecticut Post*
Bristol	*Bloomfield Journal*
Bristol	*The Bristol Press*
Hartford	*Hartford Advocate*
Hartford	*Hartford Business Journal*
Hartford	*The Commercial Record*
Hartford	*Hartford Courant*
New Haven	*Business Times*
Stamford	*El Sol News*
Stamford	*Fairfield County Weekly*
Stamford	*The Advocate*

Delaware

Dover	*Delaware State News*
Dover	*Dover Post*
Rehoboth	*Cape Gazette*
Rehoboth	*Delaware Coast Press*

District of Columbia (Washington, D.C.)

Washington	*Roll Call*
Washington	*The Common Denominator*
Washington	*The Examiner*
Washington	*The Hill*
Washington	*Town Hall*
Washington	*Voice of the Hill*
Washington	*Washington Business Journal*
Washington	*Washington City Paper*
Washington	*Washington Examiner*
Washington	*Washington Post*
Washington	*Washington Times*

Florida

Daytona Beach	*The News-Journal*
Fort Lauderdale	*City Link*
Fort Lauderdale	*Business Journal*
Fort Lauderdale	*Promenade Newspaper*
Fort Lauderdale	*Sun-Sentinel*
Jacksonville	*Florida Times-Union*
Jacksonville	*Jacksonville Daily Record*
Jacksonville	*Jacksonville Business Journal*
Miami	*The Community News of Miami*

Miami	*El Nuevo Herald*
Miami	*Miami Herald*
Miami	*Miami New Times*
Miami	*Miami Today*
Orlando	*Central Florida Advocate*
Orlando	*Orlando Business Journal*
Orlando	*Orlando Sentinel*
Orlando	*Orlando Times*
Orlando	*Orlando Weekly*
Panama City	*The News Herald*
St. Augustine	*The Saint Augustine Record*
St. Petersburg	*St. Petersburg Times*
Tallahassee	*Tallahassee Democrat*
Tampa	*Tampa Bay Business Journal*
Tampa	*Tampa Tribune*

Georgia

Athens	*Athens Banner-Herald*
Atlanta	*Atlanta Business Chronicle*
Atlanta	*Atlanta Daily World*
Atlanta	*Atlanta Journal-Constitution*
Atlanta	*Fulton County Daily Report*
Atlanta	*Georgia Latino News*
Augusta	*Augusta Chronicle*
Columbus	*Columbus Ledger-Enquirer*
Columbus	*Columbus Times*
La Grange	*La Grange Daily News*
Macon	*The Macon Courier*
Macon	*Macon Telegraph*
Macon	*The Georgia Informer*

Savannah	*Savannah Morning News*
Savannah	*The Business Report*
Statesboro	*The Statesboro Herald*
Woodstock	*Lakeside Ledger*

Hawaii

Honolulu	*Hawaii Reporter*
Honolulu	*Honolulu Star-Bulletin*
Honolulu	*Honolulu Weekly*
Honolulu	Pacific Business News
Oahu	*Kaleo o Ko'olauloa*
Wailuku	*The Maui News*

Idaho

Boise	*Boise Weekly*
Boise	*Idaho Business Review*
Boise	*Idaho Press-Tribune*
Boise	*The Idaho Statesman*
Montpelier	*News-Examiner*
Twin Falls	*The Times-News*

Illinois

Champaign	*The News-Gazette*
Chicago	*Chicago Defender*
Chicago	*Chicago Journal*
Chicago	*Chicago Sun Times*
Chicago	*Suburban Chicago News*
Chicago	*Chicago Tribune*
Chicago	*Chicago Reader*

Chicago	*Crain's Chicago Business*
Des Plaines	*Journal & Topics Newspapers*
Highland Park	*Highland Park News*
Joliet	*The Herald-News*
Naperville	*Naperville Sun*
Peoria	*Journal Star*
Springfield	*The State Journal-Register*

Indiana

Bloomington	*Bloomington Independent*
Bloomington	*Herald-Times*
Columbus	*The Republic*
Evansville	*Evansville Courier*
Fort Wayne	*Fort Wayne Journal Gazette*
Fort Wayne	*Fort Wayne Reader*
Fort Wayne	*Ink Newspaper*
Fort Wayne	*The News-Sentinel*
Franklin	*Daily Journal of Johnson County*
Gary	*Gary Post Tribune*
Indianapolis	*Indianapolis Business Journal*
Indianapolis	*The Indianapolis Recorder*
Indianapolis	*Indianapolis Star*
Indianapolis	*The Southside Times*
Muncie	*The Star Press*
South Bend	*South Bend Tribune*
Terre Haute	*Tribune-Star*

Iowa

Ames	*Ames Tribune*
Cedar Rapids	*Cedar Rapids Gazette*
Davenport	*Davenport Leader*
Davenport	*Quad City Times*
Davenport	*River Cities Reader*
Des Moines	*Des Moines Register*
Iowa City	*The Daily Iowan*
Iowa City	*Press-Citizen*
Waterloo	*Waterloo/Cedar Falls Courier*

Kansas

Dodge City	*Dodge City Daily Globe*
Dodge City	*High Plains Journal*
Junction City	*The Daily Union*
Kansas City	*Kansas City Kansan*
Kansas City	*Kansas City Star*
Kansas City	*The Record*
Topeka	*The Topeka Capitol Journal*
Wichita	*Wichita Business Journal*
Wichita	*Wichita Eagle*

Kentucky

Corbin	*Corbin News Journal*
Corbin	*Corbin Times Tribune*
Covington	*The Kentucky Post*
Elizabethtown	*The News-Enterprise*
Frankfort	*State Journal*

Lexington	*Lexington Herald-Leader*
Louisville	*Business First*
Louisville	*The Courier-Journal*

Louisana

Baton Rouge	*Business Report*
Baton Rouge	*The Advocate*
Jonesboro	*The Jackson Independent*
New Orleans	*City Business*
New Orleans	*Gambit Weekly*
New Orleans	*The Times-Picayune*
Shreveport	*The Times*

Maine

Augusta	*Kennebec Business Monthly*
Augusta	*Kennebec Journal*
Belfast	*The Republican Journal*
Damariscotta	*Lincoln County News*
Damariscotta	*Lincoln County Weekly*
Kennebunk	*York County Coast Star*
Portland	*Portland Press Herald*

Maryland

Annapolis	*The Capital*
Baltimore	*Baltimore Business Journal*
Baltimore	*Baltimore Chronicle*
Baltimore	*Baltimore City Paper*
Baltimore	*Baltimore Sun*
Baltimore	*Baltimore Times*
Baltimore	*The Catholic Review*
Baltimore	*The Daily Record*
Baltimore	*East Baltimore Guide*
Cumberland	*Cumberland Times-News*
Hagerstown	*The Herald-Mail*

Massachusetts

Boston	*Beacon Hill Times*
Boston	*Boston Business Journal*
Boston	*Boston Globe*
Boston	*Boston Herald*
Boston	*Boston Phoenix*
Boston	*Christian Science Monitor*
Boston	*Dorchester Reporter*
Boston	*South Boston Tribune*
Cambridge	*Cambridge Chronicle*
Gloucester	*The Gloucester Daily Times*
Hyannis	*Cape Cod Times*
Newburyport	*The Daily News*
Salem	*The Salem Evening News*
Somerville	*Somerville Journal*
Somerville	*The Somerville News*
Springfield	*Union-News & Republican*
Worcester	*Telegram & Gazette*
Worcester	*Worcester Business Journal*

Michigan

Ann Arbor	*Ann Arbor News*
Bay City	*Bay City Times*
Bellaire	*Antrim County News*
Cheboygan	*Cheboygan Daily Tribune*

Detroit	*Crain's Detroit Business*
Detroit	*Detroit Free Press*
Detroit	*Detroit News*
Detroit	*La Prensa*
Detroit	*Metro Times*
Detroit	*Michigan Chronicle*
Grand Haven	*Grand Haven Tribune*
Grand Rapids	*Grand Rapids Business Journal*
Grand Rapids	*Grand Rapids Press*
Grand Rapids	*Business Update*
Kalamazoo	*County Wide Newspaper*
Kalamazoo	*Kalamazoo Gazette*
Lansing	*Lansing State Journal*
Marquette	*The Mining Journal*
Monroe	*Monroe Evening News*
Pontiac	*The Oakland Press*
Traverse City	*Grand Traverse Herald*
Traverse City	*Northern Express*
Traverse City	*Traverse City Record-Eagle*

Minnesota

Duluth	*Duluth Budgeteer News*
Duluth	*Duluth News-Tribune*
Hastings	*Star Gazette*
Lake Benton	*Valley Journal*
Minneapolis	*City Pages*
Minneapolis	*Finance and Commerce*
Minneapolis	*St. Paul City Business*
Minneapolis	*Southwest Journal*
Minneapolis	*The Star Tribune*
Minneapolis	*Twin Cities Business*
St. Paul	*St. Paul Pioneer Press*

Mississippi

Biloxi	*The Sun Herald*
Jackson	*Jackson Advocate*
Jackson	*Jackson Free Press*
Jackson	*Mississippi Business Journal*
Natchez	*The Natchez Democrat*
Oxford	*The Oxford Eagle*
Tupelo	*Northeast Mississippi Daily Journal*

Missouri

Bowling Green	*Bowling Green Times*
Bowling Green	*The People's Tribune*
Branson	*The Branson News*
Branson	*Branson Courier*
Columbia	*Columbia Daily Tribune*
Columbia	*Columbia Missourian*
Jackson	*Cash-Book Journal*
Jefferson City	*Jefferson City News Tribune*
Joplin	*Joplin Business Journal*
Joplin	*Joplin Globe*
Joplin	*Joplin Independent*
Kansas City	*Dispatch Tribune*
Kansas City	*Business Journal*
Kansas City	*Kansas City Star*
Platte City	*Platte County Citizen*

Platte City	*The Landmark Newspaper*
Poplar Bluff	*Daily American Republic*
Springfield	*Community Free Press*
Springfield	*News-Leader*
Springfield	*Springfield Business Journal*
St. Louis	*Chinese American News*
St. Louis	*St. Louis American Newspaper*
St. Louis	*St. Louis Business Journal*
St. Louis	*St. Louis Post-Dispatch*
St. Louis	*The Riverfront Times*
St. Louis	*The Suburban Journals*

Montana

Billings	*Billings Gazette*
Billings	*The Billings Outpost*
Bozeman	*Bozeman Daily Chronicle*
Browning	*Glacier Reporter*
Butte	*The Montana Standard*
Helena	*Helena Independent*
Helena	*Queen City News*
Missoula	*Missoula Independent*
Missoula	*Missoulian*
Sidney	*Sidney Herald-Leader*
Stevensville	*The Bitterroot Star*
West Yellowstone	*West Yellowstone News*
Whitefish	*Whitefish Free Press*
Whitefish	*Whitefish Pilot*
Wolf Point	*The Herald-News*

Nebraska

Alliance	*Alliance Times-Herald*
Ashland	*The Ashland Gazette*
Beatrice	*The Daily Sun*
Columbus	*Columbus Telegram*
Cozad	*Tri-City Tribune*
Fremont	*Fremont Tribune*
Hastings	*Hastings Tribune*
Hyannis	*Grant County News*
Imperial	*The Imperial Republican*
Kimball	*Western Nebraska Observer*
Lincoln	*Lincoln Journal Star*
North Platte	*North Platte Bulletin*
North Platte	*North Platte Telegraph*
Omaha	*Omaha Reader*
Omaha	*Omaha-World Herald*

Nevada

Carson City	*Nevada Appeal*
Las Vegas	*Las Vegas Business Press*
Las Vegas	*Las Vegas City Life*
Las Vegas	*Las Vegas Review Journal*
Las Vegas	*Las Vegas Sun*
Las Vegas	*Las Vegas Tribune*
Las Vegas	*Las Vegas Weekly*
Laughlin	*Laughlin Entertainer*
Laughlin	*Laughlin Nevada Times*
Lovelock	*Lovelock Review-Miner*
Lovelock	*The Nevada Rancher*
Mesquite	*Desert Valley Times*
Reno	*News & Review*
Reno	*Reno Gazette-Journal*

New Hampshire

Berlin	*The Berlin Daily Sun*
Berlin	*The Berlin Reporter*
Chester	*Tri-Town Times*
Claremont	*Eagle Times*
Colebrook	*Colebrook Chronicle*
Colebrook	*The News and Sentinel*
Concord	*Concord Monitor*
Dover	*Fosters Daily Democrat*
Londonderry	*Londonderry Times*
Londonderry	*Nutfield News*
Manchester	*The Union Leader*
Milford	*Milford Cabinet & Wilton Journal*
Nashua	*The Telegraph*
North Conway	*Conway Daily Sun*
North Haverhill	*The Bridge Weekly*
North Sutton	*Intertown Record*
Portsmouth	*New Hampshire Gazette*
Portsmouth	*Portsmouth Herald*

New Jersey

Allentown	*Examiner*
Bridgewater	*The Courier-News*
Cranbury	*The Cranbury Press*
East Brunswick	*Home News & Tribune*
East Brunswick	*Sentinel-East Brunswick*
Flemington	*Hunterdon County Democrat*
Hightstown	*The Messenger-Press*
Hillsborough	*Hillsborough Beacon*
Hillsborough	*Hopewell Valley News*
Howell	*Tri-Town News*
Manasquan	*The Coast Star*
Millville	*Cumberland County Reminder*
Montclair	*The Montclair Times*
Neptune	*Asbury Park Press*
Newark	*The Star-Ledger*
Newark	*Visions Metro Weekly*
Newton	*The New Jersey Herald*
Trenton	*Register-News*
Trenton	*The Times*
Trenton	*The Trentonian*
Woodbury	*Gloucester County Times*

New Mexico

Albuquerque	*Albuquerque Journal*
Albuquerque	*Albuquerque Tribune*
Las Cruces	*Las Cruces Bulletin*
Las Cruces	*Las Cruces Sun-News*
Las Vegas	*Las Vegas Optic*
Los Alamos	*Los Alamos Monitor*
Raton	*The Chronicle News*
Santa Fe	*Santa Fe New Mexican*
Santa Fe	*Santa Fe Reporter*
Santa Fe	*Santa Fe Times*
Socorro	*El Defensor Chieftain*
Socorro	*My Mountain Mail*
Taos	*The Taos News*
Timberon	*Timberon Mountain Times*

New York

Albany	*Capital District Business Review*
Albany	*The Times-Union*
Albany	*The Informed Constituent*
Brooklyn	*New York Liberty Star*
Buffalo	*Buffalo Beast*
Buffalo	*The Buffalo News*
Buffalo	*Business First*
Buffalo	*Polish American Journal*
Cooperstown	*Cooperstown Crier*
East Hampton	*East Hampton Star*
Garden City	*Long Island Press*
Garden City	*Garden City News*
Geneva	*Finger Lakes Times*
Ithaca	*Ithaca Journal*
Ithaca	*Ithaca Times*
Mattituck	*The Suffolk Times*
Mattituck	*The News-Review*
New York	*Crain's New York Business*
New York	*Gotham Gazette*
New York	*New York Daily News*
New York	*New York Post*
New York	*New York Times*
New York	*New York Observer*
New York	*The New York Sun*
New York	*Village Voice*
New York	*The Wall Street Journal*
Newark	*Courier-Gazette*
Niagara Falls	*Niagara Gazette*
Niagara Falls	*Niagara Falls Reporter*
Norwich	*The Evening Sun*
Queens	*The Queens Gazette*
Rochester	*Business Journal*
Rochester	*Democrat & Chronicle*
Rome	*Rome Observer*
Rome	*Rome Sentinel*
Staten Island	*Staten Island Advance*
Syracuse	*Eagle Newspapers*
Syracuse	*Syracuse Newspapers*
Troy	*The Record*
Utica	*Observer-Dispatch*
Watertown	*Watertown Daily Times*
Wellsville	*Wellsville Daily Reporter*
White Plains	*The Journal News*

North Carolina

Asheville	*Asheville Citizen-Times*
Asheville	*Western Carolina Business Journal*
Charlotte	*Business Journal of Charlotte*
Charlotte	*Charlotte Observer*
Charlotte	*Charlotte Post*
Charlotte	*Charlotte Weekly*
Charlotte	*La Noticia*
Charlotte	*Mecklenburg Times*
Charlotte	*Que Pasa*
Durham	*The Herald-Sun*
Durham	*The Independent*
Greensboro	*Que Pasa*
Greensboro	*The Business Journal*

Greensboro	*The News and Record*
Raleigh	*News and Observer*
Raleigh	*Que Pasa*
Raleigh	*Triangle Business Journal*

North Dakota

Bismarck	*Bismarck Tribune*
Cooperstown	*Sentinel-Courier*
Crosby	*The Journal*
Fargo	*The Forum*
Finley	*Steele County Press*
Grand Forks	*Grand Forks Herald*
Harvey	*The Herald-Press*
Lisbon	*Ransom County Gazette*
Valley City	*Times-Record*
Washburn	*Leader News*
West Fargo	*West Fargo Pioneer*

Ohio

Akron	*Akron Beacon Journal*
Akron	*Akron Legal News*
Akron	*West Side Leader/Green Leader*
Athens	*The Athens Messenger*
Athens	*The Athens News*
Cambridge	*The Daily Jeffersonian*
Canton	*The Canton Repository*
Centerville	*Centerville-Bellbrook Times*
Chillicothe	*Chillicothe Gazette*
Cincinnati	*Cincinnati Business Courier*
Cincinnati	*Cincinnati Call and Post*
Cincinnati	*Cincinnati City Beat*
Cincinnati	*Cincinnati Post*
Cleveland	*Cleveland Free Times*
Cleveland	*Crain's Cleveland Business*
Cleveland	*The Daily Legal News*
Cleveland	*The Plain Dealer*
Cleveland	*Sun Newspapers*
Columbus	*Business First*
Columbus	*Columbus Call and Post*
Columbus	*Columbus Dispatch*
Columbus	*The Columbus Post*
Columbus	*This Week/CNS Newspapers*
Dayton	*Dayton Business Journal*
Dayton	*Dayton Daily News*
Granville	*The Granville Sentinel*
Lancaster	*Eagle Gazette*
Lima	*Lima News*
Mansfield	*News Journal*
Middletown	*Middletown Journal*
Newark	*The Advocate*
Port Clinton	*News Herald*
Port Clinton	*The Beacon*
Sandusky	*Huron County Morning Journal*
Sandusky	*Sandusky Register*
Springfield	*Springfield News-Sun*
Toledo	*Point & Shoreland Journal*
Toledo	*Toledo Blade*
Toledo	*Toledo City Paper*
Toledo	*Toledo Free Press*

Van Wert	*Times-Bulletin*
Van Wert	*Van Wert Independent*
Willoughby	*Lake County Business Journal*
Willoughby	*The News-Herald*
Youngstown	*Buckeye Review*
Youngstown	*Vindicator Online*
Youngstown	*The Business Journal*
Zanesville	*Times Recorder*

Oklahoma

Boise City	*The Boise City News*
Broken Arrow	*Broken Arrow Daily Ledger*
Broken Bow	*MuCurtain County News*
Cushing	*Cushing Daily Citizen*
Durant	*Durant Daily Democrat*
El Reno	*El Reno Tribune*
Kingfisher	*Kingfisher Times*
Lawton	*Lawton Constitution*
Miami	*Miami News-Record*
Muskogee	*Muskogee Daily Phoenix*
Oklahoma City	*The Journal Record*
Oklahoma City	*The Oklahoma Constitution*
Oklahoma City	*The Oklahoman*
Tulsa	*Greater Tulsa Reporter Newspapers*
Tulsa	*Tulsa World*
Tulsa	*Urban Tulsa*

Oregon

Bend	*Bend Weekly*
Bend	*Cascade Business News*
Eugene	*Eugene Weekly*
Eugene	*The Register-Guard*
Portland	*Business Journal of Portland*
Portland	*Jewish Review*
Portland	*Portland Observer*
Portland	*Portland Tribune*
Portland	*The Asian Reporter*
Portland	*The Oregon Herald*
Portland	*The Oregonian*
Portland	*Willamette Week*
Salem	*Capital Press Agriculture Weekly*
Salem	*Statesman Journal*

Pennsylvania

Allentown	*The Morning Call*
Clearfield	*Gant Daily*
Clearfield	*The Progress*
Du Bois	*The Courier Express*
Easton	*Express-Times*
Erie	*Times News*
Gettysburg	*Gettysburg Times*
Harrisburg	*The Patriot News*
Lehighton	*The Times News*
Lewistown	*The Sentinel*
Lock Haven	*The Express*
Milford	*Tri State News*

Milford	*Tri State Observer*
Oil City	*The Derrick*
Philadelphia	*City Paper*
Philadelphia	*Business Journal*
Philadelphia	*Philadelphia Daily News*
Philadelphia	*Philadelphia Weekly*
Pittsburgh	*New Pittsburgh Courier*
Pittsburgh	*Pittsburgh Business Times*
Pittsburgh	*Pittsburgh City Paper*
Pittsburgh	*Pittsburgh Post-Gazette*
Pittsburgh	*Pittsburgh Tribune-Review*
York	*The York Dispatch*
York	*York Daily Record*

Rhode Island

Pawtucket	*The Times*
Portsmouth	*Sakonnet Times*
Providence	*Providence Phoenix*
Providence	*Providence Business News*
Providence	*Providence Journal-Bulletin*
Wakefield	*South County Independent*
Wakefield	*The Narragansett Times*

South Carolina

Beaufort	*Carolina Morning News*
Beaufort	*The Beaufort Gazette*
Charleston	*Regional Business Journal*
Charleston	*Charleston City Paper*
Charleston	*The Post and Courier*
Charleston	*Vida Latina*
Columbia	*Free Times*
Columbia	*The State*
Greenville	*GSA Business Journal*
Greenville	*The Greenville News*
Hilton Head	*The Island Packet*
Hilton Head	*Hilton Head Today*

South Dakota

Aberdeen	*Aberdeen American News*
Pierre	*Pierre Capital Journal*
Rapid City	*Rapid City Journal*
Sioux Falls	*Argus Leader*
Spearfish	*Black Hills Pioneer*
Spearfish	*Lawrence County Journal*
Sturgis	*Meade County Times-Tribune*
Vermillion	*Plain Talk*
Watertown	*Watertown Public Opinion*
Yankton	*The Press & Dakotan*

Tennessee

Chattanooga	*Chattanooga Times*
Chattanooga	*The Chattanoogan*
Jackson	*Jackson Today*
Jackson	*The Jackson Sun*
Jefferson City	*The Standard Banner*
Johnson City	*Johnson City Press*
Jonesborough	*Herald & Tribune*
Kingsport	*Kingsport Daily News*
Kingsport	*Kingsport Times-News*

Knoxville	*Hall News*	Dallas	*El Heraldo News*
Knoxville	*Knoxville News-Sentinel*	Dallas	*El Hispano News*
Knoxville	*Mundo Hispano*	Dallas	*Park Cities News*
Lebanon	*The Lebanon Democrat*	Dallas	*People Newspapers*
Lebanon	*Wilson Post*	Dallas	*The Dallas Morning News*
Lewisburg	*Marshall County Tribune*	Fort Worth	*Fort Worth Business Press*
Manchester	*Manchester Times*	Fort Worth	*Fort Worth Star-Telegram*
Manchester	*The Saturday Independent*	Fort Worth	*Fort Worth Weekly*
Memphis	*Memphis Business Journal*	Houston	*Forward Times*
Memphis	*Memphis Daily News*	Houston	*Free Press Houston*
Memphis	*Memphis Flyer*	Houston	*Houston Business Journal*
Murfreesboro	*Daily News Journal*	Houston	*Houston Chronicle*
Nashville	*La Campana*	Houston	*Houston Community Newspapers*
Nashville	*Nashville Business Journal*		
Nashville	*The Messenger*	Houston	*Rumbo de Houston*
Nashville	*The Tennessean*	San Antonio	*Business Journal*
Nashville	*The City Paper*	San Antonio	*El Continental*
Nashville	*The Tennessee Tribune*	San Antonio	*Express News*
Oak Ridge	*The Oak Ridge Observer*	San Antonio	*La Prensa Newspaper*
Oak Ridge	*The Ridger*	San Antonio	*Rumbo de San Antonio*
		San Antonio	*San Antonio Current*

Texas

Austin	*Austin American Statesman*
Austin	*Austin Business Journal*
Austin	*Austin Chronicle*
Corpus Christi	*Corpus Christi Caller-Times*
Corpus Christi	*Corpus Christi Daily*
Dallas	*Dallas Business Journal*
Dallas	*Dallas Observer*

Utah

Brigham City	*Box Elder News Journal*
Cedar City	*Cedar City Review*
Castle Dale	*Emery County Progress*
Kanab	*Southern Utah News*
Logan	*Herald Journal*
Ogden	*Standard-Examiner*
Park City	*Park Record*
Salt Lake City	*Desert News*

Salt Lake City   *Salt Lake City Weekly*
Salt Lake City   *Salt Lake Metro*
Salt Lake City   *Salt Lake Tribune*
Salt Lake City   *Valley Journals*

Vermont

Barre   *The Times-Argus*
Barre   *The World*
Barton   *The Chronicle*
Bradford   *Journal Opinion*
Manchester   *Manchester Journal*
Middlebury   *Addison County Independent*
Waitsfield   *The Valley Reporter*
Waitsfield   *Vermont Journal*
West Dover   *Deerfield Valley News*

Virginia

Alexandria   *Alexandria Gazette Packet*
Alexandria   *Del Ray Sun*
Alexandria   *The Alexandria Times*
Alexandria   *Journal Newspapers*
Arlington   *Henderson Hall News*
Arlington   *The Arlington Connection*
Charlottesville *The Daily Progress*
Lexington   *News-Gazette*
Lexington   *Rockbridge Weekly*
Loudoun   *Loudoun Times Mirror*
Loudoun   *The Loudoun Connection*
Lynchburg   *The News & Advance*
Norfolk   *Inside Business*

Reston   *The Reston Connection*
Reston   *Times Community Newspapers*
Richmond   *Richmond Times-Dispatch*
Roanoke   *Blue Ridge Business Journal*
Roanoke   *Roanoke Time & World News*
Williamsburg *The Virginia Gazette*

Washington

Bainbridge Island   *Bainbridge Island Review*
Bainbridge Island   *The Bainbridge Islander*
Bellevue   *Eastside Business Monthly*
Edmonds   *Edmonds Beacon*
Edmonds   *Edmonds Enterprise*
Federal Way   *Federal Way Mirror*
Federal Way   *Federal Way News*
Friday Harbor   *Journal San Juan Islands*
Friday Harbor   *San Juan Islander*
Olympia   *The Olympian*
Seattle   *Beacon Hill News*
Seattle   *Capitol Hill Times*
Seattle   *Daily Journal of Commerce*
Seattle   *Kirkland Courier*
Seattle   *Madison Park Times*
Seattle   *Magnolia News*
Seattle   *North Seattle Herald-Outlook*
Seattle   *Northwest Asian Weekly*

Seattle	*Puget Sound Business Journal*
Seattle	*Queen Anne News*
Seattle	*Seattle Post Intelligencer*
Seattle	*Seattle Daily Journal of Commerce*
Seattle	*Seattle Times*
Seattle	*Seattle Weekly*
Seattle	*South District Journal*
Seattle	*West Seattle Herald*
Spokane	*Spokane Journal of Business*
Spokane	*The Spokesman-Review*
Tacoma	*Tacoma Daily Index*
Tacoma	*The Business Examiner*
Tacoma	*The News Tribune*
Tacoma	*Tacoma Weekly*
Vancouver	*The Columbian*

West Virginia

Beckley	*The Register-Herald*
Charleston	*Charleston Daily Mail*
Charleston	*Charleston Gazette*
Charleston	*The State Journal*
Huntington	*The Herald-Dispatch*
Lewisburg	*Mountain Messenger*
Madison	*Coal Valley News*
Martinsburg	*The Journal*
Parkersburg	*Parkersburg News and Sentinel*
Spencer	*The Times Record*
Williamson	*Williamson Daily News*

Wisconsin

Appleton	*The Post-Crescent*
Ashland	*The Daily Press*
Beaver Dam	*Daily Citizen*
Black River Falls	*The Chronicle*
Eau Claire	*Leader Telegram*
Green Bay	*Green Bay Press Gazette*
Madison	*Capital Times*
Madison	*Wisconsin State Journal*
Milwaukee	*Business Journal of Milwaukee*
Milwaukee	*Milwaukee Journal Sentinel*
Milwaukee	*Shepherd Express-Metro*
New Richmond	*Richmond News*
Oshkosh	*The Northwestern*
Plymouth	*The Review*
Portage	*Daily Register*
Sheboygan	*The Sheboygan Press*
Stevens Point	*Stevens Point Journal*
Stevens Point	*Portage County Gazette*
Sturgeon Bay	*Door County Advocate*
Superior	*The Daily Telegram*
Wisconsin Rapids	*The Daily Tribune*

Wyoming

Casper	*Casper Star Tribune*
Casper	*Casper Journal*
Cheyenne	*Wyoming Tribune Eagle*

Jackson	*Jackson Hole News & Guide*	Worland	*Northern Wyoming Daily News*
Jackson	*Planet Jackson Hole*		
Laramie	*Laramie Boomerang*	Yellowstone	*Yellowstone Net Newspaper*

U.S. Commercial Radio Networks

Accent Radio Network

Agri Broadcasting Network

Air America Radio

All Comedy Radio

American Urban Radio Networks

Associated Press Radio Network

Beethoven Satellite Network

Bloomberg Business News Radio Network

Business Talk Radio

Cable Radio Network

Cadena Caracol Network

Chinese Radio Network

WGBB AM1240

WCBS FM101.1

ABC Radio Networks

ABC News Radio

ESPN Radio

Radio Disney

Excelsior Radio

First Amendment Radio

Fox Sports Radio

Fox News Radio

Genesis Communications Network

Jones Radio Network

MRN Radio

National Radio Network

NBC

New Northwest Broadcasters

Performance Racing Network

Premiere Radio Networks

Radio America

Radio Formula

RBN (Republic Broadcasting Network)

Salem Radio Network

Sports Byline USA

Sporting News Radio

Talknet

Talk America Radio Network

Talk Radio Network

Talk Radio Network-FM

The 1920s Radio Network

USA Radio Network

Westwood One Radio Networks

CNN Max Radio Network

Source Max Radio Network

Source Max Radio Network

CBS Radio Network

NBC Radio Network

Next Radio Network

WONE Radio Network

BLAISE

Navigator

Wisdom Radio Network

Waitt Radio Networks

State Commercial Networks

Alabama Radio Network

Florida's Radio Networks

Ohio News Network

Tennessee Radio Networks

Noncommercial Networks

National Public Radio

Northeast Public Radio

Public Radio International

Pacifica Radio

American Armed Forces Radio Network

American Public Media

World Radio Network

Public Radio Exchange

W0KIE

Public Radio State Networks

Georgia Public Radio

Independent Public Radio (Minnesota)

Jefferson Public Radio (Oregon, California)

Minnesota Public Radio

Maine Public Broadcasting Network

New Hampshire Public Radio

North Dakota Public Radio

Ohio Public Radio

Oregon Public Broadcasting

Vermont Public Radio

Wisconsin Public Radio

South Dakota Public Radio

Alaska Public Radio Network

Religious Networks

American Family Radio

Bible Broadcasting Network

Bott Radio Network

Calvary Satellite Network

CDR Radio Network

EMF Broadcasting

Air 1

K-LOVE

EWTN Radio

Family Life Communications

Family Life Network

Family Radio

Fundamental Broadcasting Network

Immanuel Broadcasting Network

Mars Hill Broadcasting

Moody Broadcasting Network

Pillar of Fire, International

Radio Maria USA

WHJM

RadioU

Relevant Radio

Sound of Life Network

Three Angels Broadcasting Network

Toccoa Falls College Radio Network

USA Radio Network

VCY America Radio Network

List of U.S. Magazines

Agriculture

Bovine Veterinarian

Citrus & Vegetable

Dairy Herd Management

Dealer & Applicator

Drovers

The Grower

Hoard's Dairyman

The Packer

Porker

Swine Practitioner

Soybean Digest

Architecture

Architects' Journal

Architectural Digest

Architectural Record

Architectural Review

ArchNewsNow

Dwell

Metropolis

Arts and Entertainment

ACED Magazine

Architectural Digest

Array

Artforum

Castle of Frankenstein

Cinefantastique

Comics Buyer's Guide

Comics Journal

Distrikt

Dwell

Entertainment Weekly

Famous

Famous Monsters of Filmland

Film Threat

Flux

theGNOSTIC

Modern Screen

Movielink's Hollywood Life

Moving Pictures

Premiere

Soap Opera Digest

Soaps In Depth

Terry Plumming

TV Guide

UnRated

Variety

Video Watchdog

Visionaire

Wizard

Written By

Automotive

Auto World

Automobile

AutoWeek

Car and Driver

European Car

Excellence

Fastest Street Car

Grassroots Motorsports

Hemmings Motor News

Import Racer

Motor Trend

OverRev

Panorama

Race Pages

Road & Track

Skinned Knuckles

SportsCar

Sports Car International

Sport Compact Car

Super Street

Building Trade

American Bungalow

Aviation Week & Space Technology

BUILDER

Building

Professional Lighting Design

volume⁵

Business and Finance

Barron's

Black Enterprise

Business 2.0

BusinessWeek

Consumer Reports

Consumers Digest

Entrepreneur

Fast Company

Forbes

Fortune

Futures

Harvard Business Review

Hispanic Business

Inc.

Kiplinger's Personal Finance

Money

Optimize

Red Herring

Site Selection

SmartMoney

Children's

Academy Earth

American Girl

Babybug

Boys' Life

Cricket

Disney Adventures

Discovery Girls

Famous Kids

Highlights for Children

Hopscotch

Humpty Dumpty

Jack and Jill

Ladybug

Lego Magazine

Mad for Kids

Nickelodeon

The Open Road for Boys

Ranger Rick

Sports Illustrated for Kids

Stone Soup

Folklore

Traditions

Viltis

Food and Cooking

Bon Appétit

Chow

Cook's Country

Cook's Illustrated

Cooking Light

Eating Well

Fine Cooking

Food & Wine

Gastronomica

Gourmet

Saveur

Taste of Home
Vegetarian Times
Veggie Life

Gay

The Advocate
Curve
Genre
GO NYC
Girlfriends
Instinct
Metrosource
Out
Out Traveler
XY

General Interest

The Atlantic Monthly
The Believer
Collier's Weekly
Full Effect
GOOD
Grapevine
Harper's Magazine
Interview
Life
McClure's
McSweeney's
National Geographic

The New York Review of Books
The New Yorker
People
Reader's Digest
Smithsonian
Today's Christian
Us Weekly
Vanity Fair
Work

Health: Men's

Men's Health
Esquire

Health: Women's

Allure
Cosmopolitan
ELLE
Glamour
Health
Ladies' Home Journal
McCall's
More
O, The Oprah Magazine
Redbook
SELF
Shape
Vogue

Health: General

Grapevine

ONE Magazine

Prevention

History

America's Civil War

American Heritage

American Heritage of Invention and Technology

American History

Armchair General

Civil War Times Illustrated

Grapevine

Leben

Military Heritage

Military History

Naval History

True West

World War II

Hobby

Airliners

Autograph Collector Magazine

Birds & Blooms

Card Player

Cigar Aficionado

Lapidary Journal

Live Steam

Numismatist

Strictly Slots

Board Game

Ares

Fire & Movement

GAMES

Games Quarterly

The General

Moves

Strategy & Tactics

Knucklebones

Stamp Collecting

The American Philatelist

Philatelic Literature Review

Scott's Stamp Monthly

Tabletop Role-Playing

Dragon

Dungeon

The Excellent Prismatic Spray

Pyramid

The Unspeakable Oath

Valkyrie

Warpstone

Humor

Cracked

The Door Magazine

Fusion Magazine

MAD Magazine

National Lampoon

Spy Magazine

Radar Magazine

Lifestyle

Cairn Magazine

Cigar Aficionado

Domino

Ebony

Jet

Lucky

Martha Stewart Living

Paper

Real Simple

Robb Report

Sunset

Literary

2River

3:AM Magazine

Adam Sanat

Alligator Juniper

The American Mercury

The American Review

American Tanka

Angel Exhaust

Antaeus

Anything That Moves

Apple Valley Review

Archipelago

Asimov's

Athenaeum

The Atlantic Monthly

The Beau

The Believer

Bibelot

BLAST

The Bookman

Brick

The Callaloo Journal

Cerebration

Chapman magazine

Clarion

Cricket

Criterion

DDT

The Dial

The Drouth

The Dublin Magazine

Eclectica Magazine

Edinburgh Review

The Egoist

The Emerson Review

Encounter

The English Intelligencer

Esprit

Exquisite Corpse

The Magazine of Fantasy & Science Fiction

Geist

Glimmer Train

Granta

The GW Review

Halifax Review

Harper's

The Harvard Advocate

Juked

Kenyon Review

The Lace Curtain

Literary Review

The Little Review

Locus Magazine

Loggernaut

McSweeney's

Mad Hatters' Review

Mid-American Review

The Minnesota Review

Mosaic

N+1

Nemonymous

The New Criterion

News from the Republic of Letters

The New York Review of Books

The New Yorker

Nineteenth Century

NOO Journal

Others: A Magazine of the New Verse

Otium

Partisan Review

Planet

Ploughshares

Poetry

Poor Mojo's Almanac

Prairie Schooner

Puck

The Quiet Feather

Ramparts Magazine

The Reader

Room of One's Own

Scripsi

The Smart Set

SmokeLong Quarterly

Southern Review

Spike Magazine

Spires Intercollegiate Arts and Literary Magazine

storySouth

Tel Quel

Times Literary Supplement

Tin House

Transition

Vedem

Virginia Quarterly Review

World Literature Today

Yellow Book

Zoetrope All-Story

ZYX

Zyzzyva

Men

Cigar Aficionado

Complex Magazine

Debonair Magazine

Details

Esquire

Gear

GQ

Giant

Men's Fitness

Men's Health

Men's Journal

Men's Vogue

Outdoor Life

PHOTO

RICH GUY Magazine

Smooth

Sly

Strut

Toro

True

UMM

Flux Magazine

Goldmine

Honest Tune Magazine

Keyboard

Guitar Player

Living Blues

Maximumrocknroll

Modern Guitars Magazine

Paste

Punk Planet

Rolling Stone

Sing Out!

Spin

The Source

Trouser Press

UnRated Music Magazine

WESU Magazine

Who Put the Bomp

XXL

Music

AP—Alternative Press

Billboard

Blender

Blues Review

CCM Magazine

Dirty Linen

Down Beat

The Fader

Filter Magazine

News

The Economist

Newsweek

Time Magazine

U.S. News & World Report

The Week

World

Parenting

American Baby

Christian Parenting Today

Parents

Parenting

Political

The American Conservative

The American Prospect

The American Spectator

The Atlantic Monthly

First Things

In These Times

Jewish Currents

Liberty

Lilith

Moment

Mother Jones

The Nation

National Review

The New Republic

Policy Review

The Progressive

The Progressive Populist

Reason

Tikkun

The Utne Reader

Washington Monthly

The Weekly Standard

Z Magazine

Pornographic

Celebrity Sleuth

Chic

Club

Gallery

Hustler

Perfect 10

Playboy

Playgirl

Penthouse

Regional

Cairn Magazine

GEMC GEORGIA Magazine

Grapevine

Religious

A Word Fitly Spoken Magazine

Awake!

Books & Culture

Campus Life

Christian Affairs Magazine

Christian Century

Christian History & Biography

Christian Music Monthly

Christian Parenting Today

Christian Science Sentinel

Christianity Today

Ensign

The Friend
Gaia
Heeb Magazine
Humanist Magazine
Improvement Era
Leadership Journal
Leben, a journal of Reformed life
Midnight Call
The New Era
Rays from the Rose Cross
SageWoman
Sojourners
Today's Christian
Tikkun
Tricycle
The Watchtower

Science

Astronomy
Discover
Infinite Energy Magazine
National Geographic
New Scientist
Popular Science
Science News
Scientific American
Seed Magazine
Skeptical Inquirer
Sky & Telescope
Wired

Science Fiction

Amazing Stories
Analog Science Fiction and Fact
Apex Digest
Asimov's Science Fiction
Astounding Magazine
Fantastic Universe Science Fiction
Fantasy and Science Fiction
Galaxy Science Fiction
Heavy Metal
If
Imagination
Invasion
Oceans of the Mind
Seed
Space Science Fiction

Spanish

Cristina la Revista
Latina
Mira
El Nuevo Cojo Ilustrado
Selecciones
Vida Latina

Sports

Dime Magazine
ESPN The Magazine
Field & Stream

Frequency The Snowboarder's Journal
KO Magazine
Pro Wrestling Illustrated
Ring Magazine
SLAM Magazine
Sporting News
Sports Illustrated
Snowboard Magazine
Taekwondo Times Magazine

Technology

2600: The Hacker Quarterly
Byte
Circuit Cellar
Computer Power User
Dr. Dobb's Journal
Linux Journal
Linux Magazine
Linux World
MacAddict
macCompanion
MacWorld
Maximum PC
Modern Electrics
Nuts and Volts
PC Magazine
PC World
Servo
Wired

Teen

Campus Life
Elle Girl
Full Effect
J-14 Magazine
Girls' Life magazine
M Magazine
Right On
Seventeen
Teen Magazine
Teen People
Tiger Beat
YM

Teen Girls

ACED Magazine
BRAVO
CosmoGIRL!
Dirt
Dolly
ELLEgirl
Faze
Girl's Life
It's HOT!
Sassy Magazine
Seventeen
Shameless
Sugar
TeenBeat
TeenVOGUE

Teen Magazine
Teen People
Teen Scene
Tiger Beat
Twist Magazine
Unish Kuri

Video Game

Electronic Gaming Monthly
GamePro
Game Informer
Game Players
Games for Windows
GMR
Next Generation
Nintendo Power
Official Xbox Magazine
Official U.S. PlayStation Magazine
PC Gamer
PSM
Tips & Tricks
Video Game Review

Women

Bibi
Bis
Bitch
BUST
Cahoots
Cooler Magazine

Cosmopolitan
Curve
ELLE
Essence
Family Circle
Flare
Girlfriends Magazine
Glamour
Good Housekeeping
Gynaika
Harper's Bazaar
Helm Magazine
Hilary Magazine
House Beautiful
In Style
In Touch Weekly
Jane
JJ
Ladies' Home Journal
Life and Style
Lucire
Lucky
Marie Claire
Martha Stewart Living
Moondance Magazine
More Books For Women
Ms.
Natali
O, The Oprah Magazine
Parenting Magazine
Playgirl

She Unlimited Magazine

Texas Family Magazine

Today's Christian Woman

VIVmag

Vogue

W

Woman

Woman's Own

Woman's Day

Women's Health

Woodworking for Women

XM West Magazine

Writers

Byline

The Writer

The WRITERS' Journal

Writer's Digest

Written By

Miscellaneous

The Colophon

Fire Drill

Giant Robot

Iris

Mental Floss

Newtype USA

Plenty

Tieng Magazine

Work

ZoraMagazine

Top U.S. Journalism Schools

American University
School of Communications
4400 Massachusetts Ave., N.W.
Washington, D.C. 20016
202-885-2060
www.soc.american.edu/
section.cfm?id=6

Auburn University
College of Communication and
Journalism
Department of Communication
and Journalism
217 Tichenor Hall
Auburn University, AL 36849
334-844-2727
media.cla.auburn.edu/cmjn

Ball State University
Department of Journalism
Art and Journalism Building
2000 W. University Avenue
Muncie, IN 47306
765-285-8200
www.bsu.edu/journalism/

Belmont University
The New Century Journalism
Program
1900 Belmont Blvd.
Nashville, TN 37212-3757
615-460-6000
www.belmont.edu/mediastudies/
new_century_journalism/index.
html

Bowling Green State University
Department of Journalism
Bowling Green, OH 43403-0001
419-372-8349
www.bgsu.edu/departments/
journalism

Bradley University
Slane College of
Communications and Fine Arts
1501 W. Bradley Avenue
Peoria, IL 61625
309-677-3707
slane.bradley.edu

California State University, Chico
Department of Journalism
Chico, CA 95929-0600
530-898-4779
www.csuchico.edu/jour

Columbia University
Graduate School of Journalism
2950 Broadway, Room 706
New York, NY 10027
212-854-8130
www.jrn.columbia.edu

Duquesne University
McAnulty College and Graduate
School of Liberal Arts
600 Forbes Avenue
Pittsburgh, PA 15282
412-396-5772
www.liberalarts.duq.edu/jma/
journalism/index.html

Eastern Illinois University
Journalism Department
600 Lincoln Avenue
Charleston, IL 61920-3099
217-581-6003
www.eiu.edu/~journal

Emory University
Department of Journalism
201 Dowman Dr.
Atlanta, GA 30322
404-727-6123
www.emory.edu

Florida A&M University
School of Journalism and Graphic
Communication
Tallahassee, FL 32307
850-599-3379
www.famu.edu

Florida International University
School of Journalism and Mass
Communications
3000 N.E. 151st St.
ACII 335/230
Biscayne Bay Campus
North Miami, FL 33181
305-919-5940
jmc.fiu.edu

Harvard University
Office of the Registrar
Faculty of Arts and Sciences
Harvard University
20 Garden Street
Cambridge, MA 02138
617-495-1000
www.harvard.edu

Howard University
The John H. Johnson School of
Communications
525 Bryant Street, N.W.
Washington, D.C. 20059
202-806-7690
www.howard.edu/
schoolcommunications

Indiana University
School of Journalism
Ernie Pyle Hall
940 E. 7th Street
Bloomington, IN 47405-7108
812-855-9247
journalism.indiana.edu

Iowa State University
Greenlee School of Journalism and
Communication
Hamilton Hall
Iowa State University
Ames, IA 50011-0001
515-294-0303
www.jlmc.iastate.edu

Ithaca College
Roy H. Park School of
Communications
Department of Journalism
311 Park Hall
Ithaca, NY 14850
607-274-1021
www.ithaca.edu/rhp/depts/journalism/

Kent State University
School of Journalism and Mass
Communications
130 Taylor Hall
Kent, OH 44242
330-672-2572
jmc.kent.edu

Louisiana State University
The Manship School of Mass
Communications
Baton Rouge, LA 70803
225-578-2336
appl003.lsu.edu/masscomm/mcweb.
nsf/index

Michigan State University
School of Journalism
305 Comm Arts Building
East Lansing, MI 48824-1212
517-353-6430
www.jrn.msu.edu

New York University
Department of Journalism
Arthur Carter Hall
10 Washington Place
New York, NY 10003
212-998-7980
journalism.nyu.edu/index.html

Northwestern University
Medill School of Journalism
1845 Sheridan Road
Evanston, IL 60208-1260
847-467-1882
www.medill.northwestern.edu/medill/
index.html

Ohio University
E. W. Scripps School of Journalism
Park Place and Court Street
Athens, OH 45701-2979
740-593-2590
www.scrippsjschool.org

Pennsylvania State University
College of Communications
302 James Building
University Park, PA 16801-3897
814-863-1484
www.comm.psu.edu

San Francisco State University
Department of Journalism
1600 Holloway Avenue
San Francisco, CA 94132
415-338-2663
www.journalism.sfsu.edu

San José State University
School of Journalism and Mass
Communications
One Washington Square
San José, CA 95192-0055
408-924-3240
www.jmc.sjsu.edu

Southampton College
Southampton Graduate Campus of
Long Island University
239 Montauk Highway
Southampton, NY 11968-4196
631-287-8010
www.southampton.liu.edu

Syracuse University
Newhouse School of Public
Communication
215 University Place
Syracuse, NY 13244
315-443-2301
newhouse.syr.edu

University of California at Berkeley
Berkeley Graduate School of
Journalism
121 North Gate Hall, No. 5860
Berkeley, CA 94720-5860
510-642-3383
journalism.berkeley.edu

University of Colorado at Boulder
School of Journalism and Mass
Communication
Armory Building
1511 University Avenue
478 UCB
Boulder, CO 80309-0478
303-492-5007
www.colorado.edu/journalism

University of Dayton
Department of Communication
300 College Park
Dayton, OH 45469
937-229-2028
artssciences.udayton.edu/
communication

University of Florida
College of Journalism and
Communications
Gainesville, FL 32611
352-392-0500
www.jou.ufl.edu

University of Georgia
Grady College of Journalism
120 Hooper Street
Athens, GA 30602-3018
706-542-1704
www.grady.uga.edu

University of Kansas
William Allen White School of
Journalism and Mass Communications
Stauffer-Flint Hall
1435 Jayhawk Blvd.
Lawrence, KS 66045-7575
785-864-4755
www.journalism.ku.edu

University of Miami
School of Communication
Frances L. Wolfson Communication
Building
5100 Brunson Dr.
Coral Gables, FL 33146
305-284-2265
com.miami.edu

University of Minnesota
School of Journalism and Mass
Communication
110 Murphy Hall
206 Church Street, S.E.
Minneapolis, MN 55455
612-625-4054
www.catalogs.umn.edu/grad/programs/
g111.html

University of Missouri
Columbia School of Journalism
Administrative Offices
120 Neff Hall
Columbia, MO 65211-1200
573-882-4821
www.journalism.missouri.edu

University of Montana
School of Journalism
Missoula, MT 59812
406-243-4001
www.umt.edu/journalism

University of Nevada, Reno
The Donald W. Reynolds School of
Journalism and Center for Advanced
Media Studies
Mail Stop 310
Reno, NV 89557-0040
775-784-6531
www.unr.edu/journalism/apUndMain.
htm

University of Southern California
School of Journalism
Annenberg School of Communications
3502 Watt Way, Suite 325
Los Angeles, CA 90089-0281
213-740-6180
www.annenberg.usc.edu

University of Wisconsin—Eau Claire
Department of Communication and
Journalism
Hibbard 152
Eau Claire, WI 54702-4004
715-836-2528
www.uwec.edu/cj

University of Wisconsin—Madison
School of Journalism and Mass
Communication
5115 Vilas Hall
821 University Avenue
Madison, WI 53706-1497
608-262-3690
www.journalism.wisc.edu

University of Wisconsin—Milwaukee
Department of Journalism and Mass
Communication
117 Johnston Hall
P.O. Box 413
Milwaukee, WI 53201
414-229-4436
www.uwm.edu/Dept/JMC

University of Wisconsin—Oshkosh
Department of Journalism
800 Algoma Blvd.
Oshkosh, WI 54901
920-424-1042
www.uwosh.edu/journalism

University of Wisconsin—River Falls
Department of Journalism
310 North Hall
410 S. 3rd Street
River Falls, WI 54022
715-425-3911
www.uwrf.edu/journalism

Arizona State University
Walter Cronkite School of Journalism
and Mass Communication
Stauffer Hall A 231
P.O. Box 871305
Tempe, AZ 85287-1305
480-965-5011
cronkite.asu.edu

Washington and Lee University
Department of Journalism and Mass
Communications
Lexington, VA 24450-0303
540-458-8432
journalism.wlu.edu

Appendix D

Further Reading

The following list contains not only the sources used in this book but also excellent sites and publications that you can use to learn more about journalism.

Books

Blundell, William E. *The Art and Craft of Feature Writing*. New York: Plume, 1998.

Feature writing is a staple for all media. This book shows you how to do it well.

Brady, John. *The Interviewer's Handbook: A Guerilla Guide: Techniques & Tactics for Reporters and Writers*. Waukesha, WI: Kalmback Publishing Co. 2004.

Brady tells how to be a powerful interviewer.

Callahan, Christopher. *A Journalist's Guide to the Internet: The Net As a Reporting Tool*. Boston: Allyn & Bacon, 2002.

Callahan outlines how journalists can use the Internet to their advantage in reporting.

Campbell, Cole C., and Roy Peter Clark, eds. *The Values and Craft of American Journalism: Essays from the Poynter Institute*. Gainesville, FL: University Press of Florida, 2002.

The authors provide a collection of strong essays from one of the nation's foremost news teaching foundations.

Carr, Monica McCabe. *You Can Write a Column*. Cincinnati, OH: Writer's Digest Books, 2000.

One of the few good books on column writing.

Craig, Steve. *Sports Writing: A Beginner's Guide*. Shoreham, VT: Discover Writing Company, 2002.

The nuts and bolts of writing sports stories.

Durso, Joe Jr. and Mervin Block. *Writing News for TV and Radio: The Interactive CD and Handbook*. Los Angeles: Bonus Books, 1999.

The radio aspect of this book offers much insight.

Fiske, Robert Hartwell. *Dictionary of Concise Writing: 10,000 Alternatives to Wordy Phrases*. Oak Park, IL: Marion Street Press, 2002.

A good guide for getting rid of jargon and learning how to write more tightly.

Harrison, Charles Hampton. *How to Write for Magazines: Consumers, Trade and Web*. Boston: Allyn & Bacon, 2001.

Wide-reaching book on magazine writing.

Papper, Robert A. *Broadcast News Writing Stylebook (2nd Edition)*. Boston: Allyn & Bacon, 2002.

A staple in the broadcast news world.

Sova, Dawn. *Writing Clearly: A Self-Teaching Guide*. Hoboken, NJ: John Wiley & Sons, 2004.

The journalist's goal is to write clearly. This book can help.

Stovall, Glen James. *Writing for the Mass Media (5th Edition)*. Boston: Allyn & Bacon, 2001.

An all-purpose guide for getting the job done well.

Whittaker, Jason. *Web Production for Writers and Journalists*. New York: Routledge, 2002.

The skills in this book will help round you out as a journalist.

White, Ted. *Broadcast News Writing, Reporting, and Producing*. Burlington, MA: Butterworth-Heinemann, 2001.

An all-purpose book about multitasking in the broadcasting arena.

Websites

About.com
freelancewrite.about.com
A great site to begin your research on freelance writing.

Absolute Write
www.absolutewrite.com
A good beginner's guide to writing and freelancing for magazines.

All Business
www.allbusiness.com/periodicals/category/40011.html
A periodical title-searching website that's priceless for researching businesses.

Editor and Publisher
www.editorandpublisher.com
This magazine and its website are a critical resource for any journalist in any medium.

The Fifth Estate
www.fifthestate.org
"An anti-authoritarian magazine of ideas and action," this site is representative of many alternative publications and websites.

Good Practices
goodpractices.com
Good information on website development.

How Stuff Works
people.howstuffworks.com/magazine-writing4.htm
A neat little site on how stuff works—especially magazines.

Indiana University School of Journalism Ethics Cases Online
www.journalism.indiana.edu/gallery/Ethics/
Some good ethics arguments online.

Journalism Jobs
journalism_jobs.tripod.com
One of the leading job posting websites as well as a good resource for industry trends and data.

Just Who Invented the Radio?
www.qsl.net/n7jy/radiohst.html
Author B. Eric Rhodes gives you more history about radio than you can possibly handle. He is an authority.

Knight Foundation
www.knightfdn.org
You won't find much more complete and timely news and data on journalism than with this organization.

Magazine Publishers of America
www.magazine.org/home
This organization is the authority on magazine publishing.

Media Bistro
www.mediabistro.com
A hotbed of media news and jobs across the industry.

Media Life
www.medialifemagazine.com
Good website to check up on the broadcast journalism industry.

Newpages.com
www.newpages.com/npguides/altmags.htm
This website has links to many alternative magazines.

Newscript
www.newscript.com
A good tutorial on writing radio news copy.

Newslink
newslink.org/rtv.html
Solid links to journalism sites.

Newspapers.com
www.newspapers.com
Search more than 10,000 newspapers online.

Open Directory
dmoz.org/Society/Politics/News_and_Media/Progressive_and_Left/
Open directory has a strong list of media links with very good untypical links.

Payscale
www.payscale.com
A great place to get current stats comparing salaries.

Pew Internet & American Life Project
www.pewinternet.org/PPF/r/189/report_display.asp
A good discussion of Internet journalism.

Presstime
www.naa.org/home/PressTime.aspx
Presstime is the magazine for the NAA, the Newspaper Association of America.

Radio Free Europe/Radio Liberty
www.rferl.org
A U.S. government-sponsored organization that "spreads democracy" through the Western world

RDN Extra
www.radiodailynews.com/index2.htm#You%20are
Good links and information in the media world.

So You Want to Write Magazine Articles?
awc.al-williams.com/magwrite.htm
Firsthand insight into how to write for a magazine.

The Socialist
www.socialistparty.org.uk/TheSocialistContents.htm
Unorthodox as it may seem, this site is representative of many alternative publications and websites.

TV Jobs
www.tvjobs.com
This site is the A to Z for jobs in the TV world.

TV Rundown
www.tvrundown.com
Good TV news database.

U.S. Newspapers List
www.usnpl.com
A state-by-state directory of newspapers around the United States, including links to the papers' websites and contact information.

USA Today
www.usatoday.com
A good online source for business and journalism trends.

W3C
www.w3.org/MarkUp/Guide/
Author Dave Raggett provides good insight on practical website development using HTML.

Wikipedia
wikipedia.org
This free online encyclopedia has a wealth of information on journalism topics and industry notes. It's a good starting point for further research.

Writer's Market
www.writersmarket.com
Good insight into how to market your work to a magazine.

Writer's Write
www.writerswrite.com/journal/nov01/burch.htm
Good firsthand insight into the world of magazines.

Writing Help Central

www.writinghelp-central.com/
income.html

A good site for what to expect when
you write for a magazine.

Index

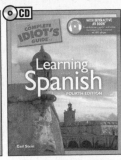

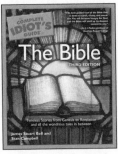

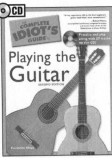